50 JOBS
50 STATES

One Man's Journey of
Discovery Across America

Daniel Seddiqui

Berrett–Koehler Publishers, Inc.
San Francisco
a BK Life book

Berrett-Koehler Publishers, Inc.
235 Montgomery Street, Suite 650
San Francisco, CA 94104-2916
Tel: (415) 288-0260 Fax: (415) 362-2512 www.bkconnection.com

ORDERING INFORMATION

Quantity sales. Special discounts are available on quantity purchases by corporations, associations, and others. For details, contact the "Special Sales Department" at the Berrett-Koehler address above.

Individual sales. Berrett-Koehler publications are available through most bookstores. They can also be ordered directly from Berrett-Koehler: Tel: (800) 929-2929; Fax: (802) 864-7626; www.bkconnection.com

Orders for college textbook/course adoption use. Please contact Berrett-Koehler: Tel: (800) 929-2929; Fax: (802) 864-7626.

Orders by U.S. trade bookstores and wholesalers. Please contact Ingram Publisher Services, Tel: (800) 509-4887; Fax: (800) 838-1149; E-mail: customer.service@ ingrampublisherservices.com; or visit www.ingrampublisherservices.com/Ordering for details about electronic ordering.

E-book versions have color photos:
IDPF epub Digital Book Format: ISBN 978-1-60509-861-6
PDF Digital Book Format: ISBN 978-1-60509-860-9

Berrett-Koehler and the BK logo are registered trademarks of Berrett-Koehler Publishers, Inc.

Printed in the United States of America

Berrett-Koehler books are printed on long-lasting acid-free paper. When it is available, we choose paper that has been manufactured by environmentally responsible processes. These may include using trees grown in sustainable forests, incorporating recycled paper, minimizing chlorine in bleaching, or recycling the energy produced at the paper mill.

Library of Congress Cataloging-in-Publication Data
Seddiqui, Daniel.
   50 jobs in 50 states : one man's journey of discovery across America / Daniel Seddiqui. — 1st ed.
      p. cm.
   Includes bibliographical references and index.
   ISBN 978-1-60509-825-8 (pbk. : alk. paper)
1. Job hunting—United States—States. 2. Occupations—United States—States. I. Title. II. Title: Fifty jobs in fifty states.
   HF5382.75.U6S43 2011
   331.702092—dc22

                                                    2010051264

FIRST EDITION

15 14 13 12 11   10 9 8 7 6 5 4 3 2 1

Designed and produced by Seventeenth Street Studios
Copy editing by Barry Owen
Illustrations and maps by Michael Andrews
Photos by Daniel Seddiqui, except page ii by Kim Hummel
Cover designed by Richard Adelson
Cover illustration by Tim Bower

To my brother, Darius. My whole life, he has coached me and
helped me find my way – whether through sports or through
work – and created the monster that could complete this journey.

And to all those who can't find a job, don't like their job,
or are just curious about what America has to offer.

Daniel A. Seddiqui

Employment Goal: 50 jobs in 50 states in 50 weeks!

ACKNOWLEDGMENTS

Thanks to my publisher for believing in my message and letting me tell my story.

Thank you to my family for being hard on me, putting pressure on me to succeed, and instilling in me the work ethic and discipline needed to make both my journey and this book possible.

Thanks to all the companies, organizations, and families that opened their doors and shared their lives. They trusted me, encouraged me, and took me in as their own. I could not have done this without the people I met along the way.

To Kristen, for believing in me when I felt that no one wanted to hear my story. Thanks also for the late nights and early mornings spent with me, fine-tuning this manuscript.

Finally, thanks to all those who let me walk in their shoes, allowing me to gain understanding and respect for what they do — and whose stories I am able to tell because of that.

BELIEVING IN MY IDEA
WHEN NO ONE ELSE DID

*"You have to go through a lot of nightmares
before you realize your dream."*

After six-and-a-half grueling laps of jumping barriers and water pits, it was down to the last lap. I was at the Pacific-10 Track & Field Championships, representing the University of Southern California in the steeplechase. It was my last collegiate race and I had been training like a seasoned Olympian in hopes of breaking the university's long-standing record. I was on the final lap of the race — a lap away from experiencing another nightmare.

I stepped onto the final barrier. My foot slipped on its slick surface. Tumbling into the water, I hit my shin. I was down. The filthy puddle splashed into my mouth, making me gag as I tried to prop myself up. I watched my competitors pass me while memories of falling during my final high school race loomed. *Same results, last place,* I thought.

My parents walked away in disappointment. My coach reacted the same way. All our hard work and scrupulous effort had been futile. I knew it: I was a loser. My defeat seemed to begin the day I finished dead last in that race, one day after I graduated from college, and it didn't cease in the years that followed.

Initially, after graduating from USC with a degree in economics, I tried to stay in Southern California. I filled out job applications, sent resumes, took aptitude tests, and knocked on doors looking for an entry-level position related to my field — from accounting to investment banking. With every interview, I was confident I had the right skill set, education, work ethic, and personality for the job. Yet despite an encouraging interview, the employer always left me with notorious words: "We went with someone else."

For months, I landed one interview after another, but never earned an offer. Each time I followed up, it was the same story — I didn't have enough experience for the entry-level position. "I hope you're not coming back to live with us," my dad emphasized. My parents grew concerned and frustrated. Still, they did everything possible to provide me with support: enrolling me in career counseling, professional interview courses, and resume-building sessions.

My dad had taught me something that always resonated with me: Be aggressive and persistent. Once, when I was in college, he dropped me off at a buffet restaurant in the hope I would find a summer job as a dishwasher. I had worked at another outlet in the restaurant chain and was wearing the company uniform and name tag. "You've got to work," my dad said as I left the passenger seat. I walked into the restaurant looking for the manager, who was confused when he saw me in full uniform, as though I had stolen it from another employee.

"I'm looking for a job here, since I worked at another location," I explained.

"I see you have the uniform already," the manager said.

"Yes, just register me on the payroll and I'm ready to start."

"Do you speak Spanish?"

"Not really."

"We're looking for someone who speaks Spanish," he reasoned. Even in a basic, entry-level position, I still couldn't land a job.

After three months and failing a dozen interviews in Southern California, I was running out of money. My mom suggested I return home to the San Francisco Bay Area, where she thought I might catch a break finding a job. *Maybe Los Angeles is too competitive,* I thought. But when I moved back home, my humiliation deepened. I was ashamed to use my parents as a safety net. I knew I was a capable college graduate, but my pride was deteriorating and my self-esteem started to fade.

I continued my job search in the Bay Area, but had no more luck than in Southern California. I would make presentations for potential employers, receive positive feedback after my interviews, and return home bragging to my parents. But as I waited for potential employers to reply, there was never an offer. After forty-plus consecutive failed interviews, I knew something in my life had to change.

My parents didn't help the situation; in fact, they exacerbated it. Both my parents had lived the American Dream, coming from nothing and working their way to success. My mom, a New Jersey native, had been working since she was a teenager. My dad immigrated to the United States from Afghanistan on his own when he was only sixteen, making ends meet to pay for his education before becoming a successful entrepreneur. I had always maintained a close relationship with my parents, which might have been the reason for their pressure and disappointment. The more failure I experienced, the more their support for me diminished. "You're a loser, a disgrace to USC," my mom would say, guilting me over the free room and board at their house. My dad would throw me out of bed at 5:00 a.m. to do chores and look for jobs. They couldn't understand why I had not found one after going on several third-round interviews and being a runner-up. As a result, our house became a war zone.

Growing desperate, I was eager to try a new career path. So I decided to channel my athletic background and love of sports into coaching. I spent two months sending over 18,000 e-mails to every collegiate coach in the country, only to earn an offer to volunteer for the women's cross-country team at Northwestern University. My parents were happy to see me off, and I moved to Chicago — supplementing the coaching position with odd jobs, from painting my landlord's houses to part-time accounting.

After the season at Northwestern, I volunteered for a position coaching with the University of Virginia's football team. When that position also failed to become paid, I knew I had to move on again. I accepted another volunteer coaching position with the track team at the University of Georgia, but soon realized that as a volunteer coach, I was swallowed up in another vicious cycle of failure: The positions never led to paid full-time. Before moving to Georgia to continue the cycle, I decided to visit Florida during spring break with the little money I had saved from working in Virginia at Bed Bath & Beyond. And that's really where it all began.

I was riding a train from Orlando to West Palm Beach, Florida, touring aimlessly around the state. Beside me on the two-hour train ride sat a gentleman who asked, "What do you do for a living?" At the time, straddling volunteer coaching and odd jobs as I was, I couldn't give him a straight answer.

"Well, right now, I'm trying to work my way up to a full-time coaching position," I told him. He was impressed with my perseverance and dedication, he told me after I shared how the past three years of my life had been such a struggle.

"I like your character. You have a lot of potential," he said. "Contact me if you're looking to work as a regional manager for CVS Pharmacies." *A job offer? A real job offer?* I wasn't even wearing a suit! I hadn't even been called for an interview! He never even saw my resume! I couldn't believe it. The job he offered wasn't coaching, and working as a CVS manager wasn't something I ever thought I'd do, but he handed me his business card as we both got off the train. He went his way; I went mine.

Staring at his card, I reflected on his proposition and my current situation, lost in my own career path — or lack thereof. I thought of how different my life would be if I moved to yet another state. I thought of the different industries and contrasting cultures throughout the U.S., and my curiosity was piqued. I had spent the first three years of college at the University of Oregon, before transferring to USC. When I lived in Oregon, I thought of the loggers. When I lived in Chicago, I always thought of the trains. Living in Virginia made me think of the state's rich history. There in Florida, I couldn't stop thinking of the amusement parks. There was so much to the country that I hadn't yet seen, and as I tried to find a career path that was the best match for my own personality and interests, there was still so much left to discover.

My mind began to race, and I had an epiphany. I thought of working a stereotypical job in each state. I wanted to live the map. As a child, I was always intrigued by maps, studying them for hours at a time, envisioning how people lived across America or how different I would be if I grew up in a different environment. When it occurred to me to work fifty jobs in fifty states, it was as though I had realized a dream I never knew I had — like waking up from a lifetime of pursuing the wrong path. Despite the struggle I had experienced since college, I had found ways to fulfill my curiosity about different cultures and environments — but this idea would also give me a chance to experience *jobs*. As my spirits lifted in excitement, I went to Georgia after spring break, as planned. In the weeks that remained until my coaching position started, I sold kitchens at Home Depot and worked vigorously on a plan to pursue fifty jobs.

I had no clue how to go about it, so I started by composing a resume of the most quintessential American jobs — one for each state, representing the culture and economy of each. It came to me like a natural instinct — without hesitation or second thoughts. Before my coaching position in Georgia even began, I knew I needed to return to California to make my vision a reality. With my college network in Southern California and my family in Northern California, I figured that if I returned to the state, I would have better luck constructing a plan, recruiting sponsors, and even selling my idea as a television show.

I left Georgia after one month. That also meant leaving Sasha. We had met in Atlanta, and she had become a close friend and ally. When I felt most alone and defeated, Sasha would encourage me to believe in myself. Though she was temperamental, I found her to be fun and kindhearted. As our friendship evolved, my feelings for her evolved too. I felt like nobody else existed when we hung out, and I believed we were meant to be together, but despite her incessant flirting, she claimed she did not want to be with me. Still, she left me with a glimmer of hope: "I would be lying if I said there's no potential between us," she told me before I left Georgia.

Sasha was the first girl to tell me she cared about me, and she encouraged me to fulfill the vision of my project. After so much adversity, I needed just one person in the world to believe in me, to make me feel that maybe, if I went for it, I could make the fifty jobs happen. Sasha was that person, that sole advocate, and in turn, I made a promise to her that I would return to Georgia a success.

I went back to Southern California, rented a car, and lived out of it until I could make ends meet. I was not welcomed back home by my parents. I shared my idea with them, but they immediately wrote it off as a waste of time, destined to fail. Though I now had a goal — my mission to work fifty jobs — I still needed to earn money until the dream became a reality. I was back to interviewing for office jobs — and back to being rejected.

After three jobless years, I found myself back to the same nightmare I had lived the last time I was in California. I bought a new suit from Macy's to wear on a job interview that "I had no real intention of keeping unless I actually got the job," I told myself. The interview was canceled as I was driving to it. That very night, I went back to Macy's to return the doomed suit. Walking back to my rental car, my three years of failure followed me like a dark cloud. I was overcome with defeat. I had no alternatives. I had no place to go, nobody to turn to. I had been sleeping in that rental car for weeks. I was hungry. I was thirsty. I was at an ultimate low, as low as a sober person could go. I didn't care about myself anymore. All I had was an idea.

I got in the rental car and pulled out of the Macy's parking lot, driving aimlessly on the freeway. Within moments, a semitruck violently cut me off, and the car swerved into a curb, nearly hitting a wall. My heart was throbbing. I was scared and felt delusional from lack of food and exhaustion. I got off the highway to park and catch my breath, but I completely broke down. Slumped over the steering wheel, I sobbed until I was out of breath. My face shivered. I had never felt such a low before or such worthlessness. I picked up the phone and called my house. My dad answered, wondering why I was crying. I explained that I almost got into a car accident.

"You don't have insurance. What are you doing? How come you never listen to us? Why can't you keep a stable life?" he scolded me. Fortunately, my mom was more sympathetic and urged me to come home and rejuvenate myself. As I returned home to the fortress of failure, I resolved that I was tired of waiting for employers to determine my destiny. I was tired of waiting for opportunities to come my way. Throughout my life, I had been given advice, strategies, tools for success, but in the end, no matter how much coaching, I was the one who had to run the race. And I was the only one who could control the outcome.

Without a penny to my name, I had nothing to lose. I had planned on turning my idea into a television show, but regardless, whether I should pursue my vision of Living the Map was no longer a question. There was no reason not to.

As soon as I made up my mind to make it happen, nothing was going to stop me. My parents weren't interested and didn't want to hear about it, so I discreetly worked on my project, developing the plan and building a web site. My uncle told me, "If the *why* is strong enough, the *how* becomes easy," and though lining up jobs was anything but easy, committing myself to making it work was.

I sat in my childhood bedroom making phone calls to employers across the country for sixteen hours of each summer day. I kept a log of every person I called, tracking responses. Some laughed at me, some hung up on me, and others made no attempt to hide their skepticism. I had heard "no" before and it didn't matter anymore. I wanted to do this, however many rejections I faced.

A big concern was how to pay for this journey. I figured it would cost well over $100,000 to fly from state to state, stay in motels, and rent cars to drive to work. But I had no money. My first idea was to find sponsors. I contacted car dealerships, figuring that if one gave me a car, it would reduce the costs. I knew I'd need a car with enough room in the back for sleeping, to avoid spending money on accommodations. I contacted other potential sponsors as well, like energy drink companies, but from everyone, all I heard was "no." So I looked for ways to greatly reduce the cost and make the journey "pay as I go." I decided to drive from state to state and plan my route strategically to make the most headway in the shortest distance. This required coordinating the jobs based on the states I'd be passing through in a logical pattern so that it wasn't too time-consuming, taxing, and expensive to drive from job to job. Even if I slept in the back of a car and avoided paying for motels, there would be substantial driving expenses, as well as other costs like food and insurance.

I knew it was critical to actually get paid, but I never outright asked employers to pay me because it was hard enough to land a job in the first place. I just wanted the job. But I hoped that if I performed well, they wouldn't let me leave without giving me some sort of compensation. I couldn't hold out any longer: I had to get out there and let whatever happened happen. I figured that if I started the journey, I could try to make ends meet on the road. Who knows? I might pick up a sponsor along the way. And even if I were to get paid, I had no way to estimate how much I would earn. But I figured that since I had been able to spend a week on vacation in Florida for under one hundred dollars, I might be able to do the same in every state. Plus, it had a nice ring to it: 50 Jobs in 50 States in 50 Weeks. I wouldn't have guessed at the time, but as it turned out, I ended up working as a volunteer in just five states.

In the meantime, my parents were on the verge of kicking me out again. "Just one more month!" I begged. I made hundreds of calls per state in the four months since I started the project, willing to work in any state with any employer who could fulfill my objective. I had invested so much of myself that even after months of more rejection, I could not surrender. I knew I needed only one break for everything to fall into place. And sure enough, it was only a matter of time before my persistence finally paid off. I found the Nebraska Corn Board Association online and called to ask if anyone there knew of farmers I could work with for a week. A staffer put me in touch with a farmer who could use an extra set of hands. Soon after, I lined up a position at a general store in Montana during that state's hunting season.

After setting up ten jobs, I knew I had to leave the house before another war broke out. I had no option but to set up the rest of my jobs while on the road. My brother opened a line of credit for me at his bank to purchase my first car. I maxed out the account with a $5,000 Jeep Cherokee. It was almost September and I was ready to start my journey, planning to hit the Midwest before the winter months. I called my local newspaper and it jumped on the story.

The article made front-page news and hit the wire to larger papers. Within days, a television producer contacted me about turning my idea into a reality show. Being the host of a television show about working across America was my dream and I was thrilled, but after giving it some thought, I realized that if a TV crew was involved, everything would change. People would treat me differently. I'd risk being scripted — or worse, I'd risk control over the project. I had already done the groundwork, lining up the first ten jobs through countless rejection. My life led me to this journey — all the failure, defeat, and struggle I'd been through had brought me here. I wanted to see it through the way I intended.

"Do you want your own show?" the producer of *Dirty Jobs* asked me. It was my dream come true — after searching for months for a sponsorship, finally, someone was interested. But this time, I wasn't. I wanted to experience America, and no network or television show would direct my journey, or even tag along for the ride.

"I'm going to do this organically," I replied, "on my own."

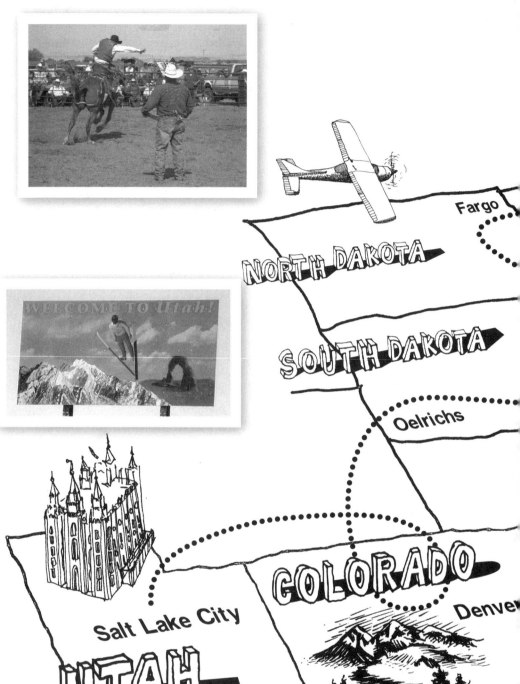

NORTH DAKOTA

Fargo

SOUTH DAKOTA

Oelrichs

Salt Lake City

UTAH

COLORADO

Denver

1 Reality Hits But No Turning Back

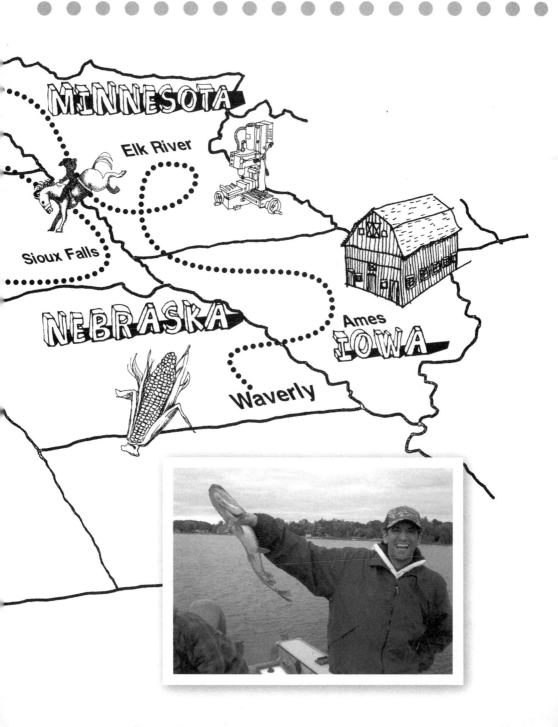

UTAH

LDS HUMANITARIAN
SERVICES WORKER

As he handed me a check for $250, my dad made no effort to hide his doubt that I could complete my journey. "See you in three weeks," he uttered skeptically. With tears in her eyes, my mom sprayed Windex across my car windows and promptly wiped the glass clean. Standing beside us, my brother videotaped my departure with the precious Sony camera I had purchased on credit just a few days earlier. I took two cases of water from my dad and put them on the floor of the car. With every move, my body shivered. Anticipating the journey ahead, I was shrouded in uncertainty. My throat choked up as though bricks were stacked from my stomach to my neck. I swallowed the emotion, climbed in my Jeep, and reversed out of the driveway.

This is it; no turning back. My mind raced as I repeated the words: *No turning back.* I was scared. I knew there was a chance I wouldn't succeed, but I had flushed the possibility from my mind. Failure simply wasn't an option, no matter what obstacles I encountered over the next fifty weeks. While I drove slowly through the familiar streets of my hometown toward the on-ramp of the highway — the on-ramp of my journey — the car was silent. I had turned off my cell phone. The radio was off. But my mind was rambling. *Where am I going to end up tonight? Where will I eat? Do I have enough money to eat? Should I cash the check my dad gave me?* Ambivalence hammered through my thoughts like static noise, and I needed to drown it out before it got the best of me.

It was a thousand miles to Salt Lake City; I was nervous and drove cautiously, trying not to let worry overwhelm me. I could not afford to have my car break down or get a ticket on top of the historically high price of gas. Before starting the climb over California's High Sierra, I pulled over at a truck stop to stretch my legs. As I headed across the parking lot, I couldn't help but notice all the different people passing through, ambling in and out of the rest room, walking to their cars. *Lots of people live their lives on the road,* I thought. *Now I'm doing it, too.* I was just starting out and had a long way to go — I knew I'd be crossing many borders. As I watched those around me, I realized that my anxiety came from anticipation of something entirely new, something I had never done before, but just because it was new to me didn't mean it was wrong, unsafe, or foolish. A sense of calm and renewed confidence replaced my stress. Driving on, as I admired the scenery, I became preoccupied thinking about documenting my journey. I thought about the web site I had recently created, and I brainstormed topics for the first entry in my online journal. I was tempted to set up my camera and chronicle the picturesque ride. In the meantime, I looked forward to staying with relatives in Utah, whom I hadn't seen in years.

To break up the drive, I decided to spend the night in Reno, Nevada. I parked the car near a university for the night and reluctantly crawled into my sleeping bag in the back of the Jeep. I had slept in the back of a car before, but this time, I was in an unfamiliar environment and was uncertain of the neighborhood just outside my car door. As I tried to sleep, Sasha called. "You're sleeping in your car?" She was concerned, but also expressed criticism. "Why are you too cheap to get a motel?"

"I don't have money for that; I need to save," I explained, not for the first time.

"Well, have a good night. Call me tomorrow." Much of the day, I was distracted by anxiety and anticipation, but as Sasha and I hung up, the noise of the day completely subsided. I was alone in a sleeping bag in the back of my car hoping all that I was putting myself through would be worth it. I locked my eyes shut to fall asleep, but

The statue of Brigham Young in front of the Mormon Temple.

every time a car passed, I popped up to check if it was a cop. I knew it was illegal to sleep in a car on the street within city limits, but I was desperate. The combination of anxiety and the chilly night air of the high desert kept me awake. After tossing and turning into the early hours of the morning, I decided to give up on sleep and start driving into the sunrise.

"Welcome to Utah." As the sign approached, I pulled over and stared contemplatively. *I made it! This is real!* State Number One, job Number One — working for the Church of Jesus Christ of Latter-Day Saints. Historically, Mormons had settled in Utah in the mid-1800s to escape the persecution they faced in other states. Given the Mormon influence, the decision to work for the LDS in that state was easy; landing an actual job, however, was close to impossible. The Mormon church typically prefers to hire Mormons. I wanted to avoid the question, "Are you a Mormon?" So I did everything I could to deflect it, answering questions conservatively and with extra courtesy. I didn't want to give any reason that might hinder the possibility of getting a job, so I didn't mention the objective of my trip. Ultimately, I settled for volunteering at the church's Humanitarian

Center. This was not my ideal choice — I didn't know how I could make ends meet by working volunteer jobs. Still, I was eager to get started, both for the week and for the year ahead. I stayed with my Uncle Mike and his wife Linda, who provided a gentle buffer as I adjusted to my new life; I knew I'd be spending many nights of the year in the back of the Jeep or in a stranger's house (if I was lucky), so staying with family was an ideal way to kick off the trip.

The Humanitarian Center is a warehouse located in an industrial part of Salt Lake City, which is nestled in the mountains. An associate was expecting me on my first day. "Thank you so much for donating your time. This is a great blessing," she stated gratefully as she handed me meal cards. *Wow, an all-you-can-eat buffet for lunch,* I thought.

"Do you have vending machines here?" I asked, curious to address a stereotype of Mormons and caffeine.

"Yes, down the hall."

"Do you have Coke?"

"Yes, we do!" the associate told me. I was surprised — I didn't think Mormons drank Coca-Cola. I went down the hall to get a drink and check it out for myself, and sure enough, there were Cokes in the vending machine — but they were caffeine-free, which made me laugh to myself.

I was set for the week, but I needed to work hard — I needed to set the tone for my trip, my project, my conscience. I knew I would have to learn this job and all my jobs quickly if I was going to make the project worthwhile. I wanted, as much as possible, to be treated as a normal employee, not as a visitor. I looked around the facility and spotted a quote on the wall: "We are to feed the hungry, to clothe the naked, to provide for the widow, to dry up the tear of the orphan, to comfort the afflicted, whether in this Church, or in any other, or no church at all . . . ." I felt humbled by these words and motivated to make my best effort for their cause.

My task for the week was to package Hygiene Kits to send to Louisiana for victims of Hurricane Gustav. The Church planned to send out 500,000 kits, each containing a comb, toothbrush, toothpaste, towel, soap, and brochures from the church. Dressed to impress in their suits and neckties, each group of associates had a quota of kits to produce; if one team slowed down, another would have to pick up the slack. I tried to keep a fast pace, but it was tedious work; I noticed I wasn't the only one glancing at the clock as the day wore on. Still, despite pressure to meet our quotas, all my coworkers appeared grateful to be working there. Only after I heard their stories, did I understand why. I was working side by side with refugees from Africa and Southeast Asia who were part of a program run by the church called "Developing Self-Reliance." The program teaches English, provides job training, prepares participants for employment, and finally — after two years — offers them job placement.

Hearing what my coworkers had been through made me reflective and subdued. Preparing for my fifty-state odyssey, I had spent energy worrying about traveling alone, being far from home, working for weeks at a time, spending money, and the general unpredictability of the year ahead. Yet here was a group of people who had fled from war-torn countries and lived through tragedy I would never know. Their experiences reminded me of my dad's family and their struggle under similar circumstances. Both had experienced corrupt governments, persecution, marginalization, and forced migration. At the Humanitarian Center, these refugees would work for two years. They had to make money for their families and acclimate to a new life — a new country, a new language, a new existence — completely foreign to anything they had ever known. We had come to this church in Utah for different reasons, though we both left home and were starting over. Nonetheless, I was humbled by the refugees. I knew the fear and concern I felt about the weeks ahead was nothing compared with what my fellow warehouse workers had been through. "We're blessed every day. We accept whatever path God chooses for us," one had explained. Despite our differences — and thanks to our similarities — I could relate. *Whatever God chooses*, I thought. *No turning back.*

COLORADO

I decided to drive through Wyoming to get to Colorado, and soon after crossing the state line, the flat, colorless landscape changed to mountains and green meadows: the cloud covering dissolved as the sun blazed in the azure sky. Wyoming's rocky terrain was overcome by enormous snow-covered mountain ranges and I wondered if every state would transform as swiftly when I entered. I wondered if I could transform that way, too.

As I approached Denver, I called Katie Thomas, a fellow USC alum, to let her know I was on my way. I found her through a college alumni network on Facebook. Though we'd never met, she was willing to let me crash on her couch for the week. When I arrived at her apartment an hour later, she had just returned from a 10K race. "There's always some athletic event in this city," she explained. When she took me to a city park to play football with her friends, I realized I was having trouble adjusting to the higher altitude: I had a bad headache and suffered shortness of breath. Still, I couldn't help but notice the prominent bike lanes and throngs of joggers everywhere. Everyone seemed so active and energetic; I could understand why Denver is rated one of the healthiest cities in the U.S.

My first weekend in Colorado was relaxing and fun. The calm, pleasant atmosphere eased my transition and I was excited about the week ahead. Katie was welcoming, her apartment was comfortable, the scenery was beautiful, and I felt right at home in an active community of runners and outdoor sports. The concerns I had only a week earlier began to subside as I looked forward with relief and excitement to working as a hydrologist with the U.S. Geological Survey (USGS) at the Denver Federal Center. I had secured an internship with the agency after calling both private and federal organizations. Water is an essential life resource — we need it to live, it's critical to irrigation, and it provides habitat for animals. To assure safe, clean water needed to survive, it's vital to have information on water quality and composition. That's where the USGS comes in. The agency works to protect us by studying water and providing scientific information others can use to purify and protect the water we consume.

I chose hydrology in Colorado because the state's rivers, which originate in the Rocky Mountains, are a significant water source for much of the West. Half our country's drinking water comes from rivers, and the other half comes from aquifers, which, like oil reserves, are underground. Once depleted, they are difficult to restore.

After a few days, I understood from experience at least one of the things hydrologists do: hike on trails with ski poles and water containers to collect water samples from reservoirs, canals, and rivers. Every morning, my colleagues and I put on waders (waterproof pants and boots) and life vests and drove deep into the mountains on some of the highest roads in the country. After driving as far as we could, we hiked in farther and waded into rivers to collect samples. It wasn't *that* simple — the current was often so powerful, I was knocked off balance, nearly dropping the bottles and testing equipment. Once the samples were secured, we tested them on-site for oxygen content, turbidity, and pH before submitting them to water treatment centers. In addition to sampling, we measured discharge rates (flow volume). Taking samples was a long, monotonous process. To avoid contaminating them, we had to be very cautious, wearing rubber gloves and quickly securing the samples into Ziploc bags. Despite the tedious nature of the work, I loved trudging through the streams. I loved the cool air, warmth of the sun, and working outdoors. My coworkers were friendly, inviting, and informative, which made the job even more pleasant. One of the interesting things I learned from

Carefully measuring the discharge rate every three feet, across the Big Thompson River.

them is that when rain hits the surface of a river or other body of water, the chemistry of the water changes instantly. Jason, one of my colleagues, told me, "If you're interested in hydrology to strike it rich, you'd be in the wrong profession." It was clear: Everyone there was genuine and committed to ensuring the water we drink is clean and safe.

I didn't see Katie much because my work hours were so long (mostly due to the two-and-a-half-hour commute twice a day). I continued to have trouble sleeping — but this time, it was because my mind raced with excitement. I was in stimulation mode: Everything was new, interesting, invigorating. At night, I couldn't wait for the next morning, to start over and take it all in again. Each evening, when I was preparing for the next day, I took a few minutes to catch up with my biggest fan: Sasha.

"What's going on tomorrow?" she asked.

"Research in the watersheds!" I was excited — after only a few days as a hydrologist, I was scheduled to attend a national conference with all the experts. Everything was going better than I imagined, I told Sasha, with only one exception. "I'm really concerned about my web site," I confessed. This was important to me because the web offered the best way to stay connected during my trip. I had been relying on my cousin to keep my site updated, but it had become stagnant.

"I can do it. I'll even improve the layout for you." Sasha volunteered, and I couldn't have been happier. Problem solved; everything was smooth and steady.

The next day, as part of the conference, we went into the field to collect more samples. We took a shuttle bus 10,000 feet up a mountain, where we rendezvoused with a group of thirty hydrologists and climbed an additional 2,000 feet to conduct research near the summit. To avoid the risk of getting my camera wet from rain predicted that afternoon, I left it on the shuttle bus. When we returned to the bus after seven hours in the field, my camera was gone. Immediately, panic set in. The bus driver told me he had left it at the conference center. I was flabbergasted — the camera was a huge investment for me and though my year was just beginning, it already carried many memories I could not get back. When we returned to the center, I rampaged through the lobby searching hysterically. I spotted the camera sitting by itself on a table. I was shocked that it hadn't been snatched up. From that moment on, it was attached to my body, no matter what. I couldn't risk losing it again.

Despite that panic, I realized as I left Colorado that my anxiety about the weeks ahead had subsided. The shock of leaving home and of my new life on the road began to diminish. Nonetheless, though everything was going so smoothly, I didn't want to get too comfortable too soon. There were many borders yet to cross. Just about everything about the year ahead remained uncertain; however, as time went on I was less afraid.

SOUTH DAKOTA

RODEO ANNOUNCER

A s I drove on Highway 20 into South Dakota, my father's parting words still resounded in my mind: "See you in three weeks." Entering South Dakota, I was starting my third week. Contrary to my father's doubts, however, I was still going strong and had no intention of turning back.

On the road, I spotted a cowboy riding atop a galloping horse, which nicely signified the start of a week working at the rodeo. Before arriving, I had envisioned vast valleys with roaming buffalo and rodeos full of cowboys competing for glory. I wasn't too far off — after making a few calls, I learned that rodeo is the state's official sport.

I searched the Internet for information and found the South Dakota Rodeo Association. I called and was connected first with bull riders, but riding a bull was out of the question. Then I talked with the Association president, Dan Pirrung, who referred me to rodeo announcers, one of whom told me he would show me the ropes.

While I pulled off the exit into Oelrichs, the smallest of small towns (population: 145), I felt really far from home and I knew right away that I wasn't going to fit in. I drove into the dusty parking lot, where hundreds of people wearing Wrangler jeans, button-up shirts, cowboy hats and boots crowded around trucks and horse trailers. My Jeep stood out from the other vehicles, and in my running shoes, T-shirt, and loose-fitting jeans, I knew I would stand out too.

I emerged from my car in search of Sugar Ray Quinn, the announcer who had invited me to Oelrichs and who was excited to be a part of my endeavor. As I walked bewildered through the parking lot, a man approached me and tipped his cowboy hat. As soon as he said "howdy," I knew it was Sugar Ray. His smooth, robust voice was enough for me to recognize him; perhaps my running shoes — or lack of a cowboy hat — were all he needed to recognize me.

Sugar Ray took me to meet the judges, timers, and scorekeepers before he climbed a ladder into the announcer's booth. Before long, I heard his velvet voice introduce me over the loudspeakers hanging from utility poles. He told the crowd about my 50/50/50 trek; as people turned to look at me, I could only smile and nod while some raised their eyebrows, some applauded, and a few gave me a thumbs up.

I became dazzled by people I met and the world around me. Above the rodeo arena, an enormous American flag rippled in the breeze, which carried the sound of twanging guitars as they came through the loudspeakers. From the shoulder of the highway overlooking the arena, a line of bikers peered down onto the cowboys standing around me. I realized there was a deep-rooted rivalry between them.

"Heya Cal-e-furnea, come on ova he-ere! Ima show ya how to wrassle a steer!" someone shouted suddenly, as I turned around to a handful of eager faces. But they weren't watching me for amusement; instead, I sensed their genuine desire to share an experience that was central to their culture. I didn't want to wrestle a steer . . . but there I was. *This is it*, I thought. *This is what it's all about.*

The cowboys brought me to a pen and showed me how it's done: Grab the steer from behind, grasp its horns, and dig your heels into the ground to slow it down. A twelve-year-old kid demonstrated the moves for me, but I just couldn't get the hang of it. I grew frustrated and coached myself out of the failure. "Let's do this!" I yelled as I chased the steer through the pen. Two other cowboys hopped in and together we got the steer to the ground. I felt a sense of both accomplishment and disbelief — it was surreal to think I was rolling around in poop chasing a steer with a bunch of cowboys. But soon enough, I would fit in easily.

"If yaw really gonna to do this, yal need ya-self some gear." Bill White had approached me earlier and commended me for my mission. Now, however, he insisted on dressing me for the role. Nothing I said could convince him it wasn't necessary. Before long, his wife

I was surprised their clothes fit me so well, although their tight Wranglers were loose on me.

showed up with boots, a belt, and five button-up shirts with fancy pearl clasps and detailed stitching. While I suited up, Bill described more of the rodeo to me — including what makes the animals buck. "There's a flank strap attached," he explained. It's a common misconception that the animals are damaged or hurt during the rodeo, he elaborated; instead, what makes them buck is a loose strap tied around the midsection. The horses and bulls buck to try and remove the strap, and once the rider is off the animal, the strap quickly releases and they stop bucking.

As the first of two days of the rodeo ended and people vacated the lots, Sugar Ray came over. He, Bill, and some others were headed to Hot Springs, a nearby town, and invited me to join them at a motel there. I was reluctant to take them up on the offer — they had already given me food and clothes, and now they were offering a place to stay. Nonetheless, after driving through the few streets in town, I knew I had little choice. I needed a good rest for my rodeo debut the next day. That evening, they took me out to dinner and urged me to try a local dish: Rocky Mountain oysters. As I stabbed the meat with my fork and took a bite, Sugar Ray confessed that it wasn't seafood. It was a local dish: bull's testicle. Like so many others before me, I'm sure, I had been fooled, and reflexively spit out my food. We laughed about it, but when I went to bed, I was still grossed out.

All night, when I anticipated my role as an announcer, my heart felt as if it would pump out of my chest. Sugar Ray made it seem so natural and easy, but I was afraid of appearing in front of crowds and I knew I'd fumble over names, numbers, and times. My mind raced when I tried to think of things I could say as filler.

As it turned out, Sugar Ray had me announce the kids' events: a three-barrel race, the youth steer-wrestling, and rodeo musical chairs. In that game, the kids circled a series of barrels on horseback, dismounted, and ran to vacant barrels instead of to empty chairs.

I spent the next two nights in Sugar Ray's house, which is filled wall-to-wall with rodeo photos. Both nights, I was entertained by his impromptu voiceovers during the television commercials. To complete my work week in South Dakota, I needed to head across the state to Sioux Falls to meet Dan Pirrung. As president of the South Dakota Rodeo Association, he had invited me to the Sioux Falls County Fairgrounds, where the rodeo state finals take place.

When I arrived in Sioux Falls, instead of meeting the locals in their cowboy hats and Wrangler jeans, I was introduced to a group of men in orange jumpsuits. Dan explained that they were inmates at a Corrections Center, but were in for minor offenses. They had been released into Dan's care for the day to help set up for the event. This source of labor kept the costs down for Dan and gave the men a chance to see something they loved. They were interested in my mission and coined a new nickname for me: fifty/fifty. Together, we spent the day preparing for the rodeo — assembling bleachers, unfolding gates, and spreading soil over the arena. That's when I got the chance to try using the tractor.

The inmate operating it looked bored, as if he had used the tractor a million times, while I was itching for the chance to try something new. I climbed up on the massive machine, whose wheels were higher than my waist. As instructed, I turned the gears, and the machine took off, spreading soil beneath it as I rolled forward. I felt like I was sixteen, driving a car for the first time – only this vehicle felt much more compact and scary. I drove the tractor through the periphery of the rodeo, which was decorated with banners from sponsors. After hours of toiling to set up for the event, I sat on the bleachers scanning my GPS, wondering where I'd stay that night. As though reading my mind, one of the rodeo guys approached to ask if I needed a place to stay. His name was Steve Klein, and he looked like a real working cowboy. He was rugged looking and covered in dirt. He had a no-nonsense way of talking that was intimidating, if not for his gentle gaze. As he stood before me, dirtier than the convicts, I wondered if he lived in a rusted trailer or a scary shack. Still, my budget was tight and I longed for a place to sleep other than my Jeep, so I agreed to take him up on his offer.

I followed Steve north to a town called Crooks. He led me off of the pavement to a dirt road sandwiched between the main road and cornfields. With every passing mile, the houses became larger and more impressive until we reached a sign that read "Klein Ranches." Within minutes, we approached a white, two-story farmhouse – Steve's home. I was shocked. My stereotype of Steve, based on his grungy appearance that day, proved to be far off base. The Kleins, Steve, Debbie and their three adult children, gracious and welcoming, were happy to host me for the rest of the week, taking me to rodeo dances and horseback riding, serving steak dinners – I must have eaten a hundred steaks while I was in South Dakota – and driving me to and from the rodeo.

My duties at the state finals were the same as those at the rodeo in Oelrichs. I announced the same events as I had with Sugar Ray. Only now, I was alone, announcing before 3,000 spectators. This time, I didn't feel like an outsider. I had acclimated to the rodeo culture and took it on as my own. Even a newscaster commended me, noting that I "walked, talked, and even looked like a real cowboy." The important thing was: I felt like one.

I was sad to leave, but I needed to get on the road to my next destination, next-door North Dakota. It had been a great week and I knew my experience in South Dakota was irreplaceable. I had pushed my boundaries and sought experiences in a place completely foreign to me — experiences available only in South Dakota; I felt positive about my project and my ability to see it through to the end. I felt confident. I wasn't yet ready to ride off into the sunset, and for that, I was thankful.

NORTH DAKOTA
CARTOGRAPHER

I took off my cowboy hat, kicked off my boots, and threw them into the back of the Jeep before driving into my fourth state. I knew there was a historic rivalry between South Dakota and North Dakota and wondered how this might affect my two experiences. I was amused to learn that many residents of both states would prefer an east-west split, using the Missouri River as a boundary. Driving north, people stared at my license plates when they passed me on the road. I don't think anyone expected a Californian to visit North Dakota, and I have to admit, I don't think I would have ever gone there if not for my objective of hitting every state. Before setting out, I didn't know much about North Dakota itself except how flat the land is. People had told me it's so flat you could see the curve of the earth on the horizon. *Even a sidewalk curb would be considered a hill in this state*, I thought to myself as I made my way to Fargo, on the Minnesota border.

Fargo is the state's largest city, and one of its biggest industries, as I learned from my research, is cartography — mapmaking. Many cartography companies are headquartered there, but I started my

job search by pursuing positions in university cartography depart-
ments. I was advised that I would do better to work with a private
company, where I could work in cartography full-time. My university contacts gave me a couple of leads, one for Ulteig Engineers,
which hired me.

A friend from home had put me in touch with the Smiths, a family
of four with two grown daughters, whom I planned to stay with while
working in Fargo. I arrived at the Smiths' house just in time for a
steak dinner. The Smiths are proud to live and work in North Dakota
and asked tons of questions about my trip and my week ahead. I had
been planning to commute forty-six miles from their house to my
job that week, but once I told them that, they insisted I stay with
their relatives, the Jones family, who lived much closer.

The next morning, I drove straight to Ulteig, where my new
boss, Mike, greeted me with the welcoming gift of a shirt, water
bottle, and other company paraphernalia. "Here," Mike said warmly
in what sounded like a Canadian accent, "the marketing team got
you this gift package," as he handed me the bundle of goods. *I
knew North Dakota was competing with South Dakota*, I thought to
myself. After explaining the mapmaking process, he took me out
of the office to have a look at the Red River Valley in which Fargo
and surrounding towns lie. As I was soon to find out, the Red
River plays a huge role in the lives of the people of that region and
figures prominently in Ulteig's business.

That evening, I drove to my temporary new home and met the
Joneses. After I settled into my room in their spacious house, Mrs.
Jones popped her head through the doorway to my bedroom: "Would
you like to come to a small function with us and meet the Governor
of North Dakota?" I wasn't much into politics, but I knew this could
be a great opportunity. Sure enough, Governor Hoeven was intrigued
by my project and asked me to explain it to his guests. "What you're
doing is so important to understanding our country," the governor
said encouragingly. We were outside, and as people crowded around
to hear about my project, swarms of mosquitoes surrounded us. One
of the guests told me there are so many mosquitoes that people joke

it's their state bird. As the week progressed, I grew accustomed to mapmaking. I spent time working on a map of wind farms and planning potential sites for wind turbines. But we focused on floodplain mapping. Because the Red River Valley is so flat, the river itself so winding, which slows its flow, and because of melting snow in the spring, coupled with natural dams caused by ice breaking up downstream, water tends to back up, sometimes disastrously, causing major floods. The worst ones are the so-called hundred-year floods, which are, as their name suggests, uncommon, but still a 1% chance in a given year. Property owners need to know the exact elevation of their houses and businesses because elevation corresponds to risk. If they're in a flood zone, they can reduce risk and avoid costly flood insurance by elevating their structures. Hence, the importance of reliable floodplain maps.

Growing up, I was always intrigued by maps and could lose myself in them for hours. Working with maps at Ulteig was fascinating, and when Mike suggested I make one of my route through the U.S., I was thrilled by the idea. Mike thought I could hand the maps out to people along the way so that they could track my progress. *Forty-six more states* . . . . My mind wandered as I created a basic map noting highways, rivers, and elevations. Later, Mike arranged for a pilot to fly me in a small plane as part of Ulteig's effort to survey floodplain. I was nervous; I don't like flying and we were in a cramped plane with winds howling at forty to fifty miles per hour. We had been advised against making the flight, but since I had only one opportunity to do it, we decided to take the chance. *That's what it's all about, anyway,* I assured myself while we flew over the valley. As we reviewed the flat land and potential sites for wind turbines, I couldn't help but think of how far I'd come in four weeks. *This is really happening,* I repeated to myself. I had never imagined I would be in North Dakota flying over flatlands. *I'm really doing it.*

Toward the end of the week, I went to the YMCA to exercise and ended up chatting with the staff about my trip and my experience in Fargo. They looked up my web site and, impressed that I had

Flying high above the Red River Valley in a small plane. I couldn't see the curve of the Earth although some had said I would.

been on the local news that week, asked to have pictures taken with me. After a brief photo session, I decided to head back to the Joneses. When I arrived, Mrs. Jones asked me about the photos I took at the YMCA.

"How did you know about that?" I asked.

"One of the girls' mom called and said she heard that the fifty/ fifty guy is staying at my house," she explained. Still I was confused, before I realized that the girl must have recognized my host from a picture on my web site, and then shown her mom. Mrs. Jones handed me the phone number of Stefanie, the girl in question, and urged me to call her. My coworkers at Ulteig were treating me to dinner that night, so I decided to invite Stefanie to join us. I found a new friend. I was happy to meet someone my age, and throughout the week we continued to hang out and build our friendship.

As I spoke to Sasha every evening and told her about my day,

I sensed her envy that I was friends with Stefanie — but it wasn't just Stefanie. Sasha seemed to grow jealous from any attention I got from other girls and would ask me about them with sarcasm. I didn't want to upset her, but I wanted to make the most of my experience. I was walking on eggshells with Sasha.

Unfortunately, I did not feel I could be open about my friendship with Stefanie, who even helped me find a place to stay the following week. She had bragged to her relatives in Minnesota that she had met me and they volunteered to host me for my week there. I wasn't sure how close my job in Minnesota would be to their house, but I didn't hesitate to accept. My time in North Dakota came to an end, but I was invited to spend the weekend with the Smiths at their Minnesota lake house, and I looked forward to the short break en route to the next stop.

MINNESOTA

MEDICAL DEVICE MACHINIST

I spent my first weekend in Minnesota at the Smiths' log cabin on one of the 10,000 lakes for which the state is famous and where I experienced my first autumn foliage. It was the beginning of October, and I had never seen the vibrant orange or blazing red leaves of a northern autumn (most of California lacks such displays). I wondered if it was the most beautiful thing I'd ever seen. From there, I made the drive into the town of Becker to stay with Stefanie's relatives, the Millers. I felt at home with them right away. Al and Margie Miller had three kids, and within hours, it was as though I had two new parents and three new siblings. They showed me around the house, gave me a key to the front door, and invited me to join them in their activities that week. I was still getting used to staying with family hosts, and it really helped to feel right at home from the beginning. To make the start of my Minnesota week even better, against all odds, my job was only ten miles away, in Elk River.

Minnesota is the leading medical device manufacturing state, so I applied to several companies before I nailed a job at Metal Craft, a family-owned company that grew from a basement operation in the 1970s into a multimillion-dollar empire. Metal Craft is a leading supplier of medical-implants and -devices.

When I arrived the first day, I was greeted by Shawn, the marketing manager. He showed me around the offices in the front of the building and then brought me to the manufacturing facility in the back. "What would you like to focus on for the week?" he asked.

"I want to try everything!" I exclaimed.

"Ah, you betcha!" Shawn replied, and with that, he made it happen for me. We set an agenda designed to give me a feel for the whole operation, day by day. Unlike the other machinists, who worked at a single station, I was scheduled to try all the stations required to make a particular product from start to finish. I experienced the whole process in five days: milling, grinding, honing, polishing, and etching. I learned how the devices made at Metal Craft help real people in the real world walk again, ski again, dance, run, think, or eat again.

It meant a lot to me to take raw metal and see it through to a completed product. This work helped me understand the meaning of it all and how small parts fit together to create a larger whole. I couldn't help but wonder if this insight had larger relevance to my trip. Perhaps on a personal level, I wouldn't understand the meaning of my journey until I saw it through to the finish. Then I'd know what it meant and why it was important.

As I was thinking about these things, a man named Scott Groit approached me, introduced himself, and told me that he would serve as my mentor at Metal Craft. Like many employees at the company, Scott was a veteran; he had thirty years of machining under his belt. He walked me through the 24-hour operation — the entire, complex, intricate process of engineering. "The main thing to remember is that the person who wrote the code for the software assumes that all of this work is done in a perfect environment. They don't account for the human element so much. They don't account for human error. This is called 'tolerance,'" he explained.

Metal Craft thought my project could bring publicity to the company and hired an outside media agency to make connections and work to get us on the national news. Everyday that week, we called the agency to see if it had found any news source willing to run my story while I was there, but each day, the reply was the same: no media attention. I decided to try to reach out on my own. I called all the Minneapolis news stations, radio stations, newspapers and the like, and finally, the day before my last, one of the most watched local stations came to Metal Craft to cover my story. Within hours, the Millers told me they saw me on CNN. My mom called to tell me she had just seen me on CNN too — the local story hit the wire, and CNN caught it and ran it two days in a row. I was thrilled! I immediately called Sasha. "This is amazing! I knew this would happen to you," she assured me. After being on CNN, I realized that I didn't need to have a television show to share my experience. I knew that I was a capable person and reaching the national spotlight was a great way to prove it. I had come a long way.

That week, Shawn did me the great honor of inviting me to my first-ever fishing experience. Once the bell rang for the lunch break, we went out to buy a license. I wasn't as enthusiastic as he was because I didn't know what to expect. While we were out on the boat, I looked up at the sky, picturing myself as a point on a map, thinking how far I had come. I felt a tug on my line within two minutes and caught a northern pike. I caught twelve fish that day, but didn't realize I had to throw most of them back — the legal limit is three. I planned on preparing the fish for the Millers, to make dinner for them as thanks for their hospitality.

As the week came to a close, I was reluctant to leave. On my last day at Metal Craft, Shawn brought me to his office and presented me with a sign to affix to my car with my Living-the-Map logo. Earlier that week, I had mentioned to him in passing that I wanted to put the logo on the Jeep, and his design was exactly what I had envisioned.

I never expected my colleagues to do that for me and was deeply moved. Together, we went outside to mount the sticker to my car. It was perfect. I came to know the meaning of "Minnesota Nice."

I felt that Minnesota would be hard to beat—the Millers and Metal Craft had shown me unmatchable kindness. I hated saying goodbye, but later that afternoon, I made the rounds at Metal Craft and said farewell to as many people as I could. Before I could make it out the door, Shawn stopped me. "There's one more thing I wanted to show you before you leave . . . ."

He led me into the cafeteria, where all the employees had gathered; Jack, the owner, stood in the middle and spoke briefly, thanking me for my efforts and wishing me well with my project. As I took the floor to speak, I looked around the room and knew I couldn't adequately express my thanks, my thoughts, or my reflections on the whole experience. I was overwhelmed by their kindness, that they had taken me in and treated me as one of their own. Jack came over and handed me an envelope. A moment later, Scott followed. After everyone had filtered out of the room, I opened the envelopes.

Sitting wasn't allowed on the manufacturing floor unless you're on break. I wasn't used to being on my feet all day, and my back ached as I was making medical drills.

I had received two checks: a check from the company as payment for my work and a second check of personal contributions from my coworkers. The folks at Metal Craft had contributed out of their pockets to give me a lofty bonus for the journey ahead.

I choked up. Driving state to state, learning from people, going into their homes and experiencing their lives, I was humbled by how much they reached out. I felt I owed *them* for what *they had* done. As I got back on the road and drove south toward Iowa, I reflected on my Minnesota experience and thought, *machining is a fitting metaphor for my project.* You start with a plan, but as Scott said, the plan doesn't account for the human element — the importance of others. However well thought out, the plan doesn't envision the people you meet along the way or the difference they might make in your life. Since I left my parents' driveway in California, all I could anticipate was related to myself — controlling my life, my decisions, my situations. But then there's the human element — how influential, how necessary, how vital other people are. And that's what makes the difference.

IOWA

AGRONOMIST

I had become far too comfortable in Minnesota and was reluctant to leave and start all over. I realized how difficult it was to say goodbye to those I met and might never see again. Plus, I had nowhere to sleep in Iowa, which made crossing the border all the more nerve-wracking. After procrastinating through the weekend, I decided to take off for Iowa Sunday evening. Just as in North Dakota, I contacted universities to find work. This time, one of them took me up: First thing Monday morning, I was to start as an agronomist at Iowa State University in Ames, almost exactly in the center of the state.

Stopping at the "Welcome to Iowa" sign, I chuckled at the clever slogan: "Fields of Opportunities." I knew I had made the right decision on a career choice in this state: Iowa's soil is considered a state treasure — "Iowa's black gold." Iowa has the world's richest and most fertile soil for farming and houses some of the world's leading agronomy institutes. There are 88,600 farms and 11,000 different types of soil in the state. Ninety percent of Iowa is devoted to agriculture — it's no wonder that it's often considered a "flyover" state. I knew agronomy was the best option for the week, but I have to admit that driving through the "fields of opportunities" was painful. The smell of manure along the way was horrific. Though I kept the windows rolled up, the stench filled my car all the way to Ames. My uncertainty about this entire venture, which had subsided, came back to me as I drove through town. It was dark outside, the street lamps were dim, and the houses big and desolate. I didn't recognize anything — there wasn't a single familiar chain restaurant, grocery store, or gas station. Many buildings were shaped like barns. Since I would be working at Iowa State University, I tried to find a neighborhood nearby that appeared safe enough to park my car and sleep for the night. I wasn't too picky, but I couldn't find a spot where I felt comfortable. I drove downtown and still couldn't find a place to park.

As drizzle turned to rain, a pit grew in my stomach. I didn't feel safe, but I had no choice. I pulled over to shift my belongings to the front of my car and prepared the blankets in the back to make enough room to sleep diagonally in the back of my Jeep. Perhaps it was the lighting on the street or movement in the adjacent houses, but I got nervous and drove another block. *This is it*, I thought, *I have no choice*. As I made a cocoon of blankets in the back of the Jeep and closed my eyes, I felt lonely and deserted. "I hope you found somewhere safe to sleep tonight," the Millers had texted me. Raindrops were pounding on the roof of my car like rocks falling from the sky. *I can't sleep through this*, I thought as my mind raced again with anxiety. *Would anyone recognize me if I told them who I am? Would anyone take me into their home if I knocked on their door?* I knew it was silly, but I was feeling increasingly desperate. I also knew it was too late to look for a better place to sleep. I just had to deal with it, listen to the raindrops, and get through the night.

Needless to say, I could hardly await 9:00 a.m. to come around so I could start my sixth job. I was eager to meet with Jamie Benning, the research assistant who was to show me the ropes for the week. As soon as we introduced ourselves, Jamie sent me to the laboratory to process soil samples. It didn't take long for the reality of the job to set in: It was tedious and I was alone. I was left by myself for hours, breaking up the soil with a sifter to the size required for accurate testing. I didn't think anyone would even notice if I was gone. *I really want to learn something.* I wasn't even sure why I was doing these tasks. The past five states had been smooth, fun, engaging, and here I was, alone in a lab doing monotonous work that I couldn't even understand. I took off my lab coat and decided to go for a walk to clear my mind. As I sneaked out, Jamie caught me in the hallway.

"Uhh . . . I'm, uh, taking a break," I told her.

"We'll have you going out into the fields if the weather gets better by Wednesday," she promised, sensing my disappointment. I couldn't help but think about the rough night I had, and I asked Jamie if she knew where else I could stay. She sent a mass e-mail to see if any students were willing to host me, but by then it was late in the day and we received no response.

I endured another night of rain pounding on my car in the same scary neighborhood as the night before. The next morning, I was exhausted and desperately needed a shower. I looked for local gyms and upon finding one was able to convince a kid working the front desk to let me sneak in. I wished I could stay at the gym a few more hours — I wasn't looking forward to going back to the lab.

Nonetheless, I resumed the menial tasks I had worked on the day before, only this time, I was joined by Charlie. He was an intern from Ecuador, and after chatting, he helped me find a place to stay the rest of the week. "People in Iowa are too nice for you to be spending nights in your car," he explained. I wish I had known that when I was thinking of knocking on doors.

A few soybeans survive in a recently harvested field as Mark, ISU's Extension Field Agronomist, examines the soil.

Charlie connected me with his friend, Aurelio, who also worked at the university. Aurelio opened his home to me and though he was busy made time to take me out to enjoy the nightlife of Ames. After staying with Aurelio, I felt rested and ready for the remainder of the week. The weather improved, so I finally had a chance to get out of the lab and drive an hour west of Ames, into the fields to analyze corn production. The plan was to work after dinner, at 1:00 p.m. "Shouldn't we have lunch first?" I asked Mark, a field agronomist. He laughed, explaining that what most of the country calls "lunch" is called "dinner" in Iowa — "dinner" is called "supper" — and we proceeded to the only place nearby that served food, a bar. It dawned on me that if a town lacks a restaurant, it would at least have a bar as a place to eat — a potentially useful discovery. We ordered the only entree on the bar's menu: Salisbury steak with peas and a slice of white bread. *Talk about a monopoly*, I thought.

When we walked out into the rows of corn, I felt nearly as lost as I had been all week in the lab. I became disoriented, so I was not too surprised when Mark told me he carries a compass to avoid getting lost in the cornfields. Thousands of cornstalks surrounded us, and to my surprise, each stalk carried only one ear of corn. As we paced through the maze, Mark instructed me to pay attention to the insects around us. He peeled open a cob and showed me nematodes burrowed into the corn. These pests can do significant damage if not controlled. My next task was to shove a three-foot probe into the dirt to retrieve soil samples. I realized that the work agronomists do, assessing the quality and fertility of the soil, is essential to cultivating crops on a large scale. At the start of the week, the work I did in the lab seemed monotonous and boring; I didn't know the meaning of any of it, how it fit in to the bigger picture. After spending time in the field with Mark, it all began to make sense, and my indifference was replaced by appreciation for our country's vast agricultural resources and those who cultivate and sustain them. I knew I could take this insight with me to Nebraska the following week where my next job was actual farming. I was relieved to be heading there, in large part because I would be staying with a friend, one fewer thing to worry about. And I was moving successfully into Week Seven.

NEBRASKA

CORN FARMER

Driving into the Cornhusker State on a two-lane highway, I was only one car in a line of many slowly following a heavy tractor that seemed to be crawling to its destination. The tractor was so wide, no one could pass, and for miles I felt as if I were in a funeral procession. To pass time, I called Sasha.

"There's something I want to talk to you about," she stated aggressively.

"What's going on?" I was nervous, but not alarmed.

"Not now, I'm with friends, we'll talk later." We hung up and my mind raced again. By now I was used to Sasha's abrasive temperament, yet I couldn't help but grow anxious as I wondered what I might have done wrong. I tried to flush the worry out of my mind and concentrate on the week ahead.

To finally arrive in Nebraska was surreal. From the outset, I planned this leg of my trip to coincide with Nebraska's corn harvest. I knew that farming is the leading industry in the state — if anyone thinks that industry is dying, I can report otherwise. True, the number of farmers is decreasing, but every farmer who remains is responsible for more land than in the past.

I didn't know how to contact farmers directly, so I arranged my Nebraska job through the Nebraska Corn Board Association, which referred me to Dave Nielsen, who owns hundreds of acres just outside Waverly, twenty miles from Lincoln. I planned to stay with my old Chicago roommate in Omaha. I was looking forward to spending time with him, but I wasn't excited about the 65-mile commute.

Throughout that day, my mind wandered until I was able to speak to Sasha again and resolve her problem. "I don't think we should talk anymore," she remarked curtly.

"What do you mean?"

"I don't feel like we can be friends, because you want something more, and we have nothing in common — there's too much of a cultural difference." Though I didn't agree, I knew where she was coming from. Until her parents sent her to Atlanta for college, Sasha's whole life had been with her family in the Middle East. As soon as school was over, she would return home. Her family would expect any man seriously involved with Sasha to return with her. In the past, Sasha had told me there was potential for us, but deep down we both knew I would never leave my family or my country to move to hers. Still, I didn't want to let her go — not just because I had feelings for her but because she had become a great friend;

after all, Sasha was the catalyst that gave me strength to embark on this journey.

I immediately tried to make Sasha change her mind, and after about twenty minutes, she agreed to keep talking to me. We had been through this before — she was hot and cold: Our friendship would be stable for a period and then she would try to end it, but I always convinced her not to. Still, we spoke every day, and I felt this latest declaration was just another episode. In any case, I certainly did not welcome the distraction; I needed to focus on my overall project, and more immediately, on farming in Nebraska.

The first few days were cold and rainy, so we couldn't go out to the fields to harvest. Instead, I spent time with Farmer Dave in his kitchen discussing his yearly operation. "I'm not only a farmer," he explained. "I also haul grain as a trucker, and I work as a financial planner, accountant, construction worker, and salesman. Working on the tractor is a very small part of the operation."

Dave took me to the local John Deere store, where we hung out for a while and everyone seemed to know everyone else. We chitchatted with other local farmers. I was impressed by Dave's knowledge — it was as if I was born yesterday and understood nothing. He knew things I'd never thought about, like the difference between sweet corn and feed corn. Dave even had a master's degree in agriculture. In addition, he built pretty much everything on his farm himself, and he taught me to become a real handyman. "It's more profitable if you're able to do things yourself," he explained.

Dave spoke openly about his family, his life, and growing up on the farmstead. I got the sense that he had a genuine desire to teach me what he did every day; he knew he was representing all farmers for my project, and I could tell he appreciated that.

Dave longed to get out to the crops and often repeated a popular Nebraska expression: "Wait five minutes and the weather will change."

Dave was right. It took longer than five minutes, but the weather suddenly became warm and sunny. We didn't waste any time and hauled 80,000 pounds of grain in his semitruck, passing endless farms, barns, silos, and water pivots on our way to grain elevators run by the local co-op. Before the co-op, AGP, paid for the grain, workers measured its moisture content, which had to be within 15 and 18 percent or Dave would be charged a penalty.

By the time we got to the fields, I understood everything Dave had explained earlier. His first order of business was to teach me to drive the auger cart, which catches the kernels dumped from the combine. "Do you know how to drive a tractor?" he asked.

"I learned in South Dakota," I replied hesitantly, as I glanced at Dave's complex machine, which was more elaborate than the one I had driven in South Dakota. I was afraid of appearing unmanly if Dave thought I wasn't up to driving the tractor. So even though I didn't know if I could operate his million-dollar machine, I decided to give it a whirl. Dave jumped into the combine and started harvesting the cornstalks while I drove alongside in the auger cart to catch the kernels. *This is so country*, I thought as I turned the radio on to a local country music station. At that moment, my dad called.

"How's everything going?" he asked.

"I'm just harvesting corn in Nebraska. Have you ever worked on a farm?" I laughed. I knew the answer was no.

"Nobody does what you do," he replied, alluding to my going against the grain, as it were.

Dave wanted to help me get some experience on a feedlot, so the following day, he arranged for me to work on one owned by Ron Raikes, a state senator. Ron knew I wasn't prepared, having never been exposed to a feedlot before. He handed me a pair of rain boots for trekking through the mud, but I couldn't tell the difference between the mud and the manure so I stepped indiscriminately in both. With my bare hands, I unloaded bales of hay, each weighing a hundred pounds, and dragged them to the feeding lines when I pulled them apart. I was constantly swatting flies off my skin and my arms were itchy and tired, my fingers aching. But despite this, I was completely distracted by the fact that I was in the middle of nowhere, completely isolated. *I never saw this coming in my life,* I

I think I know where the term "(cow)ard" came from. Every time I came close to the baby calves, they would run like the wind.

thought to myself, *breaking straws of hay in the middle of Nebraska*. It was revitalizing, and I felt I was in a place that had somehow gone undiscovered by much of the rest of the country.

Ron had mentioned that he was expecting a shipment of five hundred calves, and I knew his shipment had arrived when I saw cattle trucks approaching. The calves, separated from their mothers, moaned loudly. They would stay on the feedlot until they got good and plump, after which, their next and final destination was the slaughterhouse. "Welcome to hell," one of the farmers stated heartlessly, before spitting on one of the calves. I was overwhelmed. An hour later, Ron offered to take me out for a hamburger. Though I felt compassion for the calves, I couldn't help myself and joined him for the meal.

When I went out to lunch with Senator/Farmer Ron, a stranger came up to our booth in the diner and leaned on my chair as if he had known me for twenty years. He didn't have to be anywhere, he explained, because his land was too muddy to harvest. So he hung out with us and talked nonstop. I realized that farmers love to lean on just about any object available. Whenever I saw a farmer in a conversation, he would be leaning on a tractor tire, the hood of a truck, or whatever was in reach.

After lunch, we went back to the feedlot, and a trucker came to drop off bales of hay. I wanted to test the leaning thing on this stranger. I marched right up to his window, leaned right inside, and started talking. I don't think farmers care about knowing one another's names as long as those involved are having a friendly conversation. I hated how farmers in conversation left their truck engines running, but one explained that it takes more fuel to start a diesel truck than to leave it running.

I drove off with a tankful of gasoline fortified with ethanol, the corn-based biofuel made in the Midwest, gratified that my work on the farm would, however indirectly, help propel me through the states. I momentarily wished I could store the less expensive Midwestern gasoline somewhere, but then I noticed that with its 20 percent ethanol content, I wasn't getting very good mileage.

PUGET SOUND

WASHINGTON

IDAHO
Boise

IDAHO POTATO MUSEUM
BLACKFOOT IDAHO

2 Hitting Rock Bottom and Rebounding

WYOMING

NATIONAL PARK
SERVICE RANGER

Though I enjoyed Nebraska, I didn't mind leaving. I was passing back through South Dakota on my way to Wyoming and looked forward to visiting the new friends I had met a few weeks earlier. The Klein family was out of town on a hunting extravaganza, so I drove 550 miles straight to Rapid City to visit Sugar Ray.

It was a long drive and I couldn't help reminiscing. I thought of everything I'd been through in such a short period: wrestling a steer at the rodeo, the plane ride over Fargo, my farewell party at Metal Craft, hauling hay in Nebraska. *This is just the beginning*, I thought. I could feel myself growing comfortable with life on the road and perpetually being the new guy in town.

I was mostly lost in such pleasant thoughts, except for an aching dose of reality: I had been waiting for Sasha to return my call since leaving Omaha that morning. It was unusual and unsettling not to hear from her by midday. I knew something must be wrong, and as time wore on, I grew more concerned. I tried calling again, but without luck. I had no choice but to wait.

When I finally got to Sugar Ray's, it was like coming home to my own family again. I took up residence in the same room I had stayed in just a few weeks before, laid my bags down, and washed up for dinner. As we sat at the table, catching up on each other's lives, my phone rang. It was Sasha.

I excused myself to take her call. "Where have you been?" I asked urgently. I was still concerned that something had been wrong.

"What the hell? Why do I have so many missed calls from you?" she said abruptly. "If I was available to talk, I would have answered. You're so freaking annoying!" Her callous words shattered my heart like a rock pitched through a window.

"I was worried that something happened to you," I replied, hoping she would calm down. "I'm sorry." As my body clamped up, I knew Sugar Ray and his wife could hear our conversation from the next room. I was mortified.

"Don't call me anymore," Sasha said mercilessly.

"Are you serious? What did I do that was so bad?" I asked with desperation.

"You're a waste of time. I knew I shouldn't have been involved with you." With those words, I heard the phone go dead. I checked and realized she'd hung up on me. I tried to compose myself and sat back at the dinner table with Sugar Ray and his wife.

"What's wrong?" Sugar Ray asked. I knew I had to explain the manic conversation they'd just overheard. Sugar Ray and his wife listened empathetically.

"You don't deserve to be treated like that," they consoled me. "Move on. She sounds like a psycho." Though I knew her behavior was completely irrational, Sasha was always hot and cold and I thought I knew her better. I tried to reason with them, but they insisted that I did not deserve to be treated the way Sasha was treating me.

After dinner, I went to my bedroom to review my web site, but it didn't load. I was confused, and then noticed an e-mail from Sasha. "I deleted your web site." That was it—just one line. I couldn't believe she took it that far, and I knew there was nothing I did to warrant it. I tried to stay calm, thinking she was attempting to make a point and that it was only temporary.

"Get rid of her." Sugar Ray told me without blinking an eye. "Don't talk to her anymore. Not worth it." I went to sleep completely heartbroken. I didn't know how I could cut Sasha out of my life after the role she had in encouraging me and supporting me when no one else did.

The next morning, I wasn't ready to go to Wyoming. I couldn't put myself in another unfamiliar environment or start all over again one more time after the distress I'd felt the night before. I went to the YMCA for vigorous exercise to try to take my mind off Sasha, but ended up sobbing in the corner of the basketball court. *I've tried so hard to please her,* I thought. *There's always something wrong between us. The one person who believed in me is the one who wants to destroy me.* I couldn't believe this had happened. That night, Sasha called — twice — but I didn't answer. I was nervous, scared to be hurt again, and I knew I needed to get to Wyoming the next day and be ready to work at what I had long considered a dream job.

As a child, I always enjoyed being outside and I looked up to park rangers. Working in a park seemed like the ideal job — to be outdoors, on the trails, enjoying nature. Luckily, Wyoming is justifiably famous for its natural beauty and national parks, including Yellowstone and Grand Teton, two of the best-known parks in the country. So I was thrilled when I arranged to work as a ranger at Devils Tower National Monument in the northeast corner of the state. It was not only a fitting career choice for Wyoming, but also a personal dream come true.

The drive to Devils Tower was a metaphor for my weekend: The road was bumpy from roadkill every three hundred feet or so. As I drove farther from civilization and toward solitude, I saw Devils Tower on the horizon. I was amazed by what an impressive formation it is. I felt privileged to have the opportunity to work as a park ranger at our nation's first national monument. When I reached the security gate, I drove right through it to the ranger station where I met Ranger Julie.

"Hi Daniel. We're actually headed to rifle training today in Rapid City." I was immediately flooded with excitement.

"I'm coming too, right?" I checked to make sure.

"No, sorry, this is part of our yearly training." Just like that, my hopes shattered.

There was plenty of time to chit-chat with other rangers once the tourist season had died down.

"Well, could I go to watch?"

"No, it's on a private base."

"What am I supposed to do today?" It was pouring rain, so I knew I couldn't walk around and enjoy the grounds.

Ranger Julie was in too great a rush to care. "I'll meet with you tomorrow morning," she replied as she turned and walked away.

I sat in my Jeep bewildered and perplexed as rain crashed down on my car and the woods around me. Sasha texted me. "Please call me." I was curious. *Does she feel bad? Does she miss me?* My mind wandered, and I didn't want the questions to loom. So I called her.

"What's up?" I asked casually.

"Are you OK? I'm really sorry for what I said," she replied. I was relieved that she felt apologetic — though I wasn't entirely surprised. I had to walk on eggshells during our whole friendship. While I was shocked that she had taken it so far, it wasn't completely out of character for her moods to be extreme. Sasha continued: "I don't think we should be friends. I'm not a good person." Then she abruptly hung up the phone.

Though I felt defeated and alone, I didn't want to sit in my car all day. So despite the rain, I decided to go for a walk. I took the trail that circled the tower. I stepped off the marked path and made my way through some trees. With every step, my head pounded, my body ached, and emotion flushed through me. I looked around: I was completely alone. I felt immersed in defeat; my conversation with Sasha had conjured all my old feelings of loss and failure. Tears welled in my eyes as I stumbled to a rock, collapsed, and broke down in grief.

The stress and anxiety of the past weeks — the past years — came to the forefront of my mind: failing my last collegiate race, struggling to gain my parents' approval, getting back on the road, and striving to pull it all together. Everything I had ever been through raced through my head. I thought about my parents. *Why were they so hard on me after college?* I thought of my friends. *Would they recognize me like this?* I thought of Sasha and I felt entirely alone. *You think someone cares about you, and it's all a lie.* I couldn't breathe. My face was tingling. I sat on the rock in the rain until my head ached from weeping.

When I finally stumbled back to my car, I headed toward Hulett, the nearest town (population: 350), to find something to eat. After driving for thirty minutes, I found a bar and pulled over. As I walked in, the place fell silent. I could feel the stares of the patrons as I told the bartender my order.

"Where you coming from, honey?" The waitress asked.

"I'm working at Devils Tower for the week," I replied.

"Oh, you'll be here a week! You staying at the park?"

"No, I don't have a place to stay. There's no hotels around." I stated hopelessly.

"Hmm. Wait just a sec, OK?" she said before quickly walking away. In a few moments, she returned with the owner of the bar, whom she introduced to me.

"Where you planning to stay tonight, in your car?" Dean asked.

"Well, yeah. It's not that cold yet," I reasoned.

"It's going down to seventeen degrees tonight. Look, come back after 10:00 p.m. and I'll show you a place you could stay," he instructed.

I had nowhere to go, so I remained at the bar and digested the atmosphere, observing the locals who had spent the day working at the sawmill. Finally, Dean came back and took me to his truck, and we drove down a dirt road toward a trailer. "I bought this a couple years ago, but I never set foot in it. I thought it'd be a good invest-ment," he stated as we walked in — no key necessary. The windows were taped up, and as we entered the trailer I could feel it sway-ing back and forth from the wind. "You can stay here all week. It's better than staying in your car," Dean told me. In terms of comfort, I knew he was right; in terms of safety, I wasn't sure. To be honest, I was terrified.

When Dean left, I brought in my sleeping bag and unraveled it on the floor. I tried to fall asleep, but Sasha called again. "Did you see that your web site is back up?" she asked.

"No, I won't have Internet access for the next week or so." I told her.

"Well, I'm done helping you on it. No more updating it," she clarified frigidly.

"Listen, I'm really hurt," I tried to explain, before Sasha cut me off.

"Yeah right. You're such a liar. Have a good rest of the journey. Maybe I'll see you in Georgia." And with that, she hung up.

Sleep seemed my only refuge from the reality that had harshly settled in over the past few days. *Life on the road is lonely*, I thought. *Maybe this isn't what it's cracked up to be. What if I am a failure?* I was overcome by cynicism and defeat. There was nothing I wanted more than to my close my eyes and make the day end. As I tried to sleep, the door to the trailer kept slinging open, and I jumped up every time to make sure I was safe. *If someone killed me, no one would know*, I thought.

But I woke up the next morning and returned to Devils Tower, where I met Ranger Joe. He was from North Carolina. He took a position at Devils Tower to escape from society and retreat to nature. *He came here to escape, and I'm desperate to leave*, I thought, as we went to work patrolling the National Monument boundary. As we walked, I was mesmerized by the park's beauty, the vast grounds and swift rivers. We approached sections of the park that had been marked with flags, and Ranger Joe explained that the area remains a spiritual place for Native Americans, with specific areas designated for their ceremonies and rituals. Moving along, he asked me to check for holes in the fence from animals or illegal hunters. At times, we found the corpses of animals that had tried to leap over the fence, got stuck, and died.

I'm not sure I would have stayed if I had known what was in store for me the rest of the week. Ranger Julie wanted to show me what the maintenance crews did, so for the last few days, I was given a tiny broom to sweep the two-mile path around the tower. This was a tedious task — I had to sweep pine needles lodged in crevices of the winding path completely away. I worked for nine hours without a break for food or water. It was October (not the tourist season), so there was no one to break up my day. Spending my time in complete isolation, I reflected on how everything I'd been through with Sasha ruined my ability to enjoy Wyoming. In fact, my experience that week as a ranger crushed my childhood dream of working in the parks. The fantasy job I had envisioned was not, in reality, engaging or fulfilling to me. It was too cold to enjoy nature and too lonely to enjoy the rest. The wind blew every leaf and pine needle I swept from the path right back onto the pavement. In a way, this reminded me of my relationship with Sasha: No effort was good enough. Every time I tried to make things right, she threw the needles right back on me. Despite being hurt and confused, I was ready to sweep the memories of Wyoming behind me.

MONTANA

GENERAL STORE CLERK

Fishtail, Montana, is so small that few of the state's natives have ever heard of it, but that's where I was headed. As the road narrowed, I had a strong feeling I'd end up in a smaller town than I had ever been in. My premonition proved accurate. When I arrived, it was impossible to miss the Fishtail General Store — its sign is as big as the area's welcome sign. Fishtail boasts of thirty residents and the store is right in the middle of town. I knew right away that it is the lifeblood of the community. Montana is full of rural towns like Fishtail, where people rely on small businesses like the general store to provide for the community and help it thrive, saving the locals from having to drive many miles to larger towns to shop.

I didn't want to arrive even one day too soon. After what I'd been through in Wyoming, I was jaded and hesitant. When I finally got to Fishtail, my identity was obvious — everyone knows everyone in town, and I was clearly an outsider. Katie, the owner of the store and a ball of positive energy, welcomed me and gave me an apron for my duties in the kitchen. *I guess I won't have much time to settle in,* I thought to myself. *Then again, there's nothing to settle into — this store is the whole town.*

Katie handed me a sharp knife to cut chunks of beef for stew. "You're going to love this stew. Are you good in the kitchen?" she asked.

"I've never really cooked before," I confessed.

"Great! You're going to learn a lot this week, then!"

I continued preparing the stew as the other employees came to bake the desserts. I noticed I was the only male and mentioned it to one of my coworkers. "Yep, you're it!" she replied. "We prepare breakfast and lunch for the palladium miners who come through every day. You'll have to be up tomorrow at 4:00 a.m. to make breakfast burritos for them," she explained.

"I hope I'm not cooking all week," I replied with hesitance but my coworker's reply reassured me right away.

"You'll probably be doing everything, like all of us do. Katie's a real workhorse and makes us work at rapid speed." Though I was exhausted from the draining week preceding my arrival, I welcomed the busy atmosphere at the general store. I welcomed anything to distract me and help me move past the drama I had experienced in Wyoming.

A few hours later, Katie's husband Bill asked me to take a break so he could bring me to my room. Bill had moved to Montana from California because he liked the slow pace and the scenic outdoors. As it turned out, he and Katie gave me my own two-bedroom log cabin. "My parents used to live here, but they passed away just in time for you to stay," Bill explained. I thought back to the trailer I slept in the previous week and appreciated the extra space of my new accommodations. But regardless of size, I was without Internet access yet again. It nagged me to think about my web site—still stagnant. And I had no cell phone reception, so if Sasha even wanted to call, I wouldn't know for days. But there wasn't time to worry about this. I had to head back across the street and return to work. Bill warned me that bears lurked in the area, so I sprinted from my room to the general store to avoid any run-ins.

I worked until the store closed at 10:00 p.m., cooking and taking inventory (as I did all week), but couldn't leave until I also vacuumed, mopped, and closed out the register. Then, I had to cover the Halloween pumpkins outside the front of the store so they wouldn't freeze overnight. Finally, I returned to my cabin to retire. My energy was depleted from the drive, the long workday, and of course, the previous week. I couldn't wait to sleep. Memories of Sasha still haunted me, and since my contact with the outside world had been cut off, I was left alone with my thoughts. I knew they would likely

It didn't take long to meet everyone in town. Many locals stopped in every day to shop, eat, and socialize.

torment, but I had to get through them, reconcile myself to reality, and move on. Sasha had been a huge part of things, but the journey was still for me to fulfill. I knew every day would get better, and nothing would be as bad as the week I had just gone through. I understood, though, that I had to move forward one step at a time, even as I kept the big picture in view. I was exhausted, but keeping busy would be good for me.

Nonetheless, I didn't really want to wake up at 4:00 a.m. the next morning to open the store. But that's what the job required. When I arrived, I learned that forty to fifty miners were on their way to pick up breakfast. I realized that since I was the one who had prepared all the those meals, I would hear about it the next day if they turned out bad. Fortunately, I didn't screw up breakfast, but I did ruin dessert. My coworkers told me to make a pie and left me alone to follow the recipe. It was the first time I had ever made a pie from scratch, and I was quite pleased with myself when I pulled it out of the oven and saw that it was in perfect shape. I decided to have a bite, but instead of key lime pie, it tasted like bland lime pie. "Whoa — is it supposed to taste like this?" I asked a coworker. She agreed that the pie tasted funny, and pointing to a bag of sugar on the counter, observed, "You forgot to add the sugar." I should have known that my first-ever pie was unlikely to be perfect.

Since I had started work so early, Katie gave me the afternoon off and scheduled a horseback-riding trip with a neighbor for me. If I hadn't practiced riding in South Dakota, I would have been nervous about the terrain. At some places along the way, I had to get off and walk the horse up the steep, winding slope. We went straight up on icy paths, eventually climbing to a view overlooking the Beartooth Mountains. Montana's big skies seemed to stretch out for eternity. It felt therapeutic to be disconnected for a moment, away from the noise of the store, and the noise of my own thoughts. There was nothing to do but absorb the world around me. I felt humbled by the mountains and calmed by the atmosphere.

Unfortunately, the moment was fleeting as I returned straight to the store for the evening. The same customers would come in all week, and we became friendly with one another as the days passed. Nonetheless, there wasn't much to do in Fishtail, especially at night. Since it was the opening of hunting season, the store was unusually busy and I helped Katie keep the shelves stocked. Once a week, she drives to Billings, the largest city in Montana, to buy supplies, so I joined her for that outing while I was there. She enjoyed bragging to her vendors that I had chosen to work with her. In Billings, we visited Mennonites for eggs, went into twenty-degree freezers for poultry, and picked up bread from the baker.

Before the week ended, Katie set up another adventure: hunting with her friend Rick and his son. They were selective about what to shoot, and we waited for hours before they finally decided on the right buck. They were intent on choosing one big enough to make the hunt worthwhile. After they finally bagged the animal, we made deer stew in the store kitchen. As a parting gift, Katie gave me a free tank of gas, and I headed in the dark toward Idaho. I had arrived that week feeling demoralized and disheartened, but my time in Montana was calming and proved therapeutic. As I navigated through parades of deer on the road, I reflected on the week and felt my spirit was renewed. Montana had a healing effect; my energy was restored. I was ready to move on, and I looked forward to Boise, where I'd be staying with some college friends.

IDAHO

REAL ESTATE AGENT

I didn't expect my next destination to be so distant, but the highway twisted and turned before spitting me out in Boise. It was a tense 620-mile drive plagued by storms and semi-trucks. I drove slowly and cautiously; I even pulled over a few times so the trucks could pass. The storm, on the other hand, would not subside. I had to take my chances to make it to Earl and Kayla's before dark. I was excited to see them again — we had been friends since college, and they were still the easy-going, down-to-earth, bohemian type of people I first knew in our student days. There was no question that I'd feel at home staying with them.

As soon as I arrived, dinner was prepared. Without a doubt, the meal included potatoes. Knowing that Idaho is famous for potatoes, I was surprised not to see potato farms on the way to Boise. I did spot a potato museum and a Heinz Ketchup factory. After the meal, I couldn't resist: I dug into the trash searching for the potato sack to see where the potatoes had come from: Oregon. I searched the pantry for a potato chip bag to check on their origin: Washington. *I guess Idaho exports its crops*, I thought to myself.

Potato farming was a predictable career for Idaho, but I did not want to repeat farming. After learning that Boise has the most booming real estate market of any city in America, with three thousand licensed agents, I figured I had a good chance of getting a job in that sector. I connected with brokers who helped me network with agents. Ultimately, I found Megan, an agent with RE/MAX, who allowed me to jump on board with her for a week. It was the first job on my trip requiring that I dress to impress. I had to dig deep into my suitcase for something decent to wear.

When I met Megan, she didn't fit the stereotype of an agent. Most agents I've known were middle-aged, but Megan was only nineteen. After talking to her, I learned many people in Idaho, like Megan, marry while still in their teens and start families early. I was under the impression that most agents practiced real estate as a side job, but Megan works at it full-time. She was thoroughly professional, actively marketing herself and relying on a web site she designed that attracts clients from around the country. As we drove together to check on a current listing, Megan received calls from Alaska, Montana, Arizona, and California. Most clients were from California. The flood of outsiders fueled a boom in Boise that occurred over the course of Megan's life. For much of that time, many homes were investment properties, but by the time I arrived, quite a few were listed as short sales or foreclosures.

Megan taught me that you need to be flexible in the real estate business — there are no set work hours. Your success depends on how much effort you put into the business. During the week, Megan had me take measurements, snap photos, and make estimates on the selling price. We spent hours showing homes to families from out of state. Megan told me she showed forty-seven homes to the same person in one day, and he didn't consider buying any of them. In contrast, she once showed one client a single home and he bought it immediately. It all depends on the buyer.

That week, I enjoyed staying with Earl and Kayla — I could unwind with them every evening, and my troubles seemed to grow more distant. I knew each day would bring another opportunity to move on from my plummet in Wyoming. I felt a sense of accomplishment

Agent Megan Schomer showing this beautiful mansion to potential buyers in Boise.

with real estate, too — a competitive vibe that I welcomed. It wasn't difficult to focus on enjoying the week and trying to make a sale.

Toward the end of my tenure in Boise, a local news team came to cover my story and arranged to film Megan and me at an open house. Megan scheduled a one-hour event especially for this TV segment. I had asked Earl and Kayla to stop by and pose as potential homebuyers, and showed them around the house as the news team shadowed us.

Because of our efforts to get a sale that week, sure enough, we closed a deal, selling a home to a real family of four. I felt accomplished to have a part in the sale. I knew it was legit when Megan marked me down as coagent. To celebrate, she took me out in her monster truck for an ice cream potato: vanilla ice cream covered with brown powder and shaped like a potato. The whipped cream on top emulated sour cream. With that, I finally got to eat an Idaho potato.

WASHINGTON

MARINE BIOLOGIST

As soon as it started raining, I knew I had crossed the border into Washington. Doug Myers was the head biologist of People for Puget Sound, and I was eager to get to Olympia to meet him. We had been in touch by phone over a period of ten weeks as I prepared for a job as a marine biologist, but before I started, Doug suggested that I sit in on a hands-on class at Pierce College.

The class was "Introduction to Marine Biology." I knew it would be tough to immerse myself in a new academic discipline and learn new terminology quickly. After spending time in the classroom, we went out to the water in waders to collect fish. This reminded me of my week as a hydrologist, only the sea water wasn't as rough as the fast-moving high-mountain streams of Colorado.

I chose marine biology for Washington because the state is known for its commitment to conservation and environmental protection. I was aware that its great inland bay, Puget Sound, is threatened by development and that biologists are playing a central role in the fight to protect it. I wanted to be a part of this effort and learn more about how people working together can change public policy. By cold-calling companies and organizations, I eventually found Doug. Curious about where my project would lead, he proved eager to contribute. Weeks before, Doug had offered me a place to stay, so after class, we drove to his house, and I settled in. I wasn't surprised to find an aquarium there.

That night, my parents called. "What's going on with your web site? You haven't had an update in weeks," my dad asked.

"Yeah, I just haven't had time to work on it; my cousin flaked out and I'm too busy," I explained. I didn't want to confess that Sasha had helped me up to now. Thinking about it still stung. It reminded me of how much I had relied on Sasha and of the void left by her not wanting to be a part of my project — or my life.

"Why didn't you tell us? We'll help you find someone to take it over," my mom offered, suggesting I hire a web designer to maintain the site. After I was featured on CNN, my parents were on board with my project and wanted to help me succeed. The void Sasha created when she abandoned my site was filled by my parent's support when they helped me get it back up.

The next morning, I woke at 4:00 a.m. to search for future jobs in upcoming states. At that point, it was the norm to get so little sleep. The pressure was on to line up work, and I needed every spare moment to research prospects and compile notes and contact lists to reference when I made calls during my lunch hours or breaks from work.

At 6:00 a.m., Doug and I caught the train to Seattle, where his office is located. We had several meetings to attend that afternoon, including a very rare one: The People for Puget Sound board of directors was gathering to revise the organization's Action Agenda. This critical meeting, which sets priorities for the decade and is the basis for seeking grants that fund the work, is informed by ten years of scientific study and, likewise, takes place only once every ten years. I felt enormously lucky and privileged to attend.

The material was over my head. Everyone spoke in unfamiliar acronyms, and during the breaks, I needed Doug to translate for me. Despite being unable to keep up, I well understood the significance of the meeting, and I wanted to contribute. But I held my tongue, aware that I really had little to add to this impressively informed discussion.

That week, I also attended a yearly conference hosted by People for Puget Sound. Doug outlined plans for restoring Puget Sound

Doug taking photo-points, pictures of the same scene at different points in time, of washed-up logs, nature's way of preventing erosion.

and encouraged the community to contribute to the effort. It was obvious that Doug loathed developments that degrade the environment, but getting contributions to remedy the damage was difficult in the dismal economy.

Initially, with all the meetings we were involved in, I was frustrated that we weren't out in the field more often, as I had been when I worked in hydrology and agronomy. I thought we would spend time in scuba gear, working underwater. But later in the week, Doug brought me to Seahurst Beach for some fieldwork. For five years, the beach had been a restoration project that aimed to undo damage from retaining walls designed to prevent erosion. Doug had me take photo-points, pictures of the same scene at different points in time, of logs that had washed onto the shore, creating a natural retaining wall. Doug also took me to see a marsh in Edmonds, which survived next to an oil refinery. The city was trying to convert the space to a parking lot for the ferry. The People for Puget Sound were trying to preserve that area for the fishery it helps support. Despite the long struggle, it appeared that the parking lot would be constructed in the end.

Later, Doug took me to see salmon spawning in a stream along a hiking trail. Salmon are born in rivers, migrate to the deep ocean, and after five years return to their place of birth to lay eggs and die. The area smelled like rotting skunk, with dead salmon washed up all along the riverbank. Still, there is something bizarrely beautiful about the life cycle of these fish. It reminded me of the saying "ashes to ashes, dust to dust," and reinforced the idea that a starting place and end-point are minor considerations compared with the journey itself — and the legacy left behind. It was an amazing experience, to gain an understanding from direct observation of the powerful role of instinct in salmon and of the vital importance of keeping our rivers, bays, and the ocean pure.

The week had been more educational than hands-on; Doug did not give me independent responsibilities, but he included me in everything he did. During downtime, I threw myself into my overall project. Every night, I wrote in my web-site travel journal, uploaded photos and videos, and researched jobs. I worked on my contact lists, sent e-mails to the Millers and Kleins, phoned Sugar Ray and Katie, and reflected on my conversations with Megan, Stefanie, Earl and Kayla. I updated everyone on where I was and what I was doing. I read materials relevant to jobs I had lined up. My spare time completely evaporated as work took over. I had already invested myself by committing to the trip, but as my week in Washington came to an end, I was giving it every ounce of energy, letting go of distractions and my emotions. This trip would be what I made it; it was all up to me. I had hit rock bottom in Wyoming — I never felt so alone as I did that day I arrived at Devils Tower. In Montana and Idaho, I was still haunted by those memories. Perhaps they will always haunt me. But from that low, I rebounded. There I was, about to start Week Twelve; I was a long way from when I started, and there was a long way left to go. I was ready.

Medford

Las Vegas

3 Turning Obstacles into Openings

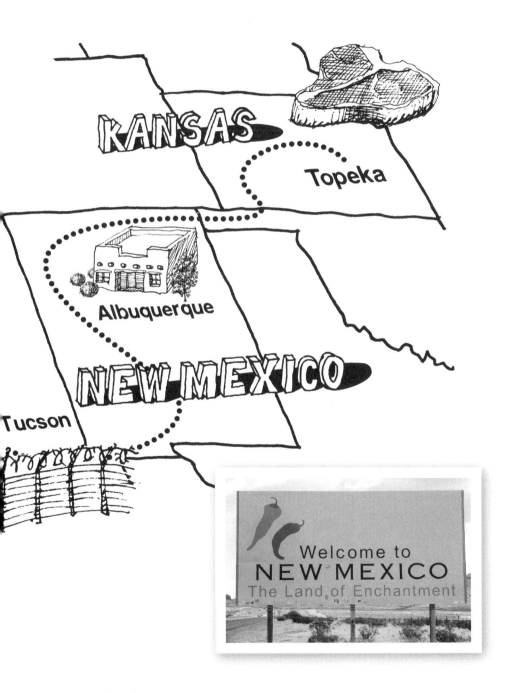

Welcome to
NEW MEXICO
The Land of Enchantment

OREGON

LOGGER

Just as I crossed the Columbia River into Oregon, my brother called. It was getting late and I didn't feel like answering, so I let the call go. The moment I heard his message, however, I was shocked at the news: I was on the front page of Yahoo!

I sped off the next exit of the highway and checked my GPS for the nearest hotel. I searched frantically for Internet access. When I arrived at the hotel, I rushed through the lobby to hunt for a computer, pride and disbelief racing through me simultaneously. Yahoo was my e-mail provider, my web-site host, my main source of news, and for years I checked Yahoo first thing whenever I went online. It was surreal to think that this time I would find myself on the front page. Beyond that, I knew that being featured on Yahoo would do wonders for the visibility of my project.

When I found the computer room at the hotel, I anxiously pushed my way to a seat. "I'm on the news!" I shouted, and as others looked on in surprise, we read the headline: "Man attempts to work 50 jobs in 50 states in 50 weeks." The article sparkled at me from the screen like a million-dollar diamond. I started cheering and ran outside. I felt a surge of confidence and energy. Adrenaline was pumping through my veins and I felt invincible. In my euphoria, I thought it was the perfect moment to call Sasha. After three anxious rings, someone answered with a foreign accent. "May I speak to Sasha?" I asked.

When she replied, "you have the wrong number," I realized I was speaking to Sasha, who was pretending to be someone else. I was hurt, but not defeated.

"Well, tell her to look at the front page of Yahoo," I blurted and hung up, hoping she would call me back.

I was headed to Eugene, my old college town — finally, a city I was familiar with. I had attended the University of Oregon for three years before transferring to USC. Six years had passed since I was last in Oregon. With not much time to reminisce, I drove straight to the Hometown Buffet, which had given me my first job ever, as a dishwasher. When I arrived, I walked straight to the back of the restaurant, eager to see if I'd recognize anyone. I immediately spotted Carlos. He was standing in the same spot washing the same plates we had washed together six years earlier. We couldn't talk much because he still didn't know English and I still didn't know Spanish — but I was moved to see him again. *Here he is, committed to the same job for six years or more,* I thought, *while I'm bouncing around from state to state.* I instantly felt appreciation for Carlos and his fortitude. Though we couldn't communicate verbally, I grabbed him and gave him a hug, and he knew I had missed him.

The following afternoon, I drove south through thick fog to Medford. Ed Hanscom, my boss for the week, had reserved a room for me at a hotel — it was my first since starting the journey. It felt strange to arrive without the usual introductions that are always part of staying with a family. My hosts always asked lots of questions and, tired from traveling, I usually had to summon the energy to answer them. But this wasn't required at the hotel. I have to admit, I enjoyed the quiet of my commercial accommodations after the long drive, especially knowing that Ed would pick me up at 5:00 a.m. the next morning to start my week as a logger.

Since the early 1900s, Oregon has been considered the timber state of the nation; there's a greater variety of tree species there than anywhere else in the country. So working as a logger was a good fit. Before departing from California, I had arranged a job working for a helicopter-logging company, but it went out of business just before I arrived. I had spent months landing the position and would need weeks at least to find a comparable one. The sudden reversal made me realize that it wasn't enough to have a job lined up; to be on the safe side, I also needed a back-up plan. Fortunately, I was spared unexpected unemployment in this case. The helicopter-logging company had thoughtfully contacted H&M Logging on my behalf, and that's how I came to hear from Ed Hanscom. It was a pleasant surprise to get the offer from H&M, and the outlook brightened further when I arrived for my first day of work.

The job was everything I wanted one to be: I was surrounded by 300-foot Douglas firs, the air was crisp and inviting, and rays of sun beamed down through the forest canopy. As I stood overwhelmed with admiration, Ed addressed safety issues. I signed a release and was issued a hardhat, thick gloves, heavy rain jacket, and pair of steel-toed boots, but no safety glasses, which surprised me. The only thing left to do was grow a beard and start working.

Ed assigned me to work with Bill, a seasoned logger, who, when we approached, was in the midst of axing a six-foot-wide trunk. I noticed a cluster of spare chains hanging out of Bill's back pocket; just as construction workers always carry a pouch of nails, loggers, I realized, always carry chains. As the tree started to sway and cackle, Bill turned to run from it. "Don't try this at home!" he warned, quickly adding that a close friend had died doing this work, after tripping on some limbs and being crushed by the falling tree.

When Bill's tree fell, the earth shook and the report echoed through the forest. After several hours with Bill, Ed returned to pick me up and take me to the skidding and stroking crew. We approached the worksite, known as the landing, where a five-man crew was enjoying lunch. It had not occurred to me to bring a lunch, so I was grateful when one of the loggers offered me donuts. I didn't realize how far we'd be from civilization and it didn't occur to me that there wouldn't even be a water fountain nearby. I decided to just sit on a stump and enjoy getting to know my new coworkers.

Stacey operated the stroker, the most expensive and impressive machine I'd ever seen. It picked up fallen trees, cut them into sections, sheared them of limbs, and placed them in a loading zone

Bill just getting started on an hour-long effort to cut down this Douglas fir. He engineers the cuts to angle the fall precisely where he wants it.

to be hauled. My job was to brand the logs according to the mill to which they were to be delivered. It was a simple task but required running in heavy boots and dodging three potentially fatal machines while watching for previously cut branches — and fast. As soon as I branded one side of a log, I had to brand the other side, and always, another log was waiting.

After six hours of branding, I couldn't wait until the horn blew to announce quitting time. At 5:30 p.m., we finally got into the trucks to leave. As we emerged from the forest, I regained cell phone reception and eight voicemails came through. To my surprise, CNN, *World News Tonight*, *Inside Edition*, and *The Tonight Show* had all found my number. I was ecstatic; my project was getting more visibility than I ever imagined. At the first opportunity, I called the networks to schedule appearances.

The next morning, Stacey and crew picked me up at 3:30 a.m. By the time we got to the forest, it was five o'clock in the morning. I was dreaming of cutting down a tree of my own, but I could barely use the three-foot, sixty-pound chainsaw. Ed came over to train me, but I couldn't even start it up. Every time I pulled the throttle, I lost my grip over the machine. So my coworkers would start the chainsaw for me and I would cut limbs off trees that had already fallen. After walking in their boots, I started to genuinely appreciate the hard work loggers do and their specialized training.

It was 6:00 p.m. by the time we left the forest. After stopping at the liquor store on the way home, it was nearly eight o'clock. Stopping at the liquor store was mandatory every day after work. It seemed like vacation time, a vital suspension from the rigors of the job. I stretched my legs as my coworkers went in to buy cigarettes and beer. They came out and we all climbed back into the truck. As they lit their cigarettes, I rolled my window down. One of them turned to me and asked, "Do you have any bad habits."

"I guess I haven't been logging enough," I teased.

When we returned to the forest the next day, it felt like I had never left. As the temperature dropped, we started a bonfire to keep warm. Employees from the U. S. Forest Service (USFS) drove by to monitor our operation, and Ed argued with them over the boundaries. We could only cut trees that were marked; otherwise H&M Logging would be assessed a $10,000 penalty per unauthorized tree. Later I spoke to Ed about the environmental hazards of harvesting timber. "It enhances the wildlife habitat and improves the quality of wood," Ed asserted. This made sense, but the positive effects wouldn't become apparent for at least fifty years.

The day wore on and I wore out. Every morning, my eyes burned from lack of sleep. My body ached for more rest; I was too drained to think logically. I couldn't imagine working another day.

Still, I woke up the next morning at the usual 2:30 a.m. to get ready for my final day of work. I went downstairs for breakfast and waited for Stacey to pull up in his truck. As I walked up to grab the door handle, I flashed on all the recent memories of working in the Rogue River-Siskiyou National Forest: running around the trees, dodging machinery, lugging the chainsaw, and the seventeen-hour workday. "Stacey, I don't think I'm going to come today." The words floated out of my mouth before I realized what I'd said. A millisecond later, I couldn't believe I had backed down on my last day work. I was ashamed. I couldn't handle a single week of something Stacey does year after year; yet I knew I truly could not handle one more day.

"All right, man; it was great meeting you. Keep in touch," Stacey shouted over the engine of his truck.

I went back to my room to lie down, overwhelmed with disappointment in myself. *I can't do this again,* I thought, determined never to back out of a day of work — ever. Later that day, I planned to head home to California for Thanksgiving break — and a break was exactly what I needed.

Thanksgiving

When I arrived home, my parents treated me like a different person. They treated me with respect. They were impressed with me. My dad expected me back after Week Three, but now that I was en route to Week Thirteen, he applauded me. When I set out on this project, my parents considered me a failure. But I defied them, refusing to accept their view. I did what I believed. I did not want to limit myself. I followed my instincts and launched my project, pushing it closer to fruition than they could imagine. Now, on my first homecoming, I knew my parents believed in me and respected me for taking control over my life. They were shocked to learn of the media interviews I had set up over the break, too. Then my mom asked the burning question: "What does Sasha think about all this?"

"I don't know. I haven't heard from her in a month," I replied. It made me sad to think that I couldn't share my experiences with Sasha, but I had to keep going. People were rooting for me, encouraging me to continue. I had received e-mails from supporters all over the world, commending my journey.

Your experience could serve the great example of human power under the economic crisis process around the world! Also You demonstrated the possibilities of american way of life-now in huge

Russia, namely in Siberia, where I am living, this experience of such mobile working, is impossible. But we hoping that You personally can show good example of optimism and skill for our young people. I wish You all the best —Irina

The encouragement I received from strangers like Irina helped fill the void created when Sasha started to ignore me. For the first time in my life, I felt wanted.

Later in the weekend, I contacted a close friend of Sasha's online. I had met him when I lived in Atlanta. Though I ostensibly called it just catching up with him, my true objective was to find out what Sasha was doing and if she had feelings for me. "Have you talked to Sasha lately, now that you're a celebrity?" he finally asked.

"No, I haven't. She doesn't want to talk to me anymore," I answered.

"Really? That's a surprise," he wrote. "She really likes you a lot." This was information that she had never admitted. I couldn't believe it. "She probably knows it's not going to work, you know, with the cultural differences," he continued. It was a familiar story, but our conversation gave me just an ounce of hope as I made my way to Nevada.

NEVADA

VEGAS WEDDINGS COORDINATOR

I was back on the road, but this time I left my parent's driveway with more confidence and certainty. The drive to Las Vegas needed at least a day and a half, so I aimed to get to Barstow, California, by the end of the first day. Wary, as usual, of spending money unnecessarily, I parked my car outside a motel. Sleeping across the back of the Jeep was starting to take a toll on my neck;

needless to say, I didn't get much rest. The next morning, I continued the drive from Barstow to "Sin City," and searched for a YMCA when I arrived so I could take a shower. I had arranged to work at a wedding chapel and did not want to show up looking like a mess.

At the YMCA, I took some time to exercise before hitting the showers. When I got back to my locker, I noticed my shoes had been moved slightly and suddenly realized that my wallet was gone. I hastily dressed and ran out to find an employee. We soon learned that my wallet had been turned into the front desk, but the money was gone. It was just another punch I had to roll with; I was trying to accept the things I couldn't change and so I made an effort not to let this incident ruin my first day of work.

When I arrived at Vegas Weddings, I introduced myself to the people in the reception area. They seemed uninterested in conversing, so I went upstairs to meet Linda, the owner of the chapel. Working there wasn't my first choice career for Las Vegas. For eight months, I tried to land a position as a hotel manager. There was not one hotel I didn't contact or one that was willing to hire me. Finally, I decided there was no better alternative in the wedding capital of the world than working at a Vegas chapel. Vegas Weddings, conveniently close to the courthouse, performs 6,000 weddings every year. The chapel is very busy and Linda always has lots to do, so she started my training immediately.

First, she sent me down to the reception area to learn about the chapel's options and rates by working with the two women at the desk, but I didn't get a good vibe from them. It was instinctual. One never bothered to acknowledge me and the other looked like she hadn't smiled a day in her life; she glared at me with disgust whenever I spoke. Nonetheless, on that first day, I experienced five wedding ceremonies, including those performed at the chapel's walk-up window and drive-thru. The first couple of the day sauntered through the lobby as if they were there to order a pizza. "What's today's date?" one bride asked as she filled out the paperwork. Despite seeming cavalier about the marriage, they ended up crying during the ceremony.

I was trying to have a good time with the job, but the negative vibes at the front desk didn't cease and were really getting to me. Beyond that, I didn't have a place to sleep and didn't even know if I would earn a paycheck. To top it all off, *World News Tonight* was planning to film me work, and I knew the publicity would benefit the chapel. As these factors gained momentum inside me, I decided to confront Linda in her office.

"How's your first day?" She asked.

"To be honest, I am not sensing good vibes here." I knew I needed to be straightforward with Linda or I wouldn't feel right all week. "The ladies downstairs are not friendly at all, I don't have a place to stay, and you guys are going to have so much publicity when *World News Tonight* comes. I'm getting the short end of the stick." It made me nervous to be so blunt with Linda, but I needed to be true to myself; otherwise, I would have beat myself up all week. I was ready to look for another chapel if I needed to.

"I am sorry you feel that way." Linda replied defensively.

"Well, do you know anyplace I could stay? Otherwise I'm going to have to sleep in my car again tonight."

"Let me see what we can do . . . . We'll take care of things." From her reassurance, I felt Linda was starting to empathize with me. I was right: Three hours later, I was sprawled across a king-size bed in a room at a hotel called The Orleans. *They sure did take care of things,* I said to myself.

Well-rested and full of energy the next morning, I was ready to take on anything. I asked if I could drive the chapel's limousine to pick up and drop off couples. Despite hesitation on Carl's part — he's Linda's business partner — Gus, the limo driver, somehow convinced him to let me do it. Driving around Vegas was much harder than it looked; luckily I had Gus to assist me through the Strip. He was so focused on making sure I made no mistakes, however, that we inadvertently dropped a couple off at the wrong hotel.

Later in the week, *World News Tonight* came as scheduled. The crew, two reporters and two cameramen, shadowed me at work. I felt pretty important with a news team following me, but I knew my

This couple was probably tired of seeing me as their one-man band: limo driver, florist, reverend, and photographer.

colleagues were looking at me and treating me differently. The way they acted seemed unnatural. Witnessing this, I knew I had made the right decision when I declined my own television show at the start of this project. I knew that the constant presence of camera crews would have affected my experience. Still, I didn't mind working with a news team for a few days, because, unlike a reality-television show, their purpose was to broadcast my mission to the country, and the visibility could help inspire others. They weren't scripting my actions. And, of course, the attention would help me with personal networking and setting up jobs down the road.

That week, Linda gave me all sorts of tasks. I went from being a florist, photographer, and decorator to a hand-biller and, inevitably, a reverend. In fact, I devoted my last two days to preparing for my big debut as a Las Vegas reverend.

I spent some time researching marriage vows on the Internet. More important, I needed to look the part. Luckily, I found a gown to wear as I made my way to the office one morning. I put it on and when I arrived at the chapel, I spotted my victims. They knew I was their reverend because of my gown, but they were surprised to find that I didn't fit the stereotype of a calm, elderly reverend. Instead, I was new, young, and nervous.

In fact, I had never been that nervous before. My heart was throbbing, my hands were sweaty, and my legs felt like Jello. There was a great deal of pressure not to screw up the wedding ceremony, and as my anxiety built up, all eyes were eagerly watching me. I pulled my notes from my pocket, my hands trembling. "He's more nervous than we are," the bride said to the groom. I managed to remember their names, but completely blanked on what came next. I asked for some assistance from Reverend Joe. "You can do it." He was right, I did do it, but I didn't do it well and was so uncomfortable with my performance, I did not care to try again.

Later, when I went to put the gown back where I'd found it, Reverend Julie ran toward me. "That's my robe!" she cried. "That's mine! I never let anyone touch my stuff!"

"Oh, I didn't know that; I thought it was the chapel's," I tried to explain. She broke down sobbing. I felt awkward and unsure of how to react, so I apologized and slowly walked away.

As the week wrapped up, I felt I had accomplished everything I'd set out to do at the chapel. I didn't care much for all the duties, but I loved the atmosphere of Las Vegas. I couldn't get enough of the lights on the Strip, the all-you-can-eat buffets, and the action around the casinos. That week, the National Rodeo Finals took place in the arena of my hotel, bringing me back to my South Dakota days. I even ran into Miss South Dakota, whom I had met ten weeks before. Oddly, though, I felt I had moved on from that part of my life. Maybe in ten weeks, I would feel the same way about Nevada. For now, I was focused on my next state, Arizona.

ARIZONA

UNITED STATES BORDER PATROL AGENT

From the beginning, I had my mind set on working on the Arizona border. As I drove from Nevada through the cool desert, I couldn't help but recall my struggle to land a position with the Border Patrol. Counting our borders with Canada and Mexico, this federal agency patrols over 6,000 miles. The Tucson sector of the border with Mexico has the highest drug and illegal immigrant traffic anywhere in the system. And that's where I wanted to work. While the choice of career was clear, however, finding a position was nearly impossible.

Nine months earlier, I called the office overseeing the Tucson sector to look into working there as an agent. I was told it takes nineteen weeks just for training. Beyond that, I'd need a background check and knowledge of basic Spanish. "If you contact the headquarters in Washington, D.C., they might be interested in helping you," I was advised. So I immediately called the Department of Homeland Security and spoke to the Head of Public Relations, who suggested I send a proposal of my objectives. When I followed up, I hit another wall: "I'm sorry Daniel, but you need press credentials to do something like this. There's a huge risk and liability unless you're a part of another entity."

I had already promised myself that nothing would stop me from working on the border. Before long, it occurred to me that I was given a press badge when I wrote for my local newspaper in California. I knew immediately that this was the ticket. I called all newspapers in Arizona and asked for a position as a reporter.

No one bought into it. The papers wouldn't even allow me to be a guest writer. Finally, after sending a writing sample to a smaller publication, *Explorer News*, I got the press badge I needed. I was excited about the week ahead: I secured the job I wanted, the weather wasn't too hot, and I would be staying with the Rafats in the mountains near Tucson.

The Rafats are part of my extended family, but they had no idea what I was doing. They thought I was moving to Arizona and, given my career choice, they were concerned for my safety. I told them I was only working for a week, but they were still confused when I walked out their front door to my first day on the job.

I arrived at the Border Patrol office knowing I might experience situations I've only seen in movies. As I waited for Agent Scioli, I filled out a release form, finishing just before he rushed in. "Come on Daniel, let's go. Hop into my SUV."

We became acquainted on our drive down to Nogales, a city split by the United States/Mexico border. Agent Scioli was young but serious, with a businesslike demeanor. He had eight years of experience on the border and came from a line of law enforcement officers in New York. "We're working the busiest border in the country. Just this sector alone, we arrest 575,000 people a year," he informed me. "We're on our way now to track two men reportedly trying to hitchhike." Within ten minutes we spotted them along the shoulder of the freeway, in heavy clothing and baseball caps. Other agents were already on the scene, so we pressed on to Nogales.

As we continued south, I noticed the kilometer signs, and reality sank in. "How far do you think those guys walked?" I asked.

"Probably hundreds of miles." Agent Scioli replied. I couldn't imagine their plight in the summer months. "They're caught now, but they'll try again once we deport them," he continued. "We keep them in the detention center until they are processed and then leave them on the other side of the line," Agent Nogales said, referring to the fence along the border. "We'll be driving that today."

When we reached "the line," we got out of the SUV to inspect the newly installed steel fence. Roughly fifteen feet high, it did not extend up into the mountains.

"Can't they hike up there and walk around the fence?" I asked.

"They could, but they would have to come back down to get into the city – and we have all of that covered," Agent Scioli replied. I spotted some men with binoculars on Mexico's side and asked about them. "Those are what we call 'scouts' or 'smugglers.' Believe it or not, but many of them are Americans who help smuggle in illegal immigrants; they get paid between $500 and $20,000 per person," he explained before suddenly urging me to get back into the SUV. As I looked around, I realized rocks were being thrown from the other side of the fence.

"This is their way of distracting us while they try sneaking over or under," Agent Scioli told me, as he leaned into the center of the vehicle in case a rock shattered one of the passenger windows.

"What do we use for protection?"

"Most of the time we don't need deadly force, so we carry a baton and a pepperball gun."

After evading the rocks, we prepared for a hike, which meant filling jugs of water. "Most of the time, especially in the summer, we capture illegals that are dehydrated from walking in this desert," Agent Scioli went on. "We're not going to let them die, so we act as a rescue team. We know 90 percent of the time, illegals are just looking for a better life. The other 10 percent are convicts, drug smugglers, murderers, and those are the ones we really try to capture.

"It's nearly impossible to spot an illegal out here because they blend in with the locals. The only thing that might set them apart is their nervousness. If people act worried or scared, that's when we bust them."

As our hike continued, Agent Scioli taught me how to track a "foot sign." Footprints could lead to an illegal immigrant, but the tracks we followed only led us to a lone tree. But it looked like illegals had been there, probably to rest in the shade. The only things left behind were clothing, water jugs, and a backpack, which held a wallet with 200 pesos and an identification card. "You can take the money if you want," Agent Scioli offered. As the first day came to a close, I returned to the Rafats relieved I had made it through the day unharmed. They were relieved too; they had been pacing back and forth before I arrived, worrying about me.

The next day, Agent Scioli and I drove back down to Nogales, and when we got there, we went underground into the sewer system. "Two days ago, we caught eighty people crawling down here," he told me. I was shocked by how dark and narrow the tunnel was — and could barely imagine trying to inch through it. "This is an easier tunnel to go through. Sometimes they dig their own hole and burrow into someone's living room, where they would camp out until they're clear," he said.

"Why would the residents take that risk of helping an illegal immigrant?" I asked.

"Money," Agent Scioli replied, matter-of-factly.

The smell in the tunnel was almost overpowering, and I felt I might vomit. I couldn't wait to get out of there, so quickly climbed the ladder back to street level ahead of Agent Scioli. As I reached the top, a Border Patrol SUV pulled up. "How's it going there?" an agent asked. It was clear that he mistook me for an illegal.

"Great, now that I'm in America," I joked. As Agent Scioli approached behind me, the agent drove off, without acknowledging my attempt at humor. Later, we visited the detention center. The cells were filled, and despite being caught, the inmates appeared to be in good spirits. When I passed by holding my camera in its case, everyone waved and posed for photos. They seemed little worried about what was going to happen to them. In the absence of harsh penalties for crossing the border illegally, it seems there are more consequences to trying to sneak into a concert than into this country.

During the week, agents trained me to use a pepperball gun, which is filled with baby powder and used to cause a distraction. It reminded me of using a paintball gun, but it has slightly more power. Toward the end of the week, I visited the dope room. Thousands of pounds of drugs may be confiscated in a single day, so the volume

Standing in the dope room with forty pounds of marijuana attached to my back, I couldn't imagine what it would be like to walk hundreds of miles through the hot desert and smuggle it over the border.

of contraband is impressive. I strapped forty pounds of drugs onto my back to test the weight; I couldn't imagine walking hundreds of miles with it in the desert. The very idea seemed outrageous.

After submitting my guest article to *Explorer News*, I was overcome with a sense of melancholy. The week had ended, but I had just started to feel at home with the Rafats. I was becoming attached. When I gave them goodbye hugs, I wanted to admit that I was scared and that I didn't want to leave; I didn't want to face another uncertain environment. It was wearing on me mentally to start over every week. As I pulled out of their driveway, my throat choked up and my eyes teared. *Don't worry, this feeling won't last*, I encouraged myself, and tried to focus on the drive ahead to New Mexico.

NEW MEXICO

LANDSCAPE ARCHITECT

During the drive, I dropped a card in the mail for Sasha. It was almost December 22 — a full year since I promised I'd buy her a scooter. *As promised, I'm sending you the key to the scooter. I'll be on CNN next week — hope you get a chance to catch me*, I wrote. Though we hadn't spoken, I wanted to stay true to my promise. Part of me hoped she'd come around or was secretly following me on my journey, and I just wanted a reason to remind her of me. At the same time, by doing this, I was letting her know I had made it, and if she didn't respond after that, then maybe she really wasn't worth it. As I mailed the card, I made the decision not to worry or stress about her anymore. Instead, I'd wait patiently till my return to Atlanta — maybe by then she'd have the space she needed.

Driving across the border and into the dusty New Mexico terrain, I was greeted by a welcome sign illustrated with chili peppers. The winds hit sixty miles per hour as I made my way to Albuquerque. I passed more signs. One warned of dust storms and another displayed martini glasses behind the strike-out symbol to warn against drunk driving. I was in no rush. I didn't have a place to sleep and wasn't looking forward to another cold night tossing and turning in my Jeep.

At this point in my journey, driving six hundred miles in one day was typical. Skipping meals to save money was the norm. Beyond that, it was common practice to spend the first night in my Jeep; I would arrive in a new place late Sunday night, sleep in the Jeep, and hope to find a place for the rest of the week. I was desperate for a good night's rest. I had a live interview with CNN's *American Morning* before sunrise the next day.

After the interview, there was more time to kill before starting work. I found a YMCA and to my surprise, some people there recognized me. I got some exercise and took a shower. When I left the gym, it was snowing outside. I was flabbergasted. I assumed the weather was always dry in this part of the country.

As I wiped the snow off my windshield, I called Jim Deflon, the head landscape architect for Hilltop Landscaping. I told him I was on my way, and he assured me I had made the best career choice in his state. When I learned that Albuquerque and Santa Fe are rapidly developing cities, I thought of working for the city's urban planning team. The department was interested, but when I said I would like to be paid for my week, I was told that there wasn't enough money in the budget. So I narrowed my search to landscaping and persuaded Jim to hire me.

When I arrived at Jim's office, everyone was friendly and ready to show me the ropes, but Jim wasn't there yet. The office itself is a massive open room. All the employees have their own elevated desks and sit on high stools to hover over their work surfaces. Blueprints covered every square inch like tablecloths. Jim had offered me a place to stay in his mountainside home that week, and I hoped he was a decent man to live with. Though I was tired of sleeping in my Jeep, I dreaded endlessly wondering how I'd fit in into the households of potential hosts.

Finally, Jim marched into the office. He was a big guy and wore a flannel shirt with his jeans and work boots. "Hey there, Daniel!" he called out in welcome. I was relieved; he seemed pleasant and inviting. We walked out to his SUV and I felt like I was back with the Border Patrol. But instead of driving around to find illegals, Jim gave me a tour of his current projects around town. He had landscaped 60 percent of Albuquerque, and his projects included parks, sidewalks, playgrounds, residential yards, and commercial parking lots. Because of water scarcity, lawns are rare in Albuquerque. Instead, what you see everywhere is indigenous rock. "There's a lot of flexibility in this business, as long as it looks nice and fits the clients' budgets," Jim explained.

"Are your designs usually the same?" I asked.

"Well, I have a philosophy: The only thing I have to do is design the projects in the scope of my workforce. It's very easy to design something you can't build. That's where you get yourself in trouble." Jim continued driving us around different properties for close-up walking inspections. I started to grow tired, having never shaken off my fatigue from the morning. I had become accustomed by this time to waves of exhaustion, but I could usually depend on the stimulation of a new environment and new people to renew me, as it did on this occasion.

Before lunch, we drove out to an Indian reservation, or pueblo, to use the term common in New Mexico, to view the landscape. I couldn't help but notice distinct differences: The homes are smaller, and the pueblo has its own schools, community centers, police station, hospital, church, and even its own laws, but its commerce is dominated by casinos. While we were there, we had one of the best dishes in America: Indian fried bread. It was soft and fluffy like a donut and covered with honey and sugar.

When we returned to the office to work on landscaping plans, I spent my time coloring the project drawings to make them more presentable for the clients. Jim sent me home early to meet his wife and get settled. The Deflon house is magnificent, and needless to say (since Jim is a landscape architect), his yard was unbelievable, perfectly manicured and maintained. He had beautiful examples of every plant indigenous to the desert. I was given my own adobe cottage one hundred feet from the rest of the house. The property overlooked the valley and the sunset was to die for. I felt like the luckiest guy alive.

I carpooled with Jim the rest of the week, which gave my Jeep a much needed rest. As we got to know each other better and grew more comfortable, I felt a pang of jealously toward Jim. He is possibly the happiest man I had ever met. Jim's passion for his work was beyond question; he knew his projects made an impact on people's lives and has truly helped make his city a great sight to behold. He couldn't wait to wake up every morning to get back to his proj-

Jim can't wait to wake up in the morning to start working on his many drawings.

ects, and he was always smiling and laughing. Regardless, he is as competitive as he is generous, as revealed by the fact that he often criticized the landscaping – or lack of landscaping – around houses and offices and in public space as we drove by them.

"Look at these yards, look at these things. It's awful! This guy has an acre and he's got his trailer on it. Would you live like that? Seriously! I have to work with this every day." I couldn't stop laughing as he went on and on.

Before the end of the day, I examined notes from a client to review what she wanted in her yard. The outline was already drawn, but I had to place trees, flowers, grass, and a guesthouse on the map. Jim and I went to visit her in person to get a better understanding of the site. The freeway near her property generated unwanted noise, so Jim suggested putting in a fountain. She agreed to all his ideas, but as with every landscaping project he works on, he had to stay within the budget. That's the hard part, but Jim loves the challenge. One of his proudest achievements, he told me, is the low-income housing subdivisions he landscaped; he created a masterpiece on the budget of a taco.

Soon enough, the week was over and Jim was advising me about the next leg of my journey, to Kansas. He cautioned me to drive carefully because of black ice on the roads. I wasn't quite sure what he was talking about, but he explained that it's transparent and a significant hazard for drivers. I left worried about the 980-mile drive ahead of me.

I wanted to get an early start to get as much daylight as possible. Driving through the mountains of northern New Mexico, I realized how different that region is from the rest of the state. As I cut a corner of Oklahoma into Kansas, a feeling of detachment overcame me. I felt I was becoming immune to worry about the weeks and work ahead. By that point, I had learned to let go of expectations and be ready for anything.

KANSAS

MEATPACKER

When I left Albuquerque, it was seventeen degrees. As I approached the middle of Kansas, the temperature dropped to nine degrees. I searched for a place to eat, but found no options along Highway 54. There were lots of small towns, but there was no place to eat. I kept hoping to get to a larger city, but Greensburg, the biggest-looking place on the map, had been demolished by a tornado the previous year. I kept driving until finally I found a bar in a town called Pratt. The bar itself reminded me of my days in Wyoming; the skimpy menu reminded me of my days in Iowa. I ordered a Kansas beef burger. I thought it was a fitting meal to start my week as a meatpacker.

My job at a meatpacking plant had been hard to come by. I tried to find work at one of the large plants, but issues around hiring illegal immigrants made companies more cautious about hiring. Further, meatpacking is a high-liability job — it's a dangerous industry with many fatal accidents each year. As I came down to the last straw, I found a small plant outside Topeka, owned by Drew Forster of Farview Farms.

After the taxing drive, I was beat and felt uneasy. My car was running out of gas, and with no idea about the area I was in, I was revisited by a sense of uncertainty and apprehension. I found a neighborhood just outside Wichita, and pulled over in front of a row of houses. In typical Sunday night fashion, I prepared for another night in the back of the Jeep — but this time, nothing could prepare me for the cold night ahead.

The weather was piercingly, bitterly, numbingly cold. I blasted the car heater one last time before turning off the engine. As I climbed to the backseat to arrange the blankets and pillows, the wind was howling, and my car rocked back and forth. I couldn't even think about opening the car door to brush my teeth or take a leak in that cold. Suddenly, a glaring sensory light came on outside a nearby house. After thirty minutes, it was still on, so I drove one hundred feet to the front of another house. I tried sleeping again, but my pillow felt like an ice cube and my blankets were stiff from the cold.

After two hours, I knew I couldn't fall asleep. I turned on my car and the temperature read "-6°." It was almost 3:00 a.m., but I was willing to take my chances on finding gas and a twenty-four-hour restaurant. I found a Denny's near the Wichita airport and passed the time there until morning. *I'm never doing that again,* I thought. I could have really harmed myself, tired, weak, and stranded in that extreme cold.

True to form, I found a YMCA for taking a shower the next morning. In the lobby, I heard the local news report that that Christmas week in Kansas would be the coldest in history. *Great! And I had to be here for this*, I thought. I had some work to do and wanted to avoid going back into the cold, so after a hot shower I used the Internet and returned phone calls from local news stations. At this point, people were familiar with my story, and stations didn't hesitate to cover me. After a few hours, I braved the cold to drive the 150 miles from Wichita to Topeka.

In Topeka, I faced another night without knowing anyone. I didn't want to risk trying to sleep in the Jeep again, so I succumbed to temptation and checked into a room at a Motel 6. For the first time in fifteen weeks, I had to cough up fifty dollars for a room. The cost was worrisome enough, but what made it worse was that staying in a motel felt contrived and inorganic. I couldn't tough it out in the Jeep another night, and I felt like a loser. "Don't worry, you'll get a paycheck this week; just work hard," my mom consoled me. At least I got some rest. The next day, I was ready to work at the Kansas slaughterhouse.

"Welcome! Are you Daniel?" a middle-aged woman asked. She explained that she was the owner, Drew Foster's, mother and that she managed administrative operations for the plant. She asked if I wanted to watch the slaughtering, which is only done on Mondays and Wednesdays. *Within minutes of being here, this is what I got myself into.* I did not want to witness the slaughter, but I knew I needed to. This is a real career real people have. And after all, I had come to Kansas to work in a meatpacking plant. I needed to get the full experience. I stood by and watched a cow stand in a small pen as a man wearing a red hardhat pointed a rifle point-blank at the animal's head and fired. The cow dropped instantly. Three other men tied chains to its hind legs and a winch lifted the animal belly up. The cow dangled upside down, and I was horrified, speechless. Next, they sawed the animal's head off and blood poured out like waterfall. It splashed all over the cement floor as the crew sawed off the limbs and butchers started skinning the animal. All this work

The scene only became more gruesome. I had to turn away.

was done by hand. The men then took the carcass into a freezer, where it would remain in storage for two weeks before final processing for market. It took about an hour to slaughter, drain, dismember, and skin a single cow at Farview Farms, compared with five hundred cows per hour at larger, more automated plants. I had to build up my courage before entering the muggy, unventilated slaughter room. I had no intention of being part of the slaughtering crew, but wanted to understand the environment and get a stronger sense of the job. The smell was horrendous; I felt as if I would contract a disease from breathing in that space. Bunny, the state meat inspector, assured me that nothing would happen to my health. She recognized me from CNN and knew my story. She offered to host me for the week I was in Kansas and even suggested I spend Christmas with her family. I was thrilled. She handed me a piece of paper with her address and phone number. "When you're done here, just swing on over."

The rest of the morning, as I worked in different parts the plant, I noticed that most of Drew's employees were high school students working part-time. I couldn't imagine working at a place like this as a teenager. I joined them in various tasks that day: packaging, labeling, meat dusting, and grinding. At first, grinding was hard to stomach. I had to shove chunks of animal into the grinder; just ten minutes earlier, I had seen their cousins flicking flies off their ears. Despite the blood squirting in my face from the grinder, it became easier after a few methodical runs to go through the motions and ignore the reality of what I was doing. In addition, I was distracted by how cold it was in the plant. By five o'clock, I had a headache and was ready to leave. I drove twenty-two miles to Ozawkie, where my new home awaited me. When I got to Bunny's, she introduced me to her husband Bob. He sat five feet from the television screen. Tubes were strapped to his nose, and he didn't turn around to face me. "Honey, this is Daniel; he's staying with us for the week," Bunny told him.

"Okay, okay." Though he had spoken only two words, I could hear his thick accent. He still didn't bother to turn around.

I started to feel I wasn't wanted. Perhaps sensing my anxiety, Bunny explained the situation: "He can't really talk now. He's hooked up to a machine because he has Type A Diabetes." We had dinner and watched television quietly together until bedtime, when I went to my room.

The next morning, I heard the television and sensed that Bob was in the living room. Sure enough, he was there, but he seemed like a different person from the night before. He got up to help me with breakfast. "I'd go outside and warm up the car for fifteen to twenty minutes," he advised. I went outside, but my windshield was frozen. I had never seen this before and wasn't sure how to handle it. I went back inside and warmed up some water on the stove to pour over my windshield and melt the ice. "No! You don't want to do that! That will crack the glass!" Bob gave me an ice scraper to use instead. I wasn't wearing gloves and couldn't bear more than a minute outside, so I did a portion of the window and drove off to work.

After driving twenty-two miles in low visibility on an unplowed road, I reached Farview Farms for another day of work. Since I was already familiar with the people and my duties, I could start and finish assignments on my own. When the news crew came in, I felt confident as a meatpacker. Turning to Drew, a reporter asked, "So what did you think when you hired Daniel?"

"I thought, is this guy for real? I didn't think he was until he showed up this week," Drew replied. After being on the air, new customers flocked to Drew's plant. I felt I had earned a good paycheck for bringing him some publicity.

By my final day at the plant, I was tired of working in the freezer. I was tired of wiping blood off my face when I ground the meat. I was even tired of listening to the slow, old-time country music that echoed through the rooms. I worked through Christmas Eve, totaling over fifty hours for the week. Having put in so many hours, and helped publicize Farview Farms in twelve different media outlets — television, newspaper, and radio — I expected to be given at least a modest check. But, in fact, I received nothing, not even a chunk of meat for Christmas.

I was discouraged and disheartened. *It seems like the harder I work, the less I get.* I decided to just let it go. After all, I'd had a good experience at Farview Farms and got a real feel for meatpacking; that was all I really needed.

My last day in Kansas happened to be Christmas Day. We all dressed up and drove several miles to Bunny's daughter's house. Susan's husband was in Iraq and she lived with her son, who was about ten years old. We had a videoconference with her husband before sitting down for dinner. With a family member in Iraq, a traditional Christmas meal, and the snow falling outside, I never felt so American as I did spending time with that Kansas family. I gave Bunny and Bob a Christmas card, and they gave me a University of Kansas Jayhawk hat, a gift card for Subway, and of course, an ice scraper.

MISSOURI

Kansas City

OKLAHOMA

Ringwood

TEXAS

Not Just about Me Anymore

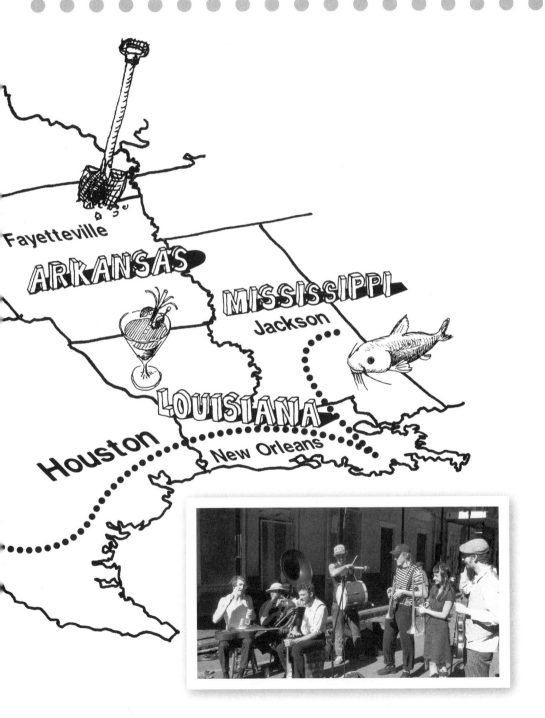

MISSOURI

BOILERMAKER

how me what you're doing here. Show me how to weld," the reporter commanded. It was my first day working for Local 83, and I had little idea about what kind of work a boilermaker actually does. Regardless, there I was standing in a welding lodge with a reporter from a local Kansas City TV station. Luckily, I had taken metal shop in high school, so I knew how to strike up a torch and cut through metal; and for everything else, I had Randy Cruse beside me to explain it to the reporter.

"We build and maintain power plants throughout the Missouri Valley," Randy noted. Randy, the president of the Brotherhood for Boilermakers, was to be my mentor for the week. "We are employed in repairing, repiping, and retubing commercial steam and hot-water boilers used for heating and domestic hot water in commercial buildings and multifamily dwellings," he elaborated. Though I grasped the basics, I was eager to know how all the pieces of this profession worked together. In many ways, the job of boilermaker reminded me of my project. Though I knew what I was doing on each particular day, I didn't always understand how everything fit into the big picture until more time passed.

The following day, I sat in a conference hall with boilermakers from Nebraska, Iowa, Kansas, and Missouri for safety training. As I took a break in the lobby, a gentleman sprung up from his chair. "Are you the guy on television?" he asked with anticipation.

"Yes, I am," I replied.

"Can you get me a job here? I have welding experience," he added with urgency.

"I'll see what I can do. I know they're always looking for new employees," I assured him. I later learned that this man is a dentist, and after being unemployed for several years, he decided to get off the couch and try something new — something he'd never seen himself doing. As we talked, I realized that if I could inspire people to move out of their comfort zones and try new things, like pursue new jobs, this would be the true direction of my project. Our conversation about his job search reminded me of my own quest to find a boilermaker job.

After doing my usual research, I learned that boilermaker is a popular career choice in Missouri, so I spent nine months trying to arrange the job. I had a difficult time securing the position, because the jobs are all controlled by a union and union members had to vote to hire me. I had felt like giving up and exploring other job possibilities, but I left myself with no other options in the state. Bottom line: I really needed the boilermaker job. Luckily, two weeks before I arrived, the union finally figured out a way to hire me as an apprentice.

During the week, I learned different techniques, including arc, TIG, and MIG welding. In the beginning, I didn't know how to use the equipment correctly: I'd ignite a rod to weld, and the whole area around me would flare up with a blinding blue light. My hands trembled, and when I placed the rod back on the table, it unexpectedly reignited, almost causing me to lose my sight. But after training from Sunday until Tuesday afternoon, I was commended for learning quickly. I was ready to go out into the field as a boilermaker.

The field happened to be a coal-fired power plant in this case. As the other boilermakers tried to locate a leak in one of the boiler pipes, I looked over the schematic prints for the boiler and I was confused by all the components. Growing up in California, the only power sources I knew were wind turbines and hydroelectric dams. The plant foreman brought me a hardhat and safety glasses and walked me around the facility to get a feel for the environment. Despite his good efforts, I didn't think I could ever get comfortable

Local 83's apprenticeship training facility, where boilermakers come for a two-week intensive classroom training (10 hours/day, 7 days/week).

working on the high catwalks — the top of the boiler at this plant was approximately 350 feet high. To make matters worse, the wind was whirling and the handrails were low. I felt I might blow right over. *I should probably gain a hundred pounds to feel secure here*, I thought as I noticed how much bigger the other boilermakers were.

At the plant, I saw some of my fellow boilermakers dangling from harnesses upside down from 350 feet, welding flawlessly. I had tried this myself the day before, but from a height of only thirty feet. As I watched them practice their art, I had a hard time grasping how they did it. I'm a baby when it comes to heights, so their ability to weld with precision and accuracy in mid-air, exposed to the elements, made me appreciate their work even more.

Later in the week, I checked my e-mail and discovered that I had received hundreds of messages. It turned out that *World News Tonight* had aired my story the previous evening and my face was again on the front page of Yahoo. People had written me from all over the country, encouraging me and praising my project.

> *I just have to say "Hats Off" to you for doing what you are. I don't have a degree like you but I was laid off in January of 2008 and haven't found anyone willing to hire me . . . Wish I had the guts you have! Let us know what job you end up with. Take care.*
>
> Diana —Allentown, Pennsylvania

> *I just got laid off last week after 5 years with the company. Reading your article and adventures has really inspired me to not limit myself on looking just for one certain type of job. Hoping for the best. I know it's a tough market out there. By the way, have you tried our Kansas City famous BBQ?*
>
> Pricila —Kansas City, Missouri

With each message, the aim of my project evolved further. I gained a new sense of fulfillment. This wasn't about searching for myself, personal growth, my own goals, or proving something. Instead, I realized how fulfilling it is to know that what I was doing helped people take action in their own lives. Their e-mails showed me that I had inspired people and encouraged them. Not only had I given them hope in their personal job search, I was influencing people to take chances and reinvent themselves.

I stayed up all night replying to every e-mail I could, eager to give people the information and support they needed. Some of them even wrote to ask for advice about their love life, and I sincerely tried to give the best advice I could. I continued to receive e-mail from strangers in the weeks that followed and continued to make every effort to respond.

ARKANSAS

ARCHAEOLOGIST

I decided to take back roads into Arkansas. When I approached the welcome sign at the border, I felt as if I were approaching a foreign country. I had never been anywhere close to this state before. *This is part of my country*, I reminded myself. *This is what my project's all about.* As I drove through the impressive Ozark Mountains, I was proud to call such a place my own. My Jeep loved the hilly terrain and curvy roads that cut through beautiful exposed rock. It was my favorite drive so far.

Up to that point, all I had to go by were stereotypes of the state, some of which I found to be true. For example, I had envisioned dirt roads where locals go four-wheeling, and it didn't take me long before I saw this for myself. Some yards were so expansive, they had their own four-wheel courses. When I rolled my window down, I could even hear the engines of four-wheel rigs running. As I expected in the Bible Belt, I saw more churches than homes and American flags flew above nearly every driveway I passed. From time to time, I passed stray animals wandering along the road. My host family later explained that, as people struggle to pay their bills, they abandoned their pets to save costs.

Entering Fayetteville, I could tell immediately that I had reached civilization when I spotted a Wal-Mart. Soon after, I saw a drive-in movie theater and countless fried chicken fast-food restaurants in a matter of blocks. I could see why some had suggested that I work as a chicken farmer during my week in Arkansas.

I was on my way to stay with the Eldriges, old family friends. Mr. Eldrige had worked with my mom in California and moved back to Arkansas when he and his wife retired. They were caring

Archaeologists posing after a long cold day searching for artifacts on an archaeological site on private property.

people with big hearts — they used their free time to volunteer at the animal shelter. Luckily, they lived relatively close to my workplace, the office of the Arkansas Archaeological Survey (AAS), the first organization of its kind in the country. After looking into different organizations in the state, I found out about AAS through its affiliation with the University of Arkansas. Like everywhere in the U.S., Arkansas has a rich history. Before I could get into the field and start to appreciate it for myself, my employer, Professor Green, suggested I attend one of his classes at the University of Arkansas.

Professor Green, who heads the AAS, thought the class would help me gain a better understanding of his organization's work and how it contributes to understanding past cultures. As I sat in the classroom listening to the lecture and glancing down at my textbook, it was hard to visualize how it would play out in the field. Luckily, I had all week to figure that out.

After class, a young student named Sarah approached me and asked what kind of work I had lined up in her home state, Texas. I told her what I was planning, and she suggested I check out a particular burger joint in Fort Worth. Though I was interested in talking about Texas, I wasn't ready to think too hard about it – my first priority was getting through Week Eighteen in Arkansas.

When the time finally came to get into the field, the archaeologists I was working with took me to explore six sites, a modest number considering that there are 43,000 archaeological sites in the state. Carrying metal detectors, shovels, and even a laser point system, we inspected a Civil War site. The temperature was twenty degrees. I reflected on how little I had cared about history. It had always been intangible, something I'd read about or heard about, almost incomprehensible. Yet walking around the Civil War site for a couple of hours, I became more engaged. Being in the field, actively absorbing the environment I'd only known through a classroom, brought to life the textbook stories I had never been able to envision. When we found an actual Civil War bullet, I suddenly imagined 5,000 soldiers shivering or sweating in the same field where we were digging – dirty for sure, probably hungry and tired, and more than a little scared. I thought of the Civil War stories I had read or seen in movies. Standing there, near the spot where perhaps a young soldier lost a bullet nearly a century and a half earlier – or maybe, where a bullet aimed at him had come to rest – was a bit surreal. I was eager to find more artifacts and soon found a horseshoe. I wanted to keep it as a memento, but was required to submit it to the curator for the artifact library.

Beyond the Civil War sites, the archeologists took me to look for artifacts in shelters Native Americans had carved into river bluffs to protect themselves in winter. We examined hieroglyphics on the walls of the shelters, and as we marveled at them, my eyes wandered just above to some graffiti: "Sasha Sucks." I could not help but feel this was a sign. *She does suck,* I thought. *It's time to move on . . . .* I hadn't heard from Sasha in months, and needless to say, this was discouraging, especially after I sent her the card enclosing a key to the scooter I had promised her. I decided I should make more of an effort to be open to other girls. So I asked Professor Green about Sarah, the student from Texas. He gave me her contact information and soon enough, we went out on a date. Later that week, another girl asked me out – and so I had two dates while I was in Arkansas.

I had covered a lot of territory and felt I had achieved intimate experiences with new places and people, but this was different. I enjoyed experiencing the local scene on my two dates, and I really enjoyed both girls' company. Not that I was seriously interested — I belonged to the road — but I wanted to be more open to possibility, to make the experience of each state as rich as possible. I wanted to forget Sasha. Up to then, I had kept myself in a bubble, hoping she would come back into my life, always trying to earn her attention. Now, girls were approaching me on their own. Finally letting go of Sasha opened me up to so many other opportunities. I couldn't resist.

OKLAHOMA

ROUSTABOUT

oon after I drove into Oklahoma, also known as "Cherokee Nation," I realized I wasn't prepared for all the highway tolls that followed. Turnpikes — toll roads — are rare in California and most of the West, and I hadn't encountered many of them in my travels up to that point. When I reached the first tollbooth, I didn't have enough cash, so I received an official notice to pay at the next one. But I didn't see a single ATM on the way. Lacking the cash to pay the toll ahead, much less the previous one, I was prepared to receive another pay-at-the-next-tollbooth notice. Instead, a state trooper pulled me over and wrote me a ticket. I tried to plead my case and explained that I was on my way to a news interview, but he didn't care.

Continuing on my way to meet a reporter in Tulsa, I passed a massive yellow statue of an oil rigger and decided that would be the perfect setting for my interview since my plan was to work in the oil fields. Oil dominates the Oklahoma economy, and drilling rigs are a common sight.

"How was your drive?" Megan, the Tulsa reporter, asked sweetly. "You must be tired," she added. I was immediately attracted to her and wanted to ask her out. I couldn't help but think of how much I'd changed and how I was looking at girls differently. Since my job wasn't near the big city, however, I decided it was enough for now just to ask Megan for her contact information

I was destined for Ringwood, where I would be staying with my employer, Arnold of A&T Roustabouts, and his wife, Rita. I found Arnold's company through simple cold-calling, dialing roustabout companies until one agreed to hire me. I had a hard time finding Ringwood — the road leading there had two names, Route 412 and Route 60 — but I was determined to get there without help. As day turned to night, I wondered if I had missed the exit, but soon spotted a rock lit up on the side of the road with words I was glad to see: "Welcome to Ringwood."

Ringwood reminded me of Fishtail, Montana, except that it is dustier, drier, and flatter. A town of only two hundred residents, it is in the heart of tornado alley. I couldn't read the house numbers from inside my Jeep, so decided to park the car and walk through the neighborhood. As I roamed the streets, I felt like I was in the Twilight Zone. They were dark and deserted, beyond a few spotlights on the driveways. The wind was howling, carrying the distorted sound of some machine in the distance. I didn't know what to expect. Suddenly Rita emerged from a house carrying a little dog in her arms. "Daniel?"

"Yes. Hi," I replied. "I couldn't see the house numbers."

"Why don't you come in!" Rita invited me. As we entered the house, I saw Arnold on the couch watching the news. I sat beside him.

"How was your drive?" Arnold asked calmly in a thick accent. From his voice and demeanor, it was clear from the get-go what a hard worker he was. He seemed focused and straightforward.

"Not bad," I told him. "It was hard finding the place; I really feel like I'm in the middle of nowhere."

"You basically are," he agreed. "There's nothing but oil fields in

At times, I just wanted to sit in the warm truck, but there was no time to waste, as when we were installing this heater treater.

this part of the state. You'll see most of it tomorrow. Get some rest; we're starting at the crack of dawn." Arnold got up to show me the guesthouse in the backyard. "You might wanna turn on the heater. It's gonna get cold tonight."

It wasn't just cold, the wind was howling. It felt like the windows would shatter from the violent gusts. And the wind was still blowing when I woke up to get ready for work the next morning. "I'll give you some boots and suspenders, but you're gonna wanna wear clothes you don't care about," Arnold advised me. I decided to wear pajama pants over my jeans — I didn't care if they got dusty or oily.

Arnold knew I didn't know much about the oil industry, but he welcomed an extra pair of hands on his crew. At work, he explained the different phases of operations, from drilling to the work-over rig to the roustabout, which was my position that week. "We're going to install pumping units and tank batteries," he informed me. As he pointed to the pumping unit, the sun rose just above it. He explained that oil trucks pick up the crude oil and deliver it to refineries, which process it into gasoline to fuel our vehicles.

We met up with the three-man crew Arnold manages, but before driving out to the oil field, we stopped at a gas station convenience store to fill up our lunch boxes, which reminded me of a field trip in elementary school; needless to say, I felt even more like a kid when Arnold dropped me off with my lunch box each day in front of the other guys. "Bye, Daddy!" one of them would say mockingly when Arnold left. I have to admit, with my pajama pants and my lunch box, I felt pretty childish.

This feeling never lingered long, though, once we headed to the work site, forty miles from Ringwood. Fortunately, there was a work-over rig operating at our site, which gave me an opportunity to see the entire process: drilling, rigging, and finally, trucking the crude oil to the refinery. The project I was working on with Arnold's crew was installing pumping units and tank batteries, which hold the crude oil. We spent every day assembling the tank battery and building firewalls around it to contain the oil in case of spills. The pumps last forty to fifty years.

The job reminded me of plumbing: threading pipes and connecting them to direct the oil. Installing the pumping units and tank batteries takes a few days, but I was amazed by how swiftly and efficiently the crew worked, and with flawless results. While I enjoyed the work and learning how to be a roustabout and learning about the entire process, that January in Oklahoma was cold and windy, and the job strenuous and dirty. I could keep up with the manual labor, but it was demanding. I wasn't used to breathing so much dust all day from the fields. My nose was stuffy, and a black residue covered my skin.

It was rewarding to complete the installation at the end of the week. As soon as we were finished, Arnold had us replace an old separator and remove one of its heaters. While we were tearing up the rusty pipelines, crude oil leaked out and formed puddles around us. Soon I was kneeling in oil. I couldn't wait to wash up. As I got up, dripping, and gazed at the oil fields around me, I was awestruck by how much our country offers. A week ago I was digging up artifacts and now I was digging up natural resources that fuel our lives.

I glanced over at Arnold and his crew, still toiling with the pipes. Their work is essential to our society, and while this fact was old news to them — part of their everyday lives — it was a fresh and profound insight to me, as it probably would be to most of America. *They're the ones who keep our country running*, I thought. *The least I can do is understand what they go through each day.* This kind of rumination was typical of my last day of work, as were thoughts of what comes next. As the oil soaked through my pajama pants, I couldn't help but wonder what Texas would bring.

TEXAS

PETROLEUM ENGINEER

I knew I had crossed the border into Texas when I noticed that the Texas state flag had replaced the American flag in people's driveways and on the rooftops of commercial buildings. *When you're in Texas, the state will keep reminding you of it*, I thought. I also flashed on how many words include the state's name: Texas T-bone steak, Texas Christian University, Texas Roadhouse Grill. *Texas this, Texas that. They might as well call the state "Texas Texas,"* I thought.

I was on my way to Houston to work as a petroleum engineer for Chevron. Texas is the country's leader in energy resources and the home of several energy giants. My experience in Oklahoma's oil industry would serve me well in my job with Chevron's offshore reservoir team, where, as I was about to find out, I was assigned to work with a group that manages a drilling site in West Africa from the Texas office.

I was staying with Tadd, the cousin of my boss at Ulteig, the mapping company in North Dakota. He's my age, and I looked forward to hanging out and enjoying Texas with him. The only downside was the thirty-mile commute to and from work each day, which required three hours. I had heard that Houston has the worst traffic in the country, and was not looking forward to experiencing it for myself.

Early that week, I was invited to appear live on *The Today Show* and then Fox News. I hoped the anchors wouldn't ask me too much about my position at Chevron, since I was still learning about the job. As I walked to my car that morning to drive to the studio, I saw a young woman in her twenties crossing the street as she spoke on her cell phone. Suddenly, a car sped down the road and made a left turn into the crosswalk, crashing into her. He hit her so hard, she flew twenty feet from the car, where her body left a dent. Sprinting to the accident, I realized I was the only witness.

When the victim tried to get up, she discovered she had lost all the strength in her lower body. "No, don't get up," I told her. The driver of the car came out to examine his bumper, and hovered over us in the street. He didn't say a word. I started to think he was more concerned about how much time this was taking out of his day instead of whether this woman would ever walk again. Within twenty minutes, the police and ambulance arrived. An officer took my information, and I was back on the road to the studio. As I drove to my interview, I knew I was terribly late, but the image of the girl being struck kept replaying in my mind. I wondered if she would be paralyzed for the rest of her life.

"Act perky! Be energetic!" the producer advised me as an assistant attached a microphone to my shirt collar. *I just saw a girl almost die*, I thought. Still, I was about to appear on national television. I wanted to inspire people, so I had to put aside the distractions of the morning. Sure enough, both interviews got me back into focus, and talking about my project left me feeling confident about starting the new job.

When I was looking for work in Texas, I tried cold-calling petroleum companies to find a position as an engineer. Chevron got wind of my effort and sought me out with an invitation to work on its offshore drilling team. I was happy to take the company up on it.

When I arrived, I met with my boss, Sue Park, to discuss her

Just outside Tadd's backyard, he takes me through a long and bumpy ATV course.

current project. She walked me to her computer where she showed me some charts and graphs related to offshore drilling, underground simulations and forecasts for the amount of crude oil and natural gas available. Sue recited her team's philosophy: "We're never right, but how close to right are we?" She told me that drilling predictions are never dead on, but if they're 98 percent close, that was the goal.

As I took it all in, I was reminded of how much I disliked office environments. It was my first office job in twenty weeks. *I'd rather be oil rigging in Oklahoma, where people can be themselves*, I thought. I felt suffocated by the office, though, admittedly, there were perks, like an expansive cafeteria and state-of-the-art workout facility. Nonetheless, throughout the week, as I attended meetings and sat at my computer making graphs and printing simulation models, that suffocating feeling persisted. By and large, my fellow office workers kept to themselves and stayed at their own desks.

Petroleum engineers are lucky in that at times they're able to go out in the field. Though I didn't get into the field myself in this case, I was able to break up the week by visiting the laboratory to review soil samples and learn a bit about how oil is extracted. I was not aware that machines could extract oil from soil itself; I always assumed that oil only came from reserves of liquid, like the puddles I'd seen in Oklahoma, except underground.

In addition to oil and Chevron, another quintessential presence in Texas is Joel Osteen, the senior pastor at Lakewood Church in Houston, a so-called megachurch. I did not want to miss the opportunity to attend one of his sermons. I went to the church, which is more like a stadium, to hear him preach. He listens to people's stories and uses them to empower others. I knew I could learn something from him about how to help those around me. As Osteen encouraged parishioners to de-emphasize the bad things in life and focus on the good, I felt revitalized, newly empowered to give my all to my project. When I started my journey at the Mormon Humanitarian Center in Salt Lake City, I read the quote on the wall — "We are to feed the hungry, to clothe the naked, to provide for the widow, to dry up the tear of the orphan, to comfort the afflicted, whether in this Church, or in any other, or no church at all" — and was energized to move forward with my best effort. After Joel Osteen's talk, almost halfway into my project and looking ahead to Louisiana, I felt renewed in my commitment to the objective of my journey, especially to my goal of inspiring people along the way.

LOUISIANA

BARTENDER

After watching the Super Bowl with Tadd and his friends, I was reluctant to leave Houston. Despite the positive outlook I was taking with me from Texas, I had never fully adjusted to starting all over again every week, leaving behind family, friends, and what I'd just begun to call home. Looking forward, my demanding daily commute in Houston made me dread driving into the craziness I expected at my next destination, the French Quarter of New Orleans. On the other hand, my timing was perfect: Mardi Gras was scheduled to begin that week. So I was a bit conflicted, but I knew it was better to get going than to linger. Driving through one bayou after another reminded me of the lakes in Minnesota; only, in this case, I could feel steamy air penetrating the atmosphere.

Despite the muggy heat, the interstate was beautiful, like driving on an endless bridge through the calm natural world that surrounded me. I had never seen swamps and wetlands, and I wished I had an airboat to breeze through them and explore close up. As I drove across the parishes — counties — of southwest Louisiana, I saw lots of mobile homes, and the landscape gradually became more urbanized as I approached Bourbon Street, the heart of the French Quarter and my newest domicile.

My specific destination was a bar called the Funky Pirate, whose owners, Pam and Earl, were expecting me. They are the proud creators of the famous "Hand Grenade," a cocktail of vodka, rum, gin, and various liqueurs. It is also a potentially dangerous concoction evidently, for a sign outside the Funky Pirate warns against drinking more than one. Considering that I had no bartending experience, Pam and Earl were hesitant to hire me. To be honest, I wasn't comfortable with the idea of bartending either. I felt pretty strongly that nothing positive ever comes from alcohol consumption, and I have stayed away from it my entire life. So morally, I didn't feel right serving drinks. It was troubling to think about being part of something I was against. Still, my project was about exploring the jobs and lives of others, and as I had discovered, if this meant going out of my comfort zone, then that was what I'd have to do. I had set a mission for myself, and staying true to that mission was more important than avoiding situations simply because they made me uncomfortable. So I was ready to start my job at the Funky Pirate, or at any of hundreds of other bars and clubs in New Orleans (though, in fact, I limited my search to blues taverns). "If it's not you, it's going to be another bar," I had told Pam before she hired me. The day I arrived, we met over dinner to discuss the week ahead.

"How about some wine with your crawfish?" she'd asked. I told her I didn't drink. "Good, now I won't have to worry about you drinking on the job," Pam laughed, "or drinking up my entire inventory!"

She walked me down the block to present me with my new apartment. We walked on Bourbon Street to a wooden door that opened onto a narrow alley; at the end of the alley was a courtyard that led to two apartments. Pam led me into one of them and then left me alone to rest for the night. From my room, I could hear the noise and excitement of the French Quarter: street traffic, music, people yelling and shouting as they stumbled from bar to bar. *Why am I always intimidated coming to a new city?* I wondered to myself. *See, it turned out fine . . . I should have come a day earlier.* I felt the energy of the city as I lay in bed, and I had to fight the urge to jump out of bed and go exploring. I concentrated on getting some sleep — I knew I had a demanding week ahead of me. It would be my first week working only at night, with days free. Since I needed to be up late, I knew I should rest when I had the chance. I needed to devote any spare time available to setting up future jobs.

As with most of my work experiences up to then, I was thrown right into the action. Pam gave me a pirate bandana, eye patch, black

Pam was right, there were lots of friendly girls. Maybe a little too friendly, trying to get the beads around my neck.

sweatshirt, and plenty of beads to wear around my neck. These were for giving away to customers at my discretion. "Trust me, there will be lots of friendly girls, so use the beads wisely," she advised. As my coworker, Dave, was explaining the different drinks and showing me where everything was stored, people began to flood into the bar. By 4:00 p.m., the place was packed. The entire street roared. It seemed as if the city was a twenty-four-hour party. In retrospect, it was silly of me to hope that customers would not ask me for anything, because within seconds of starting my shift, I was slammed.

"Can we have two Miller drafts?" my first customer asked. Dave had told me where the Millers were stored, and I reached for two of them. "Drafts, man, not bottles," my customer instructed. Unfortunately for him, I didn't know how to use the draft machine. I pulled the lever and spilled beer everywhere; the cups overflowed with foam. I told my customer that I had no idea what I was doing. Though he was patient and chuckled, I'm sure he wondered why

I'd been hired. More customers pressed up to the bar and asked for drinks, and my ignorance amused them.

"I have never had to tell a bartender how to make my drink! That's awesome, man!" someone exclaimed when I asked him how to make a Jack and Coke. Everyone was laughing and having a great time, dumping cash tips into my jar. Most of the customers tricked me into pouring more alcohol into their drinks than I was supposed to, and by the end of the night, I had groupies lined up, waiting for me to serve them.

I couldn't believe how time flew by in that environment. I was meeting friendly Southerners and listening to blues music from Fat Al (the Funky Pirate's 495-pound house musician). It didn't feel like work; in fact, it felt better than going out myself, because working at the Funky Pirate, I was the life of the party. I got to the point where I was more concerned about how my customers felt than I was about my personal beliefs. I was so consumed with making them happy that I overcame my initial discomfort. This reminded me of working at the meatpacking plant. I had to grit my teeth and focus on the job rather than allow myself to become consumed and paralyzed by duties that conflicted with my personal beliefs.

I knew it would be a crazy week, working through Mardi Gras, but it was beyond anything I expected. After just a couple days, I was exhausted; I did not understand how people could party every night. There was no sanctuary — indoors and out, roaring parties filled the air. Guys on the balconies were throwing beads and yelling down to girls on the street to take their shirts off. Every morning, I woke up to streets that had been hosed down from the lively night before. I wondered if the locals ever got tired of the incessantly busy atmosphere and endless parades.

Before I left, Pam gave me a tour of some of the damage from Hurricane Katrina. The French Quarter, which is on relatively high ground, was not badly affected by the hurricane. Driving over potholes and across canals to view the surrounding destruction was like leaving the safe haven of a bubble and getting hit by a harsh dose of reality. The hurricane had struck three years earlier, but people talked about it as if it had happened just a week before. Pam brought me to a development center where employees and volunteers hustled around urgently from one room to the next. To me, they all seemed to still be in panic mode, as if things had not calmed down to the point where they could work at ease. The solitude of emptied out neighborhoods and general devastation stifled my excitement that week. I saw water marks ten feet high on buildings I passed. The gap between the wealthy and the poor was on clear display, as the devastation had obviously had a greater impact on those who were less fortunate to begin with. The total area affected by the hurricane covered a region the size of the United Kingdom. It was incomprehensible.

Later, when I got back to the French Quarter, I talked to a local man about my drive through the damaged areas, but how much I loved my week in Louisiana. "Look man, don't give us a bad rap," he pleaded with me, hoping that Katrina wouldn't define New Orleans. "New Orleans is riding on you — you have the power," he said.

In the end, I didn't want to leave Louisiana — not because I was intimidated by the need to start over in the next state, but because I hadn't had my fill. Everyone I met that week was friendly and outgoing. The city was just beautiful; The distinctive architecture and the narrow cobblestone streets of the French Quarter were especially captivating. There was nonstop activity day and night. I was having fun and didn't want it to end. But Mississippi awaited me.

MISSISSIPPI

DIETITIAN

Like Arkansas, Mississippi was completely unfamiliar territory to me. I felt like Christopher Columbus discovering a new land. Initially, I resisted selecting a career that reflected the state's obesity problem; I didn't want to offend people. But after the two-hundred-mile drive from New Orleans to Jackson, the capital, I was confident I had made the right decision. The city is plastered with billboards devoted to obesity, and hospitals and clinics all over town offer special programs and services related to the problem. So my decision to be a dietitian seemed most appropriate.

I had looked up positions online and before long found myself talking to Urmila Mota, founder and Head Dietitian of the Jackson Nutrition Clinic. I told her how passionate I was about the field and how truly interested I was in the clinic's work. I asked if I could work with her, and she agreed right away. I assumed my job would be to help educate and motivate local people to adopt healthier eating habits, a difficult challenge in a place where most of the available food is fried.

After I arrived in Jackson, Urmila and her family invited me to join them at an all-you-can-eat restaurant to try some of the local dishes myself. If I hadn't already spent time in neighboring Arkansas, I would not have recognized any of the dishes: hush puppies, fried catfish, sweet tea, broccoli with cheese, and fried corn on the cob. When I stared down at my plate, it was filled with brown food—brown from having been deep-fried.

In addition to her role as Head Dietitian at her clinic, Urmila Mota belongs to a food-labeling committee. If "you are what you eat," as the saying goes, you need to know what you're putting on your plate. Hence, the importance of accurate labels on processed foods to understanding the nutritional value of the product.

On Monday, Urmila took me to St. Dominic's Hospital to work in the food line helping prepare meals for patients. Every meal is customized based on the each patient's needs, and patients are closely monitored to track how much they eat. I went to visit a patient in his room and noticed a bag of chips and Mountain Dew. "I just wanted a little taste in my mouth," he explained after confessing that he had sneaked it in.

In another room, I visited a gentleman recovering from heart-bypass surgery. "Oh, it's no biggie," he assured me, "this is my third time!" His wife and sister-in-law stood by his side laughing. They seemed so natural and at ease, laughing away the seriousness of the procedure. As I returned to the food line to fill and serve trays, I wondered if they truly regarded heart bypass as something routine, like having your teeth cleaned or getting an oil change for the car.

Later in the week, Urmila scheduled private consultations, which I joined. One woman came in concerned about her weight; she had gained thirty pounds in two months and couldn't understand why. In an attempt to lose the weight, she ate just one meal a day, she told us. She also told Urmila that she had a hereditary disorder that required her to take seven different medications. When she listed the prescriptions, Urmila realized that this woman's metabolism had been affected by the medications, contributing to her weight gain. We learned that she has a teenaged daughter who suffers from exactly the same problems: the hereditary disorder, drugs that affect her metabolism, and weight gain.

According to Urmila, one of the big problems in Mississippi is lack of physical exercise. She told me that exercise isn't addressed in the schools there. I was shocked; when I was growing up, physical education was a requirement. Everyone had to participate. I couldn't imagine a life without lots of physical activity. It's a pleasure, not a burden.

The coach in me was inspired to encourage Urmila's clients to be active. As I met more of them, I became increasingly invested and

Never work the food line on an empty stomach.

engaged. It meant a lot to me to understand their troubles and to encourage them to make positive changes. Many people seemed to just give up on being healthy, blaming it on genes or poverty. Working with Urmila, I came to see that we could help change people's lives in two ways: by educating them and by motivating them. The people I met had little in the way of a support system — no teammates, no colleagues, no one to push them — and in turn, they had little motivation to push themselves. Being inactive is part of the culture, and each generation seems to echo the one before it. I could see why Urmila got involved in this field: She cared about people and found fulfillment in helping change their lives for the better.

Urmila's work isn't limited to addressing obesity. Some of her patients suffer from actual malnutrition, as I discovered when we visited a nursing home close to Oprah's hometown, Kosciusko. When we got there, we examined food consumption records for the week, confirming that with few exceptions, Urmila's patients were not eating normally. They were all elderly and their bodies were failing. The malnourishment most of them suffered was related to medical conditions. Of the twelve patients we visited, only two were able to respond to our questions; the rest were too weak to talk. In those cases, we had to rely on nurses at the facility for more information on eating habits.

As the end of the week approached, I began to realize that this was very rewarding work, and I could see myself doing it for longer than one week. And I began preparing for the 1,000-mile drive to my next state, Wisconsin. I wanted to drive through the Mississippi Delta curious as I was to see a place I'd only heard about, the poorest region in America. The experience was eye-opening. I felt like I was going back in time; it was as though there existed a third-world country within our own. As I drove, the radio waves transmitted nothing but '80s soul music to my car radio. I passed endless cotton fields and uneven trailers surrounded by dirt yards filled with junk and broken-down vehicles. I yearned to do more to help these communities, but with a two-day drive ahead of me, I kept my mind focused on reaching Wisconsin. I said goodbye to all the birds that had flown south for the winter, because I was heading north.

WISCONSIN

Theresa

WISCONSIN

CHEESE MAKER

It was 9:30 p.m. when I pulled over to take a picture of the "Welcome to Wisconsin" sign. After 980 miles, the two-day drive had pushed my body to the limit. It was mid-February, and I had driven away from Mississippi's sixty-degree warmth into Wisconsin's six-degree cold. Having spent a month in the South, I wasn't prepared to face the wintry chill of the Upper Midwest — specifically, in the small rural town of Theresa, about an hour northwest of Milwaukee.

The owner of Widmer Cheese Cellars, where I had arranged to work in Theresa, had reserved a room for me at a local motel. Wisconsin is considered the nation's dairy state, and as such, produces over 2.6 billion pounds of cheese per year. Mr. Widmer, the owner of Widmer Cheese Cellars, had hired me after seeing a message from me on his desk, asking for work. The day before he got my note, his son had seen me on *The Today Show* and mentioned that I wanted to work at a cheese factory in Wisconsin. Mr. Widmer had offered me a place to stay, but his daughter contracted the stomach flu, a virus I wanted to stay far away from. That night, I walked through the motel lobby with my usual luggage: computer, camera, and toothbrush. "I'm here checking in; last name is Seddiqui," I told the concierge.

"Welcome; we've been expecting you!" she replied with an impressively thick Wisconsin accent. I burst out laughing.

"I'm sorry, I just came from Mississippi and thought I'd heard the thickest accents possible, and now I ran into you!" I explained. "Have you ever visited Mississippi?"

"No, na'chet. I haven't been out of this state," she explained. "They're all the same, right?"

If she only knew. "That's why I'm going to every state, to show how different they are." I headed to my room. It was midnight, I was delusional from the long drive, and I had to be at work at 6:00 a.m. the next morning.

When I entered Widmer Cheese Cellars the next day, Dustin, one of the employees, spotted me and rushed me to the back room to get me started. Only twenty years old, Dustin was a hard worker and an aspiring cheese master. "It's a good thing you're here," he said, "because this morning, one of our workers put his arm inside the presser and now he's in the emergency room."

"I didn't know this was a dangerous job!" I exclaimed.

"It's not. He's just a dimwit," Dustin replied. He helped find my boots and apron and showed me how to sanitize myself. We dunked our boots in blue liquid, splashed it onto our aprons, and rubbed it onto our skin. I was surprised we didn't have to rinse our mouths with it to sanitize our breath.

As I prepared for my first chore, Mr. Widmer came to introduce himself. "Hey Daniel, sorry, we had an employee go to the ER this morning," he said. Mr. Widmer took me to meet Lenny, the cheese master, and thus Dustin's mentor. He had been working there for twenty-eight years. He was intimidating and seemed too busy to be friendly.

Before I could even try to make small talk, Dustin stole me away to show me how to squeegee the cheesemaking vats to clean out the old cheese curds while waiting for a fresh vat of cheese to harden. After it hardened, we cut the cheese into curds, dyed it yellow, drained the whey out, and mixed the curds with salt before dumping the cheese into forms. I grew fatigued from lifting endless buckets of cheese — each bucket weighed at least forty pounds — and reaching lower and lower into the vat. After filling two hundred containers of cheese, we put lids on each and pressed them.

We labored for thirteen-and-a-half hours my first day, and 75 percent of that time was devoted to cleaning. We mopped the floors, scoured the pipes that carried the milk, and scrubbed the vats. Then we washed the cheese, the shelves the cheese aged on (top and bottom), and every piece of equipment used in the process. After cleaning for hours with disinfectant, my fingers started to wrinkle and my skin grew sensitive. Just before we left, we packaged hundreds of blocks of cheese in boxes for shipment. After that long day, I couldn't wait to get back to my room to rest.

The next day, I got to work at 4:30 a.m. I started early because my first job was to pick milk up from the dairy and bring it back to Mr. Widmer's. Back at the cellar, as we waited for the milk to filter through the vats, I took the cheese, which had been soaking overnight in brine, and placed it on the shelves. Cuts on my hand from the day before burned from the saltwater. I placed two hundred blocks of cheese on the shelf to age for a week. *By the time they finish aging*, I thought to myself, *I'll be on my way to Illinois for my twenty-fourth job.*

As I washed the cheese, I got a call from the national news network of South Korea, asking to follow my journey for several days. I was hesitant, for the same reason I didn't want my own television show: I worried that having a crew follow me might change the experience. Ultimately, since it would only be for a few days, I decided to go for it and stepped outside the building to coordinate details on my cell phone. When I went back in, Mr. Widmer gave me a cheeseburger from Burger King for lunch. It was drowning in cheese; in Wisconsin you could expect more cheese on your burger than in any other state.

I went to the break room, a converted boiler room saturated with cigarette smoke, to eat. As I finished my burger, I heard Lenny yell at Dustin for being behind schedule. Lenny was no-nonsense and totally invested in his work. He seemed especially hard on Dustin, constantly putting pressure on him to perform — I assume because Dustin was training to become a cheesemaster.

Before long, Lenny yelled at me too. This happened while I was planning my Illinois job for the following week. I had hoped to work

Draining out the whey from the curds. This is just the beginning of a long and physically demanding process. Widmer's Cheese Cellars produces cheddar, colby, and brick cheese.

for Metra Train, the commuter rail service for metropolitan Chicago, but nothing was definite. I was on the phone with a director from another prospect, John Deere headquarters in Moline. He was telling me the company needed a decision. I preferred to work with Metra, but wanted to keep John Deere as a backup and was trying to finesse this when Lenny came in. "Are you going to come to work or what?" he yelled.

"I'm really busy," I tried to explain.

"So are we!" Lenny shouted. I told the director that I'd call him back and hurriedly placed a call to Peg, my contact at Metra, to verify our plans. The tension increased.

"Daniel, I told you I'd let you know," Peg insisted. Between Lenny, Peg, and John Deere, I grew anxious. I called the John Deere director back to take him up on his offer.

I walked back into work with my camera to get footage of the factory. Lenny spotted me, and as he walked toward me, his anger reached a climax. He grabbed a bucket of sanitizer and abruptly slammed it to the floor.

As water splashed across the walls, Lenny yelled, "Where were you when we were working! You came here to learn, and then you're on the phone!" While Lenny stormed about, my heart was pounding. I didn't regret making the calls, but I was mortified to be the new guy, put on the spot by Lenny yelling like a lunatic. Later, Mr. Widmer apologized for his behavior.

"If he can't treat our guests appropriately, I don't want him working for me." Mr. Widmer said.

"He apologized," I assured Mr. Widmer.

"OK, let's move on. He's been here twenty-eight years. Let's forget about it. When are the South Koreans coming?" I was relieved and told Mr. Widmer they'd be there the next morning.

The Koreans met me at my motel at 4:30 a.m. to film my last day at work. It was frigid as we drove to Widmer Cheese Cellars. On the way, I realized they were as unprepared for the cold as I had been. When we arrived, I introduced them to everyone and explained the cheese process as though I had been making cheese for years. In fact, of course, I had been there just five days, and that afternoon, my coworkers would once again become ex-coworkers.

Despite the long hours and occasional tension, I regretted having to leave. Over the week, I had come to identify with all my colleagues and had grown attached to them. As the workday ended, we said goodbye. Dustin walked over and shook my hand. Then Lenny approached us. "I'm sorry for how I acted. Could we put this behind us and be friends?"

"Of course." I was happy to leave on a positive note. And though I hated saying goodbye, I was excited about spending the weekend in Green Bay with my friend's dad, Mr. Osterloh, who had promised to take me ice fishing. The Koreans followed me there, but by the time we arrived, they were exhausted and needed to catch up on sleep, so we arranged for them to join me the next morning when Mr. Osterloh planned to take me ice fishing.

When the time came, Mr. Osterloh and I drove through thick snow out to the lake, where we set up a floorless tent to shelter us from the wind and snow. Mr. Osterloh set up a small space heater to keep us warm, but I worried it might melt the ice. I also pictured the ice cracking. "Calm down Daniel, it's four-feet thick. It's impossible to break," he assured me. Sure enough, it took five minutes to drill a hole through the ice. We sat on stools in the tent with our fishing lines immersed in the water until we caught something. The South Koreans were exhausted and arrived late, but I didn't mind as long as they filmed me catching some lake perch.

After ice fishing, Mr. Osterloh treated us to the best appetizer I ever had: fried cheese curds. I needed to get to Chicago, so I thanked Mr. Osterloh for a great weekend and started on my way. Ten minutes later, I wanted to turn around. The snow fell so heavily, I couldn't see in front of me, and every now and then, the car threatened to swerve out of control. I must have hit some of that black ice Jim Deflon, the landscape architect in Albuquerque, had warned me about before I headed off to Kansas what seemed like ages ago.

Wisconsin was no breeze. If it was a breeze, then it was a harsh snowstorm breeze. The job was as daunting as driving on an unplowed highway. I thought I had avoided the Midwest winters, but doubted that Illinois would be any different.

ILLINOIS
TRANSIT TICKET AGENT

My body was sore, my neck and back still ached from cheese-making, and the snow continued to fall as I drove into Chicago with the South Koreans right behind me. My windows were as foggy and unclear as the twenty-fourth job. I still wasn't sure where I would be working that week. Though I had accepted the position offered by John Deere in Moline, I had not given up on Metra. Chicago has long been a transportation hub, first for ships and railroads and later for interstate highways and air travel. After living in Chicagoland, as locals call their sprawling metropolis, for two years, I knew that you didn't need a car to get around in that city. The train could take you anywhere and everywhere, and it affects the locals whether they see it, ride it, hear it, or even smell it. I had hoped that Metra would pull through with a position for me in time, but I arrived in Illinois still waiting for confirmation.

Meanwhile, John Deere was expecting me. The company had featured me in its newsletter, planned my work schedule, and even arranged for accommodations. It was ready to welcome me and give me the star treatment, but I remained mentally committed to Metra; I just felt it embodied Illinois perfectly.

I needed to stay true to my project's mission by working a job that best represented the culture and economy of the state. Throughout my journey, I had declined job offers that I felt strayed too far from my purpose. So on Sunday night, I regretfully e-mailed John Deere to say I wouldn't be working there that week after all. In reply, a spokesperson noted the company's disappointment, but was diplomatic and wished me well. I felt guilty for leading John Deere on. On the other hand, since I had turned down John Deere, I felt pressure to work things out with Metra.

The presence of the South Koreans added more pressure to make things work with Metra. They wanted to get more footage, but were staying for only a couple more days. So we brainstormed ideas for filling my time in lieu of a job that had not materialized yet. Frustrated by the delay, I decided to take matters into my own hands.

"Let's just go over to the main office and figure this out once and for all," I told them. We showed up at the lobby of the Metra building and asked the security guard to buzz my contacts, Peg and Jeff, the marketing directors.

"What are you doing here?" Jeff asked after coming down on the elevator. "You can't just show up with cameras. We told you we'd get back to you. It's probably going to be midweek," he scolded before ushering us out of the lobby. *This should have been the easiest job to land*, I thought to myself. I was overcome with remorse about the South Koreans. They had come so far, and I was not able to give them a complete story.

Two days later, the news crew left and I was still jobless. I thought I would have to stay in Chicago another week to get the Metra job. *It's not fair to cut the week short*, I thought. Fortunately, I had a place to stay in a friend's condo, and as usual, plenty to do with my free time – namely, looking for jobs. The most immediate job search, in next-door Michigan for the following week, was proving difficult. I wanted to work for General Motors. The company was interested and came close to offering me a position, but couldn't justify hiring me after laying off so many people. Not sure what to do, I spent my days calling auto mechanics in Detroit. I called hundreds of shops, but it seemed as if everyone in Motor City was unemployed.

Maybe this is bad karma for leading John Deere on, I thought. I had trouble looking at myself in the mirror. I was stressed out. All the money I had earned so far was consumed by car insurance, health insurance, my cell phone, my web site, and gas. I didn't even have money for food. I was thin and my energy was waning.

Metra finally called Wednesday morning, instructing me to meet with the marketing manager for training. When I met Jeff, he handed me a beautiful blue Metra shirt to wear in my new position as a ticket-agent trainee. I familiarized myself with routes and schedules, and when I started actually selling tickets in a booth, I made an extra effort to be as kind and courteous as the best sales people are. My coworkers were middle-aged Metra veterans from the Southside who had been working in ticket booths since they were teenagers. They had grown accustomed to standing behind bulletproof glass, talking through a vented window, and exchanging money through a tight slot. They explained the cash transactions to me as though I had never handled money before. It was clear that they were step-oriented, well-trained, and very knowledgeable. But

I studied rigorously to provide passengers with assistance.

after working half a day as a ticket agent, I had the position down and was ready to tackle another.

My next assignment was the information booth, where I was to give directions to both locals and tourists. There was a constant stream of people who didn't know where they were or how to get to where they wanted to go. Luckily, I knew Chicago well and was able to help confused Metra passengers quickly. My coworker liked to check out girls walking past the booth while he was announcing track numbers as trains arrived and departed. Hearing his voice echo through the station, I grew jealous. His job reminded me of my time on the microphone at the rodeo in South Dakota. "Could I try?" I asked.

"Sure, but you have to make sure you read this line and number." He handed me the microphone, and I started to get nervous and confused. Thousands of people rely on station announcements to make their trains. The pressure was building. My eyes scanned the station and noticed people standing against the walls, sitting in the lobby, hovering over the information desk, all waiting for me to call out the track number.

"Your train to South Chicago is boarding on track number four — ahh, I mean six,"

"Say the time!" my coworker commanded.

"Your 1:30 train to South Chicago is now departing on track number six," I recited. He gave me a thumbs up, and I was ready to give the next announcement.

"I hope he's not taking my job," he joked to the marketing manager. "It's easy but it pays the bills!"

More than anything, I wanted to be a conductor on a train or sell tickets on board, but from the start, Metra had been concerned about liability and was too institutionally conservative to take any chances with my safety. "Can I work Saturday too?" I asked Peg over the phone. I hoped to work through the weekend to compensate for the delayed start.

"No, just return the shirt. You know you've been a bigger pain than anything," Peg said tersely. I felt horrible. My return to Illinois wasn't as pleasant as I'd expected. It was snowing, gloomy, and the job struggle continued to prove frustrating. I knew I had blown it with John Deere. I was so focused on working with Metra that I closed myself off from what could have been a great opportunity. I loved Chicago, but the week hadn't agreed with me. As I approached the halfway point, people told me it's all downhill from there. *Maybe Detroit will be better*, I thought.

MICHIGAN

AUTO MECHANIC

Driving into Michigan the first week of March, the snow didn't ease up, and with it came the two-degree temperature. I could feel a head cold coming on, on top of feeling worn out. I had been offered several places to sleep for the night, but none were close to my destination: Detroit, headquarters of the "Big Three" American carmakers. Recalling the impossibility of sleeping in my car that cold night in Kansas, I knew better than to try to sleep in my car here. I reluctantly opted to spend scarce money on a motel.

The next morning, I drove to Speedy Mechanics to meet with Mohammad, a thirty-something man who had recently moved to Michigan from Lebanon. After searching frantically, calling hundreds of auto repair shops, I had finally reached Mo. "Sure, no problem, Daniel. We'll help you out," he'd told me.

It was cloudy and still below freezing as I drove through the inner city of Detroit, with its barred windows and barbed wire fences. Most of the cars I passed were rundown; most people, it appeared, hold on to their vehicles, fixing them up as needed rather than buy new ones. When I reached Mo's, the garage shop doors were closed, presumably to keep the cold out. I parked my car, walked through the door and spotted him immediately. "Hey, Daniel," Mo greeted me from behind the counter, recognizing me right away, probably because I was a minority in that area. "How you doin'? How's everything?" Mo asked. His face reminded me of Sylvester Stallone.

"It's brutally cold outside!" I exclaimed, though to my amazement, it was even colder inside the shop.

"I know; you came on a bad week — our heater is broken, too. We have a little foot heater on the floor if you want to warm up," Mo offered, pointing to a small space heater.

"Yes, I'm going to get more clothes from my car too," I said. Before I could turn to head back to the Jeep, Mo handed me some mechanic's clothes, including a jacket with the name "Robi" embroidered on it.

"By the way, I was wondering where you're staying while you're here?" Mo asked.

"I'm not sure yet."

"Well, no problem. You can stay at my ma's house this week," Mo offered. It was clear that Mo wanted to help me. Perhaps it was Arab hospitality, but whatever the explanation, I quickly noted and even more quickly appreciated how kind and generous he was.

Mo introduced me to Frank and then Robi, Mo's brother-in-law. Both were busy working on cars in the garage. "Hey guys, this is Daniel. Have him help you," Mo told them. I walked over to see what they were working on.

"What are you guys doing?" I asked.

"Ah, just working on the same old stuff," Frank said, as a car pulled up to the shop riding on a flat tire. "Why don't you help that lady with her flat?"

I was too embarrassed to admit that I'd never changed a flat tire, but everyone could tell after I tried jacking up the car. Mo came outside to show me how to remove the tire from the rim, replace it, and put it back on the car. I thought all of this had to be done manually, but fortunately, an automated rotator device was available to handle the work. "Hey, could I do an oil change on my car as well?" I asked. I figured this was a good opportunity to finally do some upkeep on the Jeep as I was likely to encounter.

"Sure, do you know how to do that?" Mo asked.

"No, but I can figure it out," I replied confidently.

Mo wasn't fooled. "I'll show you that, too."

I was learning the basics quickly, but carburetors, engines, axles — those were another story. I'd try to learn as much as I could about them in the week before me. In the meantime, when customers approached, I decided to stick to basics: fixing flats and changing oil.

You can see they offer lots of services. A mechanic doesn't want to turn away customers by telling them he doesn't do a particular service.

I shivered constantly all day from the piercing cold, which persisted into the afternoon. "Sit by the heater," Mo urged after I confessed that I was getting a sore throat. I crouched by the space heater and didn't get up until the shop closed. I felt helpless and at times, worthless. I couldn't wait for the day to be over so that I could follow Robi and Mo back to Mo's mom's house. We drove several miles to Dearborn, the Arab capital of America, where I met my hosts for the week, Mo's Lebanese family.

Mo's mother wore a headscarf and spoke no English (something I was used to with my own grandmother). The house was packed — his mother, brother, sister, and sister's husband and children all lived there. Mo lived down the street with his family, but they spent lots of time at his mother's. Down in the basement, friends were playing poker and smoking. It was an animated, even boisterous, domestic scene and reminded me of the TV show *Full House*. "Sit down Daniel, we're going to have dinner," Mo's younger brother instructed me.

On my plate I saw a raw ball of meat accompanied by rice, vegetables, and seasoning. "Is it OK to eat raw meat?" I asked.

"Of course; we've been doing it for years, especially back in Lebanon," Mo's sister answered. I couldn't help but think of Sasha. It broke my heart to realize that my hands were tied, that I couldn't call her to share my experience with her. I wanted to tell her I was living with a Lebanese family and that even though our cultural backgrounds are different, we could still care about each other. But it was out of my hands — we had become strangers.

"Saha, saha . . ." Mo's sister cooed as she patted her little girl's back. Signs of Sasha seemed to be everywhere that evening.

"What does that mean?" I asked.

"My daughter is sick so I'm telling her to cough." That explained it, but the reminder of Sasha drove me nuts.

Mo's brother offered to sleep on the couch that week so I could have my own bedroom. I felt motivated to work the next day, but when the time came, I was overwhelmed by exhaustion and the cold. *Another day of not contributing*, I thought, yet again disappointed in myself. Still, I got up, got dressed, and drove to the shop. "We're going to take you to smoke hookah tonight with my in-laws," Mo told me. He was aware that I wasn't feeling well and praised me for making it to work. That day, as much as I wanted to help, I still felt sick and decided to take it easy, hovering close to the little heater. Later, I did get up and while wandering around the shop, I noticed a shotgun behind the door.

"What's this for?" I asked Mo. He told me that everyone carries a gun in that part of town. He had never fired it, but it came in handy for scaring people away if they appeared threatening, he added, and as I was about to discover. For soon enough, a black Mercedes SUV pulled into the driveway. A woman emerged from the passenger seat.

"Mo, I want my money!" she demanded.

"I told you I'm waiting for the check to come in. I told you yesterday. Don't come back here," he replied calmly.

The driver of the SUV rolled down his window. "Look, man, don't mess with my family. That's my money!" he shouted.

I couldn't understand what was going on, but as soon as I saw the guy clenching his teeth, I knew he was about to explode. "Don't yell. Get the hell out of here," Mo said as he approached the car window. "I told you I'll let you know when the check comes in."

I could see the driver reach into a bag behind the seat and knew instantly that he was reaching for a gun. Mo didn't show any sign of weakness as he continued to urge the visitors to leave. Frank grabbed the shotgun from behind the door, waiting to react. "I'm coming back tomorrow; you better have the money," the driver said before speeding away. The scene seemed totally unreal. I felt as if I were in a movie, but I should have expected something like this to occur in one of the most dangerous cities in America. Though police were roaming the streets, Mo explained that guns are so common in the middle of Detroit that cops don't bother to respond when they hear gunshots. If you're lucky, they will come if someone is shot.

That afternoon, we went home to clean up before going out to the hookah bar. I washed the grease off my hands, but as I stood over the sink scrubbing the oil off my pants, my head throbbed. I felt weak and my body ached. By the time we sat down for dinner, I knew I had a fever. "I'm sorry," I told Mo's family, "I have to lay down." No sooner had I slumped on the bed than I bolted up to rush to the bathroom. I vomited as if I'd been holding it in for years. Outside the bathroom, Mo's entire family was listening and talking to me through the door. "I'm fine," I reassured them. I wanted to be brave; I was embarrassed to be sick as a guest in their home.

I went back to my room, collapsed on the bed, and desperately tried to will myself to get better. Despite the effort, over the next few hours I was constantly rushing back to the bathroom. In the darkness of the early morning, I woke Robi up and said, "I think I need to go to the ER." As he prepared to take me, I quickly changed my mind. "Maybe take me to a pharmacy instead," I asked. When we arrived, the pharmacist told me that only time would treat the virus. We returned to the house, and my vomiting continued; my stomach ached from the constant contractions. The next morning,

Robi's five-year-old daughter came into my room. "I heard you're sick . . . can I lie down with you?" she asked with endearing eyes.

Her mother quickly swooped in to get her. "You're going to get sick," she warned.

"I don't care, I love him."

"Don't worry, I'll get better tomorrow" I told them. "I never miss work."

OHIO

METEOROLOGIST

I had regained my health and left Detroit behind, though the weather followed me toward Cleveland. I wasn't sure how consistent it would be. I knew Ohio had the most unpredictable weather in the country, due to the effects of the Great Lakes. While driving through Toledo, a weather alert came over the radio, and I was hesitant to continue driving. I decided to check into a motel for the night. As I stepped outside the car, I heard deafening sirens screaming through unseen speakers. My first thought was: prison break! I dashed into the motel and ran right up to the clerk. "What's that noise?" I asked urgently.

"Those are tornado warnings," she informed me. "There's one that's going to rip through Toledo tonight." I couldn't help but notice her casual tone. It was unsettling.

"What should I do?" I pressed her. Growing up in California, I'd never experienced tornadoes. I was completely dumbfounded.

"Just stay indoors; it will pass."

I took refuge in the only shelter available to me, my motel room, where I anxiously remained glued to the local news for much of the night. I wondered where the tornado had touched down. As I listened to the weather updates, I wondered what I would be doing that week myself as a meteorologist for NBC Cleveland. *How fitting this position is*, I thought. From the beginning of my planning for the trip, I longed to be a meteorologist in Cleveland. Miraculously, several local news affiliates offered me a position in the weeks preceding my arrival. I decided to be fair and go with the station that contacted me first: NBC affiliate WKYC Channel 3.

I didn't know much about the weather; in California, it's always seventy degrees and sunny year-round. So I didn't make a habit of paying much attention until I moved to Chicago. After a single night in erratic Ohio, though, I could see the importance of weather forecasts. The alarming drama of the tornado warning was followed by a beautiful day, sunny and clear, as though nothing had happened. It was still bitterly cold, but I knew that's typical for March.

When I arrived at the WKYC newsroom, it was like walking onto a movie set. There were several news desks, each one an epicenter surrounded by cameras and by dozens of lights hung from the ceiling and pointing in every conceivable direction. Everyone was well dressed, so I was grateful that my dad had given me a suit jacket weeks ago to make me more presentable. Before starting to work, I was invited for an on-air interview with the anchors, an odd experience since they were about to become my coworkers.

"We've been following your story for several months," Casey started, "and now you're here!"

"Thank you, I've been looking forward to this week for a long time," I assured her.

"Tell us, tell our viewers, what we have you doing here," Casey urged in an apparent effort to build suspense.

"I'm going to be the weatherman for *The Morning Show*," I said enthusiastically. By this point, I had become an expert in masking any hardship I'd endured over the previous twenty-five weeks. I expressed excitement and curiosity as though Ohio were my first state. It had become natural to act a certain way when the spotlight shined, the microphone was propped before me, and the camera stared back. It was as if nothing mattered except that moment.

A. J. shows off his goofy personality before going on air.

I realize that everyone assumes a similar persona in front of the camera. Whatever their usual personalities, people tend to become perky and upbeat when the spotlight is turned on, a curious contrast. I had previously thought that live television required lots of people working around the studio to support the effort. But that's not the case — in my interview, and typically, there were only a camera controller and the anchor. It was very different from the lively atmosphere of announcing before an audience, as I had done at the rodeo.

After my interview, I observed my mentors, Holly Straino and A. J. Colby, performing their weather reports. Both had their own styles but were equally informative and pleasant to watch. As I had observed, when preparing behind the scenes for their brief time on the air, newscasters and weather reporters take great care to look just right, strategically positioning every strand of hair and adjusting and readjusting their clothes in the mirror as they waited for their moment in the video spotlight.

The Morning Show was the venue for my debut as a weatherman. "It's much more open and relaxed; we don't really do the hard news," the station producer told me. While hard news — like murders and house fires — was not typical fare, *The Morning Show* did cover pressing topics. The Ohio job market, for example, was at an all-time low, so my weather report was squeezed between stories on the economy, job fairs, and unemployment. After hours of practicing in front of the green screen, I went live and gave a five-day forecast based on the slides A. J. had prepared for me. This is standard procedure: A. J. and other TV meteorologists pull data together from the National Weather Center to create slides for their forecasts. A. J. succinctly explained to me where weather comes from. "The sun is one heat source, but since the earth is spinning around its axis, the sun heats the earth unevenly," he explained, "and weather is the mechanism by which the earth equalizes that uneven heat."

Not surprisingly, if unfortunately, *The Morning Show* was broadcast daily at 5:00 a.m. I would have done anything for the noon or evening time slot. I had fallen so far into sleep deficit that, given the chance, I could have become a modern Rip Van Winkle, and slept for twenty years. I was so exhausted that once during the week, I even dozed off on the floor of the newsroom.

Tired or not, after four days on the air, my job that week ended with a bang: I appeared on a national network, *The Weather Channel*. "That's the pinnacle for a weather forecaster," A. J. told me. "Most of us strive for that position. I never will even get a minute on that show," I was wiped out, but I felt great. I was never nervous. If anything, being on the air was a constant high.

As usual, however, the real world intruded. Three weeks had passed since I last updated my journal on my web site. And I had not taken a single picture. I was burned out, and I knew I couldn't continue my trip in that state of mind. My mom had been pressuring me to take a break, and though I did not want to accept her advice,

Thirty seconds before the camera turned to me to read the five-day forecast. The adrenaline rush of being on air overcame my fatigue.

I knew I needed one. I had completed more than half of my journey, and looking back on the past few months, I couldn't believe that what was once only a vision had become the norm. Still, "normal" is not the same as "routine." I was mentally drained and physically depleted, and so, happy to acquiesce to my mom's importuning, I drove to Cincinnati to catch a flight home to California. The week I was home wasn't much of a vacation; I used my time to set up more jobs and work on my web site. But the familiar surroundings and change of pace were good medicine. I appreciated being able to slow down and even relax a bit before hitting the road again. After all, most people take at least two weeks of vacation, so I figured I deserved one week of downtime — just this once.

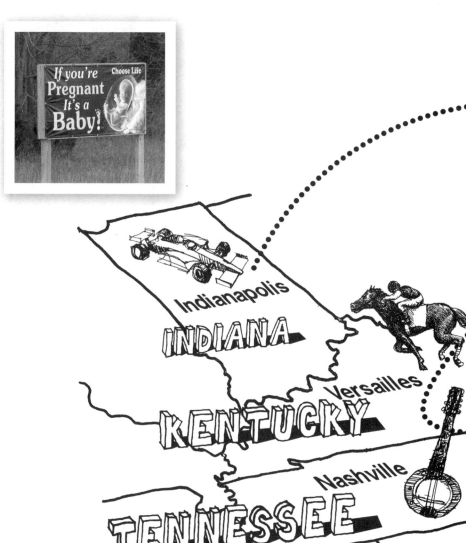

If you're **Pregnant** It's a **Baby!** Choose Life

Indianapolis

INDIANA

Versailles

KENTUCKY

Nashville

TENNESSEE

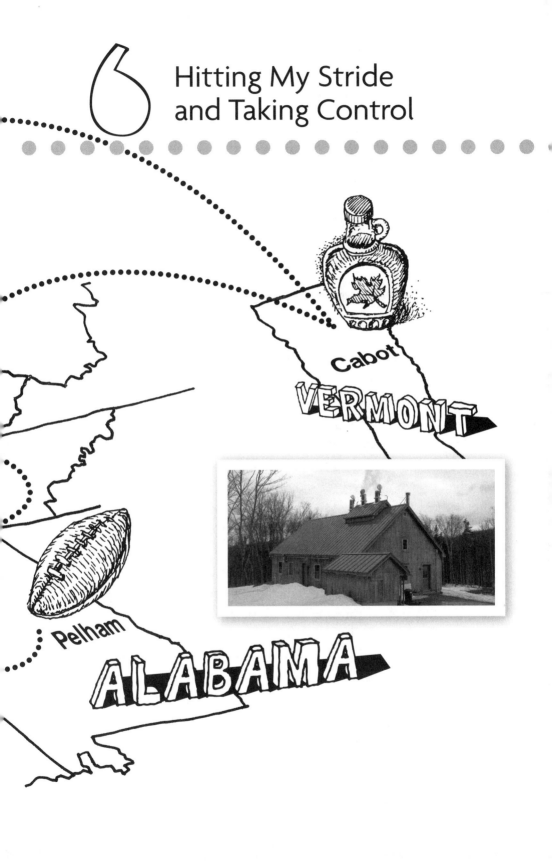

Cabot

VERMONT

Pelham

ALABAMA

INDIANA

RACING PIT-CREW
MEMBER

Memories of rednecks, four-wheeling, shooting guns, and grilling corn ran through my mind as I crossed the border into Indiana. It had been only two years since I last visited the state, and I was eager to experience it all again. One thing had obviously changed: The town of Milan, where the movie *Hoosiers* was filmed, had become a metropolis — at least in my eyes. When I last visited the Tush family in Milan, located in southern Indiana, I couldn't fathom living in such a rural hamlet. But after staying in even smaller places in Wyoming, Montana, and Oklahoma, Milan didn't seem so tiny after all.

I was in Milan to visit Amy Tush, the former track coach at Northwestern University in Chicago, and spend the weekend with her family. I had been Amy's assistant coach a few years earlier, and we had become close friends. Her family knew I was excited by my return to Indiana, and remembered how much I enjoyed four-wheeling the last time I visited, so they prepared another weekend of wheels for me. As we drove together to their friends' backyard ATV course, I was once again struck by the endless parade of pro-life billboards and American flags. Along the way, we saw children fighting over whose turn it was to play with a wheelchair, an odd but telling reminder that cars, motors, and wheels seem ingrained in the culture of Indiana. When we arrived at the enormous farmhouse where the Tushes' friends live, they strolled right over to offer us cold beers. "How ya been, Danny?" Marvin asked. "We've been following you on the news." "Doing great! Looking forward to riding again," I replied. Though he was a grown man and father, when it came to motors, Marvin was as excited as a kid.

"I'm just fixing up yours right now," he said, referring to the ATV assigned to me. Do ya wanna beer? Oh, never mind! That's right; you don't drink." I recalled that on my previous visit, when I first told Marvin I don't drink, it was like a culture shock to him. He couldn't make sense of it. It was as if I told him I don't believe in taking showers. As we grilled corn, I teased him, claiming that Californians never eat corn on the cob, either; everything comes from a can.

While we waited for my ATV to be readied, we warmed up with go-carts. I drove over the train track and through the neighborhood, passing children in every driveway. They all played with something that had wheels or a motor. It was no wonder that the Tushes were jealous of the job I had secured in their state.

Panther Racing, a competitor in the Indy 500, had invited me to train as a member of its pit crew. Everyone, of course, is familiar with the Indianapolis 500, including those who aren't interested in car racing. Not caring for it myself, I had never attended a racing event, and always flipped past races when I came across them on television. I simply never understood the appeal and so always wondered why it was considered a sport.

After my fun weekend, I drove to Indianapolis to start the new job, my twenty-seventh. As soon as I arrived, I was introduced to Lance, the pit-crew coach. He is a typical strength-and-conditioning coach, strong and serious, and he told me right away that he planned to spend the week training me. Our first stop was the body shop, where engineers design race cars for upcoming events. A model IndyCar with all four tires attached was available for practice. "Have you played any sports before?" Lance asked, obviously unaware of my background. I told him all about my experience as an athlete and coach, which seemed to have a positive effect on him, maybe because he saw in me a kindred spirit, broadly speaking, and imagined that his job would be easier than expected. "Let me get you knee pads and gloves, and we'll get started."

The pressure was on. Time and time again, my biggest problem was when the tire rolled away in front of the car. Sometimes even the lug rolled away.

When he got back, Lance told me to imagine waiting in the pit stop as a car raced straight toward me at 250 miles per hour, slowing abruptly to sixty before skidding forward, its tires nearly hitting me. Pit-crew team members working the outside tires of a race car must wait on the track itself and are constantly at risk of being struck by their team car as well as by competitors.

Lance instructed me to kneel as I held a twenty-pound drill. The drill was attached to a long hose, which constantly got in the way as I attempted to position it precisely in the center of the tire to remove a giant lug. Even on that first try, I could feel stress building as I imagined the pressure of changing tires during a real race. Typically, millions of dollars are on the line. For the pros involved, drivers and pit crew, I realized, the Indy 500 isn't a hobby, it's their life.

After I practiced removing the oversized lug again and again with the monster drill, Lance got me started on a more critical job in the pit crew, removing a forty-pound tire as fast as I physically could. The tire actually came off easily, but putting it aside without it rolling in front of the car was very tricky.

With each critical technique I learned, my perspective on the sport of car racing changed; I realized it is a *sport* and deserves respect as one. Pit-crew team members not only have to be physically fit to handle the work, they have to be precise, consistent, and fast. I couldn't imagine what the race car driver must go through. My reverie came to an end when Lance crouched behind me with a stopwatch. He wanted to time my work.

He hit the timer. *On my knees. Pick up the drill. Hit my target — miss the lug. Try again — miss again. Getting frustrated. Look over at Lance.* "Keep going," he commanded. *Remove the lug; tire slips off. Throw it to the side; it rolls away. Grab the new tire. Shove it on; doesn't go on. Push it harder. Tire clicks on. Pick up the drill; hit the center. Drill lug back in.* "Total time: 12.47 seconds."

"What does the average crew member get?" I asked immediately.

"Five seconds," Lance replied. I was not surprised by the big gap, since that was my first timed try. My view: There was plenty of room to improve.

"I want to try again," I said earnestly.

Second run: Lance hit the timer again. *On my knees (knees hurting despite kneepads). Grab the drill, hit my target. Perfect hit. Remove the lug; tire slips off. Tire rolls away — try to stop it. Roll new tire toward me. Prop up tire to lug it on; drop the gun to stop the clock.* "Total time: 7.89 seconds."

As the week went on, I kept training. On my last day, CBS planned to record my performance live. I wasn't satisfied with seven seconds; I had to prove I could be in the five-second range. As an athlete, I always put pressure on myself to perform, and my competitive nature served me as I strived to beat my last performance in changing the tire.

During the live newscast, I wore an earpiece to hear the anchor start the time. "Go!" *On my knees (knees bruised from the kneepads). Grab the drill. Hit the lug precisely; put drill down, remove the lug. Tire slips off. Prop new tire into position. Pick up the gun; missed the target. Stay calm. Try again. Nail it.* "Stop. Total time: 5.86 seconds. Lance was so impressed, he offered me a position as an alternate for the pit crew. *Thanks Lance*, I thought. *My work here is done.*

VERMONT

SUGAR MAKER

If it weren't for my boss, Mr. Widmer at Widmer Cheese Cellar in Wisconsin, I would not have made a timely detour to Vermont. I knew that Vermont is the leading U.S. producer of maple syrup and I had planned to find a job in the state's syrup-making business when I got to New England. But that was still in the hazy future, and pressed by more immediate concerns, I hadn't gotten around to my job search in Vermont yet. Mr. Widmer shared some critical information: Maple syrup is made for just a few weeks in the spring during what's called sugaring season — and sugaring season was rapidly approaching. If I wanted to make maple syrup in Vermont, I couldn't wait any longer to nail a job there. Thank you, Mr. Widmer.

So I called the Vermont Maple Sugar Makers' Association and got the phone numbers of members. Then I made cold calls until I found someone willing to hire me. That someone turned out to be the Denton family.

And so it happened that distant Vermont followed Indiana. I booked a flight to Burlington, where I was met by Ellie, the youngest of the Dentons. *Just when the weather starts to get nice in the Midwest, I leave for a gloomy, overcast day at my new home*, I thought, as a chilly late March shower threatened. My mood lightened as Ellie drove me on winding roads through the scenic landscape. I noticed the pegged snow tires on her car, but ever-changing views of the hills, rocks, and church steeples took my mind off the weather. Looking out the car window was like looking at a Thomas Kinkade painting. It was idyllic, except for warning signs along the highway to beware of falling ice. Buildings are so close to the road and their rooftops so steep that ice inevitably crashes down onto the pavement. I was without my Jeep for the first time since I bought it and felt like I'd lost my protective bubble, my coat of armor, my safety net.

Ellie brought me safely to the Dentons' sugarhouse in the woods of Cabot Hills. I saw steam blowing out of a rustic wooden house. Though it was surrounded by winter's skeletal trees and a blanket of snow on the ground, the sugarhouse seemed a picturesque refuge from the cold. I climbed out of the car and into the crisp air, which reminded me of being in the forests of Oregon. I was immediately struck by the scent of syrup. It was as if the air had been caramelized. I inhaled deeper and deeper, over and over, savoring the fragrance and wishing it would last longer with each breath. I walked into the sugarhouse to see a busy group of workers, otherwise known as the Denton family.

"That's my dad and mom, Ken and Marcia," Ellie told me. "Those are my two friends; that's my older sister, Janice." As my eyes wandered around the sugarhouse, nothing looked familiar. I had never heard of a sugaring arch — the boiling rig — much less seen one at work, boiling maple sap, and the process seemed pretty complex.

"Want to try a shot of syrup?" Marcia asked, handing me a shot glass of the viscous liquid. It was piping hot, fresh from the valve.

"Whoa, that should be a regular drink!" I cried. It tasted like melted caramel.

The Dentons and their friends continued to bustle about me, intensely focused on their work. "Daniel, grab some of these labeled jugs and seal the caps of syrup. Once the water evaporates from the sap, we have a strict deadline before the syrup loses its sugar."

Though I didn't understand the process, I knew it would come together before long. The truth was, I didn't know much about making syrup in general. I wasn't even sure of what the job was called until that evening, when I learned we're called "sugar makers." To me, none of this mattered; I knew by now that I could tackle any job, even if I didn't know what the job was.

As always, I came unprepared in terms of clothing; Ken handed me a pair of snow boots and a waterproof jacket. "Check how much sap is in the large milk trucks outside," he said. "That will let us know how much more we have to boil tonight." I took a measuring stick from him, walked outside, and climbed the ladder to dip the stick in.

"Two feet!" I shouted, unaware of how much time that meant.

"We have about two hours left to boil and about an hour of cleaning," he replied. On the third hour, when the tanks finally ran dry, I took care of cleaning. "Wash out the tanks with the scrub brush and bring the water hose in with you," Ken instructed.

Feet first, I crawled into the tank through a narrow opening. Working in the dark, I misjudged how deep the tank was. Attempting to climb in, my legs dangled, struggling to reach the floor; I was stuck, hanging from the rim, and my arms were getting weak. Within a few moments, Ken came out to give me the ladder and a headlamp. Unbeknownst to me, I needed these tools to clean out the tank.

Ken had seen what happened, but before he could offer assistance, I found the strength to pull myself back up. Embarrassed, I tried to give the impression that everything was fine. Ken wasn't fooled. "Did you try to go down without the ladder? I've done that before, too," he laughed.

Midnight passed, and we continued working. I was eager to get some sleep. "You can take the four-wheeler up to the house," Ken offered.

"Yeah, it's really muddy here," I muttered.

"That's our fifth season in Vermont, the mud season," Ken explained. As I drove a quarter mile up the Dentons' driveway, I realized I had lost cell phone reception. *Not this again*, I thought. When the rest of the family arrived home, Ken turned on the radio to listen to the weather report, wondering if temperatures were high enough for sap to flow through the pipes. The Dentons don't own a television; they're too busy running their sugarbush, also known as maple woods that are tapped for sap to make syrup. The following morning, Marcia cooked pancakes and left five types of graded syrup out for me to try. I felt like a taste-tester.

Ellie and her sister take off during the week, so it was just me and

Sniffing the boiling sap. I couldn't get enough of the scent.

the parents for the rest of my stay. It was a quiet week — especially on my birthday. I was lonely, but to celebrate, Marcia and Ken took me to Montpelier for dinner, where I was able to receive several text messages and voicemails. It helped alleviate the loneliness to know that others remembered me on my twenty-seventh birthday.

Earlier that day, TV reporters came out to the sugarhouse to meet me and watch me work. Vermont is a small media market, so "local" news runs statewide; we were pleased to learn that my story would be seen all over. They spent the entire day with us, and I noticed that their pace was more laid-back than I was accustomed to in the cities and towns where I had worked to date. "He's a quick learner," Ken and Marcia told them. I was grading syrup based on the color of the samples. "I thought this would've been a lot to train him, but luckily, he jumped right in," Ken added.

At one point, Marcia made us all a dessert from snow and hot syrup. She simply poured the syrup onto the ice, and it hardened immediately. It tasted just like caramel. I couldn't help but notice how everything I ate that week involved syrup — even the vegetables are sautéed in syrup.

"Why don't we go out on the snowmobile to check our taps around the sugarbush?" Ken suggested later that week. I was thrilled. I had wanted to ride a snowmobile since I was born. "We have about 4,600 tapped trees covering five miles. There's a lot of work to do," Ken explained. It was cold, but it was better than scrubbing knitter, syrup residue, from the bottom of the boiling arch; it was better than cleaning out the filters; and it was better than working with a 209-degree liquid.

When we climbed onto the snowmobile, Ken let me drive. Once we started moving, however, I hit a snow patch and fell off the vehicle. I was hesitant to drive with Ken on the back, afraid my driving might hurt him. "Let's take the snowshoes," Ken suggested. I had just as much difficulty with the snowshoes, falling countless times as we trekked between trees. "If you fall down, just get back up," Ken encouraged me. *Theme of my life*, I thought.

As we schlepped through the forest, we checked every blue tube tap attached to every tree. Unlike the old-fashioned drip method, the tubes suck sap from the maple trees like a vacuum; it then flows down to collect in milk trucks. Part of our job was to look closely for taps that had disconnected from the tree trunk due to weather or disturbance by animals.

Toward the end of the week, Ken again asked me to measure the sap in the milk truck. "Around eight inches," I reported. *Not enough to boil*, I thought; *less work for me!* I was selfishly happy — I didn't want to clean anymore; I'd done enough equipment cleaning for a lifetime when I was a Wisconsin cheese maker.

Before I could return to Indiana to pick up my car and resume the journey where I had left off, Metal Craft flew me from Vermont to Minnesota for the grand opening of its new facility. I had been invited to be the honored guest and cut the opening-day ribbon before flying on to Indiana to pick up my Jeep and continue on my way. As I left Vermont, I knew I wouldn't miss the gloomy, frosty weather. But I would certainly miss the caramelized air, and the maple syrup sidewalk sales — the Vermont mud season equivalent of a lemonade stand in the summertime.

KENTUCKY

HORSEMAN

Almost immediately after entering the Blue Grass State, I passed white picket fences enclosing green pastures where kids were riding on horseback. I could not have imagined a more fitting scene for Kentucky or a more reliable indicator of what was coming. Still, I wondered why it was called "blue grass" instead of "blinding green grass"—the fields and pastures of Kentucky were like a great green carpet laid out everywhere, covering every inch of ground.

I drove through the extravagant gate of Three Chimney's Horse Farm near Lexington, in the north-central part of the state. Tony, the head horseman, was waiting to meet me. He wore a huge smile and was neatly dressed, his unbuttoned shirt collar resting flat on top of the lapels of his suit jacket. I was eager to learn what he planned for me to do on the farm. "You're going to love it here," he stated confidently in a thick Southern drawl. I knew he was right. Kentucky is horse country and I really wanted to work with horses while I was there. I contacted hundreds of horse farms until finally, Tony and his staff hired me. The minute I passed through the gate and first caught sight of the grounds, I could see it was an outdoor palace: Everything was perfect. I felt like each blade of grass was worth a hundred dollars. I hadn't seen the horse stalls at that point, but I knew they are worth millions. "We'll have you muck stalls, take the horses out to graze the fields, and give them a rinse," Tony explained.

Never having worked with horses, I was slightly concerned about the learning curve, but Tony made it worse: "This is breeding season," he warned, "so the mares are really protective. They could kick and get aggressive." *Good thing I paid my health insurance,* I thought. As I led the horses out to graze, I observed the other employees walking horses gracefully through the fields. I realized confidence is the key to working with thoroughbreds; otherwise they might be tempted to assert control. I would have to be the boss and maintain dominance over them.

Confidence didn't matter, however, when it came to mucking stalls. Instead, it was a test of my patience. The foul smell of horse piss and manure infiltrated the beauty of the stalls as I cleaned out the excrement and replaced the straw bedding. The consolation was being able to watch the studs, "Smarty Jones" and "Big Brown," breed with the mares.

It was a lucky coincidence that my workweek at Three Chimneys was in the breeding season. The critical importance of successful breeding became apparent when I attended a horse show early in the week. I learned that stud fees are astronomical. And at the show, two-year-old thoroughbreds were sold for $200,000 to $500,000. Every horse is an investment, and breeding strategies are all geared toward a single goal: conceiving a million-dollar race horse.

Horse breeding plays a key role in Kentucky's economy. Apart from the value of the horses themselves and employment created by the business, tourists are drawn to the state to see the blue-grass countryside and visit the lavish horse farms. During my week, tourists even showed up at Three Chimneys to witness breeding in action. The action, however, isn't overtly sexual or intimate; nor is it quite natural. Instead, breeding is a precise, elaborate, and care-fully orchestrated procedure that requires efficient preparation and methodical performance. It is so complex that most horse farms rely on artificial insemination, which is much simpler.

Breeding sessions occur fifty times a day and are aided by a group of employees to speed up the process. First, the mare's vagina is washed thoroughly with hot water to attempt to arouse her. If the mare is confronted by a stud before she is ready, she'll kick back, which could kill the stud. To avoid such a catastrophe, a "teaser horse" is introduced to determine if mares are in the mood to breed.

Teaser horses, not surprisingly, are worth only about $10,000, a pittance compared with a million-dollar winner like Smarty Jones.

The teaser wears a harness, which serves as a contraceptive to ensure that it doesn't actually impregnate the mare. Once the teaser is introduced to the mare, the employees know the mare is ready for breeding if she doesn't kick back to defend herself, but instead, urinates and farts, which are signs of excitement. If this happens, the staffers walk the mare into a rubber-padded room and then bring the stud in to start the session. The employees, who are outfitted with helmets and padding to ensure they don't get kicked or otherwise hurt during the procedure, surround the horses. They bring the stallion to the mare and guide their intercourse to assure that the procedure happens safely and efficiently.

That week, the owners of Three Chimneys let me stay in a six-bedroom house right on the farm. No one was living there and it was completely furnished; it was unbelievable. One night, as I got ready for bed, Tony called. "Daniel, get ready! I'm picking you up!" I wasn't sure why he needed me, but as soon as he arrived, he drove me to the stalls. As we approached, I heard a couple mares moaning. We parked and walked in. Right in front of my eyes, both were about to deliver. One of the veterinarians had his arm shoved up one of the mare's you-know-what. I wasn't sure I could bear to watch. "Do you want to do this?" the vet asked.

"Um . . . ." My eyes dilated and darted around the stall as I took a deep breath and laughed nervously. I thought he was joking, but he stared back at me seriously.

"Get him a plastic sleeve!" the vet yelled.

"I don't know guys; I don't think so." I trailed off, knowing no matter how much I didn't want to, I couldn't say no when my journey led me to new experiences. From meatpacking in Kansas and bartending in Louisiana, to delivering a colt or filly in Kentucky, my journey was testing all my limits. I slipped the glove on, my anxiety undisguised as I imagined the inevitable next step.

"Just reach on in there. Feel around. Make sure that colt is coming out straight," Tony instructed me.

That pretty colt was born seconds before I shot this photo, and is getting a kiss from mom.

"How can I tell?" I asked. I had never felt so uncomfortable in my life. I never thought this was coming. There I stood with my arm extended inside an animal, feeling a baby horse waiting to be born.

"You'll feel the head and legs in there." He was right. I felt the animal inside coming closer and closer toward me. As my arm stretched inside her, the mare plopped on the ground and turned on her side.

As the newborn emerged, the mare sighed deeply and I wondered how bad her pain was. The vet and I grabbed the front legs of her baby, trying to provide assistance as she gave birth. It got gruesome as all sorts of fluids flowed out of her. The vet's grip slipped and he fell to the ground. I realized I needed to pull as hard as he had, until finally, the infant, a colt, squeezed through, and with one last push, popped out.

We wiped the colt aggressively to clean him; as he struggled to get up, its umbilical cord snapped off and hit the wall. The colt scrambled to raise itself on trembling legs and tried to take a step before buckling back to the ground. Watching the colt attempt to rise and start moving was a wondrous and powerful experience. I had just witnessed the birth of a beautiful creature, the start of a new life — and, potentially, not just a life, but an award-winning horse. I couldn't believe I had been a part of it.

Before leaving the state, I was invited to join a group of thirty Kentucky natives to watch a race involving thoroughbreds from all over the world. I felt out of place dressed as I was in jeans and a T-shirt, a vivid contrast to their suits and summer dresses as they chewed on frog legs and sipped on Ale 8s. Everything was new to me — the food, the dress, the way people talked. I wondered if I was as exotic to the other guests as they were to me.

After the race, I had to make my way down to Tennessee. I did not want to trade this week for anything, but I loaded up the Jeep and slowly headed to Nashville. On the way, I stumbled upon Abraham Lincoln's birthplace, a tiny log cabin set in acres of yellow fields. As I walked through the cabin and read about his experience, listening to the informational video playing in the background, I was reminded of my connection to Old Abe. He faced one rejection after another and yet made his way to the highest office in the country, the presidency. What I'd been through was nothing compared with his experience, but visiting his humble birthplace and reflecting on his life gave me confidence. *This guy came from a log cabin in the middle of the woods of Kentucky*, I thought, *and went on to become President of the United States.* I knew that if he could do that, I could take whatever Tennessee, Alabama, or the other eighteen states before me had in store.

TENNESSEE

MUSIC STUDIO TECHNICIAN

Driving into the hazy skies of Nashville, a.k.a. Music City USA, I knew I would experience a real cultural immersion that week. I hadn't been a fan of country music thirty weeks ago, but the limited radio stations on my drive through the Wild West, the heartland, and now the South forced me to adapt, however slowly. Country music was starting to grow on me, but could I handle a full week's worth as a studio technician at the largest music recording studio of the Southeast?

I met with my boss, Ira Blonder, owner of "The Sound Kitchen." Ira had sought me out and recruited me to work for him during my week in the state. He was in his mid-fifties, and his energy and excitement conveyed the message that he was young and hip. "You couldn't have picked a better week in the year," he told me. "We have a ton of events this week, and I've hooked you up with some sponsors. You're going to stay at A-Lofts Hotel, and Whole Foods is setting you up with a week's gift card." Everything was flawless and beyond ideal. I couldn't have planned it so perfectly.

Ira asked me to settle in right away, because he needed help setting up a charity event at the studio that night. "I'll settle in later. Let me help now," I told him. Ira was surprised I was so eager to help. *He's not familiar with my work ethic*, I thought.

His event attracted a slew of professional singers and songwriters. Many are iconic in their genres. But unfortunately, I'm not an avid fan of country, blues, gospel, jazz, or even bluegrass. Still, Ira made everything exciting for me. "You're going to have a great time and we'll introduce you to the crowd," he said, as he walked me through his seventeen-room recording studio. Hundreds, maybe thousands, of big-time artists have recorded there, from Tim McGraw and Miley Cyrus to Taylor Swift and Dolly Parton.

"Are any of them coming tonight?" I asked with anticipation.

"You'll meet some . . . Taylor Swift's guitarist . . . . Maybe Toby Keith and Faith Hill will come," Ira replied naturally.

That day, I helped set up the stage and learned how to work the soundboard. It records vocals and tracks and is used for everything music-related. It's worth thousands of dollars and has thousands of buttons to show for it. As musicians took the stage to do a sound check for the charity event, I was in the studio with Shawn, the sound technician, making sure the sound was all right, since we would be recording the event live. In the meantime, Ira interviewed applicants for an internship at the studio. I noticed a trend in his selection of candidates: pretty girls, who were also starving musicians.

Ira asked me to help with the interviews, so I got to meet most of the girls. *I've never been on this side of the interview*, I thought, as I asked each one questions about her musical background and motive for working at the studio. As I interviewed the girls, I couldn't help but remember how I often felt when I sat in their chair. The candidates were all so polite and professional, I wondered about their real character, since I knew first-hand how restricting the process could be.

At one point, Ira came in and asked me to come into his office to introduce me to one candidate in particular. A smiling college girl sat in front of his desk. As I began to conduct the interview, Ira looked on eagerly before suddenly blurting out: "Daniel, do you have a date for tonight?"

She knew what he was getting at, and agreed to the invitation. She was a redheaded country singer, and when we talked, her confidence showed; it was obvious that she felt she was a talented musician. Still, whenever I spoke, she looked up at me with wide eyes like I was a star. In fact, lots of people in the area were familiar with me and my story. I was working in a celebrity-driven industry, and I felt like I was being treated like one.

It takes longer than a week to learn how to work this soundboard.

That night, I met up with my date to walk into the event. A stage was set up in the largest room at the studio, while artists and bands rotated through sets. I could see the work we'd put in throughout the day came to fruition, as everyone was enjoying the music, the food, and the energy. As for my date, I discovered she had a boyfriend, but that was fine — I wasn't sure a country singer would be my type, anyway.

In addition to the countless events of the week, I helped Shawn on the studio equipment — dials, knobs, levels and the list goes on. My welding skills even proved useful as I soldered cable to reconfigure some speaker wires. Shawn was a great instructor; he guided me precisely and didn't allow me to make mistakes.

That week, the music never stopped. Regardless of the time of day, even when I left the studio to explore Nashville, there was live music wherever I went. I heard it in every bar I went into and in nightclubs downtown. I heard it when I went to other charity events with Ira. I went to a hoedown and heard banjos, and of course, I heard music in the studios, which bands and solo artists rented from Ira by the hour.

By the end of the week, the tangling guitars that once drove me nuts inspired appreciation; the harmonicas, the violins — I felt could have been me, my music, and that the life I was experiencing could have been my own. From that perspective, California was a different world. I'd never seen anything like this, where people who are the age of my parents acted like teenagers, dancing and singing along without a care in the world. Despite initially not liking the music, I had a blast in the atmosphere. I was feeding off everyone's carefree vibes. Immersing myself in the culture, I understood why so many people like country music; I started to appreciate it, and this made me feel like I'd been missing out for so long. The music brought a sense of comfort, like home.

And after being around talented musicians all week, I knew I couldn't miss the opportunity to record my own track. Shawn and I set up microphones in the singing booth to track my vocals and employed a surplus of equipment to make my voice sound polished when it flowed through. Just as CBS captured me changing the tire in Indiana, the local news showed up to witness my first recording. I knew that if instruments cover up my vocals, I sound fine. But this time, it was just me and the microphone, with silence all around us. I was nervous, but I'd been practicing, listening to and singing tunes in my car for weeks; now it was just time to track one. Everyone suggested I choose an upbeat song, so I decided to record "Kissing Games," an early '90s R & B tune that suits my voice.

When I was finished with the four-minute song, Shawn worked his magic to make my voice more bearable. My nasally off-pitch vocals were like the wails of a bird in distress until Shawn used compression, digital effects, reverbs and delays to build over my voice and make it sound professional. *Now I can listen to my own track on the way to Alabama*, I thought, despite the fact that my car didn't have a CD player.

"SWEET HOME" ALABAMA

HIGH SCHOOL
FOOTBALL COACH

I never thought this time would come, but there I was: State Number Thirty-One. As with Arkansas, I had been antici-pating Alabama since the day I started. I always envisioned it far in the future. It seemed like a distant country. I had never met anyone from Alabama or anyone who had even been there. I was excited by the prospect of experiencing the state and thrilled by the job I had arranged: working as a football coach at Pelham High School outside Birmingham.

I had hoped to get a coaching position during spring training and had called every high school in Birmingham. Most could not fit my schedule, so I expanded my search to the suburbs, and found Pelham. When I called Coach Burnett, Pelham's Athletic Director, it was an easy sell; I told him about my experience coaching at North-western and the University of Virginia, and he hired me before we finished the conversation.

During the drive from Tennessee, I noticed I had missed a call from Coach Burnett. I had left him a message to confirm our meet-ing time Monday morning. In response, his message was unsettling: "I'm sorry Daniel. I thought it would be all right for you to work here, but the principal thinks it will be a distraction." Ordinarily I would have panicked, but I had made it through thirty jobs already. I felt calm. Though I was supposed to start the next day, Monday, I was confident. I called Coach Burnett back right away to explore a solution to this unexpected obstacle, but he didn't answer and I had to leave a voicemail.

The Norwoods had seen my story on the national news and offered me a place to stay that week. "I am intrigued by what you are doing," Mrs. Norwood had e-mailed me. "I see that you are headed to Birmingham, AL. If you need a place to stay, give me a call. I am an over-fifty working mother." A tornado warning was in effect, so I decided not to waste any time in taking Mrs. Norwood up on her offer. I arrived during a pounding thunderstorm to the sound of a tornado siren. If I hadn't experienced that noise in Ohio, I wouldn't have been so relaxed driving through it. When I got to the Norwoods, the warning had passed and I explained my predicament at Pelham High School to my hosts. Mrs. Norwood suggested other schools, but I wasn't ready to give up yet on Pelham.

At seven o'clock the next morning, I made my way to Pelham. When I arrived, I parked the Jeep and went straight to the principal's office — I was ready to sell my idea, for the thirty-first time.

Principal Levett barely looked up at me as he shuffled through papers on his desk. He reminded me of a girl playing hard to get; he acted like he had no idea who I was or what I wanted. "Look, I never knew about this until last Friday. I have no idea who you are; I don't know if you're a child molester," he reasoned.

"Have you been to my web site to see the objective of my project? I came all the way to Alabama because of this position, and I was told I had the job until yesterday."

When Principal Levett asked, "What do you want to do with my program?" I knew I had him right where I wanted. I told him I wanted to coach Pelham's team. "I'm going to need to see some references. I still have no idea who you are. Give me four references by 2:00 p.m." I smiled graciously and ran out to update Coach Burnett. I was determined to be on the field at team practice that afternoon. There were eight previous employers I could count on to be at their desks for quick references, and I immediately contacted all of them.

In a sense, I could understand why Principal Levett was hard on me. In the first place, he was concerned about student safety, which is his job. In addition, I knew I was trying to break into a very selective profession. Becoming a high school football coach in Alabama is more difficult than in most other states for the simple reason that high school athletic programs are run like collegiate programs. Coach Burnett was recruited from Kentucky and chose to bring his staff with him to Pelham. He had a winning record and was chosen by the football committee to coach at Pelham High School.

With several hours until practice, I returned to the Norwoods' to search for future jobs. For my next state, Georgia, the following week, I was hoping to set up a position at CNN. I had exchanged e-mails with the producer of Kyra Phillips's show, but never received a confirmation. I had to put the pressure on, and decided to e-mail Ms. Phillips directly, since I had been a guest on her show. Within ten minutes she replied with a position for me, lifting a great weight from my shoulders. More than any other state, Georgia and Florida were sentimental to me, and I needed everything to work out as planned. For my week in Florida, I had Sea World and Universal Studios competing for me, and as I headed back for Pelham's practice, I felt great.

No sooner had I arrived at the field house than Principal Levett called to tell me he only received two of my references. "I was copied on all the e-mails, I'm pretty sure six employers wrote you," I replied.

"I didn't get them. Just have Coach Burnett call me." Principal Levett was back to playing hard to get. I ran to his office, and his secretary told me he was meeting with the coach. I paced the halls and before long, Coach Burnett emerged.

"I was finally able to convince him!" he exclaimed with relief. "Finally!" Together, we walked to the football field to start my first practice.

The ninth graders took the field to start practice at 2:00 p.m. sharp. In Alabama, there are two coaches per position, which makes it seem like there are more coaches than players. I helped warm up the linebackers with Coach Danny. When the whistle blew to start the scrimmage, I was assigned to coach the defensive backs. I made sure my lines of backs were parallel with the receivers. "Watch the eyes of the quarterback!" I shouted. During the first play, the ball was thrown to the receiver my player was covering. The receiver ran diagonally, and my player didn't follow him; he thought it was someone else's assignment. "That was your play! Every play is your play!

Spring training: varsity boys hit the weights for an hour before putting on pads and taking the football field.

Don't be lazy!" I coached. Throughout the game, I called some plays for defense. After the scrimmage, Coach Burnett asked if I wanted to see the University of Alabama the next morning. I thought it would be a great chance to get an inside perspective to the campus, and agreed to go.

That day, on the way to UA, Coach Burnett took me to appear on *The Rick and Bubba Show*. They are two of the most recognized radio personalities in the South, and they always record before a live audience. "What are the most unique things you've seen here in Alabama?" Rick asked.

"Almost every kid at Pelham has the same fluffy, parted hair; I think it's called the 'frat swoop.'"

"A lot of us in the South have that!" Rick exclaimed. I glanced over at one of the coaches, who had the craziest frat swoop I'd ever seen.

For lunch, the coaches took me to "Dreamland," the most famous barbecue in the state. Ever since I had barbecue in Kansas City, which was the best I ever ate — and is widely considered the best in the country — I've been eager to compare it with others. When we arrived, there was no menu, just towels on the table and piles of ribs and white bread. One thing I learned about the South is that it's all about pork. I love barbecue beef ribs, but I don't eat pork, so as the coaches sat beside me eating slabs of it, I was stuck eating loaves of bread. Luckily, the meal was followed by banana pudding, a very common dessert, and this one, at least, turned out to be one of the best dishes I'd had in 31 states. In the South, sweet tea is just as popular as banana pudding. It's sold everywhere and consumed with every meal; I saw it so often that I wouldn't have been surprised if it came out of the water fountains.

After a forty-five-minute drive, the coaches brought me to the AU's athletic facilities. Since Alabama is in the SEC conference, I knew it would be an athlete's heaven — and indeed it was. We walked around the "Bear Bryant Museum," but not for long; we had to head back to Pelham in time for practice.

When we arrived at the school, the ninth graders were in full pads and uniform, ready to play their final game of the year. The bleachers were packed with parents and students. As we prepared for the game, I was struck by what seemed like a lack of aggression on the part of the players. They were very quiet, soft, and intimidated. I wasn't surprised. Southern kids are so polite, constantly saying "yes ma'am" or "no sir." But that courtesy and respect is what the coaches love. It helps them develop the players to reach their full potential in the four years of high school available. They use it to shape players into more competitive athletes during their four years of eligibility.

When the scrimmage was complete, I helped Coach Mac collect equipment from the players. Coach Mac has retired, but loves to be around the game. "It really keeps you hanging on to your youth. I couldn't see myself being around any other kind of work," he explained. "Hooo! Keep the line straight!" he shouted to the players, who couldn't stop laughing at his voice. I suspected that Coach Mac used that deep, resonant voice of his in some other way, and confirmed my suspicion when I heard him belting gospel music in his car, and later, when he invited me to sing in the choir at his Baptist church.

Coach Mac's church is nicknamed "Jesus looking down on Six Flags" because of its size and its playground like an amusement park. As we settled into choir practice, I realized that although my voice is the opposite of Coach Mac's, there would be no problem if I didn't know the words or sang off key: The choir had 250 people in it and their enthusiastic singing would easily mask my tuneless voice.

In Alabama, you could go from singing in a Baptist Church choir to attending the Talladega 500. Coach Burnett suggested I experience the largest "redneck convention" over the weekend, and gave me two tickets to the Sunday race. I decided to invite Kaley, the daughter of one of Coach Burnett's friends. Tailgating there reminded me of the rodeo in South Dakota, but with lots of flannel shirts, jean shorts and tank tops instead of pearl-buttoned shirts and cowboy hats. After stepping onto the racetrack, I could understand why 200,000 people attend Nascar events. It's thrilling, and hearing the race cars whiz by left me breathless. And I enjoyed seeing the skills I had learned in Indianapolis put to work by other pit-crew members.

After a short while, I turned to Kaley and suggested we leave early to beat traffic. I still had to drive her back to Birmingham, and then I was off to Georgia. The whole time we were at Talladega, I couldn't get my mind off Atlanta. This had been the light at the end of the tunnel. It had been twenty-four weeks — nearly six months — since Sasha and I had spoken, and that night I'd be headed back to where I met her and where she still lived. After all the time and space between us, I couldn't stop wondering about Sasha, and what would happen there.

GEORGIA

Colquitt

7 Returning a Different Person

FLORIDA

Orlando

GEORGIA

PEANUT SHELLER

The illusory exchange of "will I ever see you again?" still resounded in my mind. A year had passed since Sasha and I exchanged those words outside her apartment complex. Back then, nothing was certain, but I knew I had to leave. I knew I had to retreat to California and figure things out; perhaps, I thought at the time, I could return to Atlanta as a successful, more stable human being.

At the time, I wasn't fit to stay in my job selling kitchens at Home Depot. I was too shy, too insecure to talk to strangers about something I knew nothing about — countertops, cabinets, and faucets. My salary was 100 percent commission, and on a good week, I would earn twenty-five dollars. I was too ashamed to admit to Sasha that I was running dry. I couldn't afford to live in Atlanta anymore; I couldn't afford to be her neighbor.

The truth is that back then, I had nothing going for me. I had no direction. The money I had saved was being chewed away by my lackadaisical life. With every day that passed, I had less money for rent and food, and I was losing weight from skipping meals.

Will I ever see you again? It's such a loaded question. Sometimes it's empty. Sometimes it's a diversion, a distraction, a way to mask indifference. Other times, it's a genuine plea: "Don't let this rendezvous be our last." *Will I ever see you again?* Just before I departed, Sasha handed me a bag with a meal she had prepared: "You're going to be able to do this," she said compassionately, "I know you will." Then, at last, I left Georgia.

Back then, her words hit a nerve in me, speaking to my soul. I felt a surge of confidence, that I could achieve my goal of working fifty jobs in fifty states and make my journey into a reality television series. Hours before I left Atlanta, I walked into Turner Headquarters, approached a security guard, and anxiously inquired: "How do I pitch a show? I've got an idea."

"You can't do it like this, just walking up here."

"Come on! I'm sure you know producers and directors who come through here all the time!"

"Yes, I do. There's a process though."

"Look, I don't have much time. I'm leaving Atlanta in a couple of hours," I pressed, hoping he could give me a contact.

"I'll take your name and number and if I come up with something, I'll let you know."

"You'll see me here again!" I promised, before walking away.

● ● ● ● ●

Exactly one year to the day I left, I was on my way back to Atlanta. I was painfully disappointed that CNN had withdrawn its offer to let me work with Kyra Phillips. After first confirming the offer, the network apologetically rejected me within days of my return to Atlanta, citing conflict of interest. My disappointment was completely outweighed, however, by the anxiety relating to confronting my memories. For months, I had been waiting for this moment for my triumphant return to Atlanta. I had been waiting for this moment to prove to Sasha that I did it, to show her what I had made of myself, what I had earned, and who I had become. Beyond Sasha, Georgia churned up memories of hard times in my life. I had looked forward to a new beginning, to overwriting the bad memories with a new script in which I was the hero, the star.

So far on my journey, my confidence had grown as plans came to fruition. Months ago, Sasha deserted me; I secretly thought that maybe now, once I returned to Atlanta, things would change. Still, so many questions had been left unanswered. I had an alternative job in southern Georgia and would pass through Atlanta for one night on my way there. I knew that on that night, I could find the answers I had been waiting for.

My heart was pounding and my body trembled too much to make the call. Instead, I sent a text message — two words: "I'm here." It was late in the evening, and I drove around looking for a safe spot to park. Naturally, I returned to the neighborhood I once called home. I found a spot on a narrow street, reminding me of the days I used to walk through the area with Sasha.

I went to the back of the Jeep in my usual routine, arranging the array of pillows and blankets to sleep for the night. As I tried to close my eyes, I finally got a response. The instinctual pit in my stomach warned me it wouldn't be good. It had been twenty weeks with no contact; things could have changed dramatically for her, as they had for me. I braced myself as I looked at my cell phone. "I told you not to contact me," her text message read. "I'm engaged."

That was it. My heart plummeted. I knew I should have known better, and my mind started turning, wondering about this engagement and how long it had been in the works. I was crushed, but there was nothing I could do. There was nothing left to say. There was no point in responding. I was done.

I was exhausted physically, but even more so emotionally. I had an interview the next morning with Fox and would have done anything for a good night's rest. CNN had been following my journey for its parent, Turner Broadcasting, and had invited me to give a talk the next morning. I was thrilled to return to Turner Headquarters, keeping that promise a year ago to the security guard that I'd be back. But now, more than anything, I needed to rest and be alone.

As I lightly dozed in and out of sleep, I was suddenly alarmed by an incoming text. "Well, aren't you going to congratulate me?" *She can't be serious*, I thought. There's nothing in the world I wanted to do less.

"Yes, congrats," I replied. That whole year of waiting came down to that. I had looked forward to returning to Atlanta and seeing Sasha again — if not romantically, then at least as friends. I wanted to bring her around the city with me, catch up with her, and take her to hear me speak the next day. If we couldn't do that, then at least I wanted some answers, some closure, some respect to dignify the friendship we once had. But a year later, after months of neglect from someone I had once felt close to, she slaps me in the face. Finally, for the last time, I was ready to forget and move on. It was one thing for her to be engaged, but quite another for her to demoralize me and rub it in my face. Enough was enough. She was not worth it.

Despite everything, I had to stay focused. I couldn't let these thoughts hinder my project. I had Georgia this week and seventeen more states to cover. Nonetheless, that night, it was one hindrance after another: First Sasha, and then the police.

Around 3:00 a.m., I saw the lights of a patrol car flaring alongside my Jeep. I popped my head up and noticed the officer lurking. Afraid of getting a ticket, I immediately opened the back door. The cop was alarmed to find someone inside. "Sir, what's going on?" I asked in a daze.

"You're parked in a handicap spot," he stated matter-of-factly.

"I'm sorry, I didn't notice it. It's dark," I tried to rationalize.

"What are you doing in your car?"

"Sleeping." I knew I couldn't lie, since it was so obvious. "I'm really tired from driving. I'm on my way to Colquitt . . . ."

"Oh yeah? What's going on down there?" he asked skeptically. I briefly explained my project, and the cop suggested I get a hotel for the night and be safe. I simply thanked him and drove off to find another spot to park and sleep for the remaining hours of the night.

The following day was jam-packed, which kept me distracted from the defeat of Sasha. I had my morning interview with Fox; I gave the lecture at Turner Broadcasting, and then I was headed to Birdsong Peanuts in the southwest corner of Georgia.

Georgia produces 45 percent of our nation's peanuts; so after CNN fell through, I called around to peanut farms. I was connected with Kevin Calhoun, director of the shelling plant. Only months before I arrived, the peanut industry had come under major scrutiny, suffering a major recall due to concerns about salmonella poisoning. I thought working on a peanut farm would be a great chance to get the inside scoop, in addition to learning about an industry that helps fuel the state's economy.

On the drive through the humid Georgian forests, bugs kept hitting my windshield and splattering like raindrops. I called Kevin for more specific directions. "I can't find your plant," I told him.

"Wah you neow?" he asked. I couldn't decipher a word he was saying. His accent was like no other I had heard; it was thicker than peanut butter itself.

"Could you e-mail me the directions?" I tried not to be rude, but I couldn't puzzle out the meaning of his words. He understood me, though, and sent the directions, so I was able to meet Kevin at the shelling plant in Blakely as planned. Directly across the street stood Peanut Corporation of America, which had been shut down permanently due to recent contamination charges. The town seemed to exist on peanuts alone and was drastically diminished by the closing, which left hundreds of local people jobless. If a small town relies on a single industry, there are no alternatives when it stops operating. People had to relocate.

Though Birdsong had nothing to do with the salmonella outbreak, its reputation was in turmoil simply for being in the industry. Kevin handed me a "Peanut Proud" T-shirt and guided me around the plant; I hadn't realized it was such a big operation.

"Lat's heed ova to Colquitt wha ya ken cheek into ya hotel and get stotted on the gigging machines" he proposed.

When we got there, Kevin showed me how to use a probe to take samples of the peanuts from the top of the uncovered trucks on the way to discharge their loads. I stood in a moving cage, hovering over 20,000 pounds of peanuts to take the samples. With the probe, I measured moisture, meat content, the size of the nut, and removed rocks, weeds, and other unwanted material. That week, planting started and I learned how to package seeds. All the seeds, which are just regular peanuts, were treated with fungicide in preparation for planting back into the ground.

As the week wore on, my body wore out. One day, while I was working at the peanut farm, I developed a fever that quickly pro-

Sliding down a pile of peanuts. Maybe that's how I got sick. If I'm allergic to peanut dust, I had no idea.

gressed. I was freezing, shivering, sweating at the same time. I felt an overwhelming sense of weakness. The peanut farm had booked me a room in the only hotel in town. I knew I needed to go back there and rest. I couldn't focus on anything.

I couldn't breathe — with every inhalation, my chest cringed in pain. Every cough felt like I was destroying my lungs and throat. I felt so weak I could barely keep my eyes open. As it turned out, swine flu made its world debut that very week, soon becoming a global pandemic. As my health rapidly deteriorated, I knew I had all the symptoms of swine flu. When I watched the news and learned that the virus had claimed many lives, I wondered if I would suffer the same fate.

Kevin offered to take me to the hospital, but I was no longer covered by health insurance, so I thought I could wait it out and take care of myself in the meantime. My mom called, but I was too weak to talk. She was alarmed and sprang into action, calling every hotel in the area to figure out where I was staying. Once she found the manager of the place where I was staying, she sent him to my room to check on me. I heard his knock on the door, but was too weak to get up. My chest burned like an oven, and it was too painful to speak. Finally, the hotel manager called Kevin to pick me up.

From outside my door in his thick, southern accent, Kevin told me he was there to take me to the hospital. I slowly sat up from my bed, wondering if I could muster the strength to get dressed. As I pushed the blankets to the side, my shivering intensified. Thirty minutes later, I was in the local emergency room.

Several of my coworkers stood before me. I was surprised to see everyone there so late into the night. *Southern hospitality*, I thought. There was one other patient in the emergency room and only one doctor; an hour passed before he could see me. My body continued to ache and sweat, and my heart pounded heavily in my chest. After having been in contact with so many people, driving through so many states, I thought for sure I had swine flu. I dreaded the formal diagnosis. Two hours later, I was finally tested, only to learn I had bronchitis. I was relieved; I wasn't sure what caused it, but I was ready to try to get to work the next morning.

I wasn't back to normal the next day at work, and the humid, muggy air didn't help. I needed to be strong; otherwise my contribution at work was minimal. Reflecting on Georgia, the one state I had looked forward to most, I couldn't deny what a disappointment it had been. But as I struggled through the final days at work, mustering the strength to commit to my project — a purpose greater than myself — I knew I had to maintain that philosophy in the following weeks.

FLORIDA

THEME PARK ENTERTAINER

The last time I was in Florida, I was on a spring break vacation — not a break from school or work, but from life. I slept on the beach, met strangers, skipped meals, and lived like a breeze until vacation ended. That's when I conceived the idea of Living the Map, before heading to Georgia, and then California, to make it a reality. Over a year later, as I arrived at State Thirty-Three, I felt sentimental returning to the place where it all began. Luckily, compared with Georgia, I had everything worked out to ensure a pleasant week. I had stoked competitive tension between SeaWorld and Universal Studies, and even Disney World was contending for me, hoping to hire me as a park entertainer. I knew by then that I was a walking billboard and the theme parks of Orlando would do anything to stand out from their competitors.

I chose Universal Studios, but the company wasn't sure what it would have me do. When I arrived at the theme park, I met with the marketing team to go over possibilities. "We're going to have you become a grouper and greeter (groupers help keep lines for the rides moving), and we're hoping you'd be interested in becoming King Tiron for the Revenge of the Mummy ride." I sensed their excitement, but I didn't understand everything behind it until they mentioned that the King Tiron job required walking on stilts. Though the excitement was infectious, I wasn't sure what to expect. As we left the meeting, I noticed a line of job applicants. *I found another way*, I smirked to myself. After two days of greeting guests at "The Simpsons" ride and grouping lines at "The Hulk" ride, I was more than ready for my debut as an Egyptian stilt walker.

I checked in at the employee entrance and proceeded to the

locker room, where the outfits are marked according to their corresponding rides. The marketing team had designed a customized costume for me. "Do you mind going shirtless?" they had asked earlier. I didn't mind, until I saw the other stilt walkers — muscular and tan. "I'm really white, and skinny," I told them. The designer's solution was to craft a tight-fitting gold shirt for me, with a headdress and long pants. It took forty minutes to simply put it on, and another twenty-five minutes to apply the makeup.

Before I could show off my new look, I had to learn how to walk on stilts. Regular employees take two weeks to train. I had about two hours. Ben, a professional stuntman, was my trainer. He had me stand on a chair and show him how I would ordinarily fall. I stood and braced myself for the fall by extending my arms to catch myself. "Wrong!" he shouted, explaining that that's the worst way to fall as a stilt walker. If you're falling from twelve feet high, you can break your wrists and other bones if you try to catch yourself the instinctive way. Ben demonstrated the proper fall: Squat and rotate the body to land on the shoulder. I practiced falling until I matched his demonstration. "You're ready to put on the stilts!" he said proudly. "We'll start you off real low."

I strapped the stilts on, attaching them to my shins and ankles as I sat on a bleacher. When Ben asked me to stand, I felt like Yao Ming towering over him. But my legs wobbled, and I was losing my balance. I didn't want to take a step — I just wanted to stand. Otherwise, I knew I would fall. "How high are these stilts?" I asked.

"Only three feet. We'll have you up on six feet," Ben explained.

"What! No way!" I didn't think I could do it, not at first. Ben had me walk around the carpeted floor, close to an oversized, insulated padded gym mat where he pushed me. Instinctively, I extended my arms to catch myself.

"Wrong!" Ben shouted again, with disappointment. He helped me back up, and I wandered around again. I started getting the hang of it and tried bending, walking backward, and doing 360-degree spins. That's when Ben graduated me to the six-foot stilts.

Moments later, we were outside on the pavement. There was

I wasn't supposed to touch the visitors, but a couple times I needed to keep my balance. Every time the wind blew or someone got too close, I was terrified of falling.

nothing to protect me if I fell. If I was lucky, Ben could catch me, but he told me not to count on it. "If you don't pass this test, we can't have you going out in the park. There will be kids tugging on your pants, wanting your autograph, trying to make you fall, and if you do, you might injure them. We can't have that," he explained. I felt the pressure to perform as I slowly made my way, step by step, across the parking lot, up the sidewalk curb, through grass and gravel. Ben kicked some gravel and walked in my path to distract me.

Learning how to walk on stilts was demanding, but learning how to play my character was also a challenge. When I met with my fellow stilt walkers, I saw how well they played their roles. As a character on stilts, I could not talk or smile; I had to look scary, and come up with weird poses when guests took pictures. Admittedly, I had a hard time keeping a straight face; as I stared past my metallic gold leotard to the tops of guests' heads at the park, I couldn't believe how bizarre the scene was. Fortunately, I had a bodyguard to make sure no one got too close or tugged on the eight-foot silver-striped pants that covered my stilts and legs.

As the day wore on, I had to deal with exhaustion, even though I got a thirty-minute break after every half-hour of performing. The break room was far away, and the heat and humidity were killing me, especially with my elaborate costume. But once I got past the break room to the cafeteria, it was like walking onto the set of *Pee-wee's Playhouse*. All the park entertainers sat at tables and wandered around in full costume; I saw Hulk, Bart Simpson, Harry Potter, Shrek, and Spider-Man lined up at the salad bar or sitting at a table with their costumes' heads beside them. Hulk didn't have as much on his plate as I thought he would.

By the end of every performance, I prayed I could make the walk back to the break room without falling. As I raised a steel-framed stilt with every step, my legs felt heavy and I grew more tired. I desperately tried to take a short cut, but the wind blew my pant leg into the path of my foot. It got caught. I was tumbling toward the popcorn machine. I felt I was falling in slow motion. I landed on my wrists — exactly as I had been warned against. And I ripped the costume. But the show had to go on, and the next day, I was up on the stilts again.

WEST VIRGINIA

Campbells Creek

New Curves and Bumps in the Road

DELAWARE
Wilmington

MARYLAND
Baltimore

Charlottesville

VIRGINIA

Greensboro

NORTH
CAROLINA

SOUTH
CAROLINA

Kiawah Island

SOUTH CAROLINA
GOLF CADDIE

Driving up the coast of South Carolina's Lowcountry, the region between the hilly Piedmont and the Atlantic Ocean, I could barely tolerate the humidity. I was sweaty and sticky, and at times, the sun was so bright, I felt like I was getting a tan inside the car. But sunshine alternated with dangerous thunderstorms, as the radio kept warning me, and several times I had to pull over to the side of the road to brace myself for the high winds and pouring rain. Thanks to Mother Nature, it wasn't necessary to pay for a car wash.

I had planned on making a brief stop in Savannah, Georgia, but the city is too beautiful for a passing glance. The neighborhoods are shaded by ancient weeping willows, and everywhere you look, there are outdoor cafes, courtyards with fountains, and well-kept parks and public squares. The residential streets are lined with elegant southern mansions I'd only imagined before arriving in Savannah. So I decided to spend the night and even contemplated staying the weekend. But I knew I had to keep moving to get to South Carolina to start my next job. South Carolina's welcome sign greeted me as I crossed the border: "Smiling Faces, Beautiful Places." Perfect. It *was* beautiful, and feeling lighthearted, I was smiling from ear to ear as I drove through the marshlands and waterways, watching egrets flying above. I drove toward the coast to reach Kiawah Island Resort, where I was scheduled to work. South Carolina is known for its tourism and resorts, so I had arranged to work at one of the state's — and the country's — most prestigious golf courses.

Upon reaching my destination, I met Jessie Watts, the employee recruiter for the resort. In pursuit of the job, I had sent a bulk e-mail to dozens of people all over the state, and Jessie agreed to hire me. She was waiting for me at Kiawah's five-diamond-rated restaurant. "Welcome to the resort!" she said as I approached. Jessie was well dressed, pleasant, and polite. I had become accustomed to such courtesy, having been in the South for weeks. And the island is paradise. I was breathless with delight: the palmetto trees along the driveway, the blooming indigenous flowers, the beach that stretched along the Atlantic coast, and of course, the resort's Sanctuary Hotel.

"This is too early for a vacation," I joked to Jessie, as she ordered various seafood appetizers, hearty entrees, and dessert. Together we reviewed my meal plan and accommodations for the week. The resort would be hosting me in one of its premier rooms. "How much do these rooms go for per night?" I asked curiously.

"Yours is roughly $1,000, but we have a presidential suite that Will Smith just checked out of for $5,000." In that moment, I couldn't prevent the places I had stayed before from flashing in my mind: a trailer in Wyoming, an adobe house in New Mexico, a cabin in Vermont, and now a resort. I was lost in reminiscence when Jessie interrupted.

"I'll take you to Golf Digest's number-one rated toughest golf course in America, the Ocean Course, tomorrow to caddie golfers." Despite the beauty and the charm surrounding me, I knew better than to get too comfortable too soon. *Nothing has been relaxing on my journey; why would it start now?* I thought. I knew to be ready for anything.

The next day, Jessie picked me up to get me started at work. On the way to the clubhouse, she abruptly stopped her car for a turtle crossing the road. "Pick it up and bring it to the side," she requested. I casually went outside, not quite sure how to handle a turtle. I grabbed its brown shell, until the turtle began hissing violently. I dropped it and ran back to her car. Jessie went out to remove it herself.

"Don't blame me," I said, trying to deflect embarrassment. "You're used to this."

"I just wonder what you're going to do when you see alligators crawling around the golf course!" Jessie laughed.

When I got to the clubhouse, I met the rest of the caddies. "Do you know how to play golf?" one of the employees in the pro shop asked.

"Yes, I play," I replied. I knew that knowledge would be instrumental, since caddies not only carry bags, but recommend clubs, cite yardage to the pin, point out hazards, and, in general, know the ropes of the course.

"We'll have you start with one bag."

I went to the bag drop, where players meet their caddies. I immediately spotted a man wearing a University of Virginia baseball hat as he emerged from his car. When he approached me to check in, I couldn't resist mentioning my connection with the university.

"I used to coach at Virginia!"

"Oh, great! What were you doing there?"

"Strength and conditioning for the football team. How about yourself?"

"I work in the peanut industry," he said casually. I recalled that Birdsong Peanuts was headquartered in Virginia. I wondered if he might have heard of the company I worked for only fourteen days earlier.

"I worked in the peanut industry two weeks ago in southern Georgia," I mentioned.

"Are you the fifty-jobs guy? I'm Mr. Birdsong!" the gentleman exclaimed. I couldn't help but laugh.

"What a small world! Now I'm working for you twice!"

Within minutes of starting as a caddy, I realized it's like coaching: Though you're not playing yourself, you are invested in the player's every move, every swing. I felt even more invested, knowing I'd earn at least seventy-five dollars in tips for a four-to-five hour

A brutal sand trap on Golf Digest's #1 most difficult course in America: Kiawah Island's Ocean Course.

round of golf. In the extreme heat and humidity, I couldn't imagine carrying two bags crisscrossing the fairways. After only one round, I felt as if my shoulder would break off from the weight of the golf bag. Yet some caddies go multiple rounds, walking fifteen miles per day in the heat, carrying the same weight.

Though working on the golf course was my primary job, Jessie had me take on other tasks as well. I washed dishes at the restaurant, served as a kayak instructor, and was a nature guide for the local elementary schools. I managed the tennis courts, and I was even a pool boy. I didn't have much time to relax or enjoy the amenities of the resort myself.

"Do you want to come to downtown Charleston with us tonight?" Jessie asked toward the end of the week. This was tempting since I had not had a chance to explore that renowned city, and my time was growing short.

"I don't know, I have a lot of work to do," I replied with regret.

"Well, if you change your mind, just give me call."

I wanted to go, but I was beating my head into the ground trying to line up jobs for the following weeks. I had been working on the coal-mining position in West Virginia for months, and since I planned to be there a week after next, time was running out. Still, in my heart I knew that this was probably the last opportunity I would have on the trip to see the city with a personal guide. *I can't miss out*, I told myself. I called Jessie and drove into Charleston to meet up.

At the restaurant, Jessie and her friends were happy to see me. "You're so lucky to be doing this journey! It sounds like fun!" they all agreed. I tried to be diplomatic, compose myself and agree with them, but I couldn't help but reveal how I really felt. I was stressed and exhausted; I had been on a physical and emotional roller coaster since day one. I told the group that it's not as fun as it seems.

"I sleep three to four hours a night, I am stressed about finding a job for West Virginia, I get rejected all the time, I have to update my web site, market my project, and live frugally — it's not what it seems," I confessed. Their faces immediately changed from pleasant excitement to awkward, as they exchanged glances and stared back at me apologetically. I could tell I had destroyed their happy mood, but their southern kindness didn't waver.

"You'll figure it out!" one encouraged.

"Let us know if you need help!" another said. "We hope you get it all taken care of."

Their offers and encouragement were sweet, but they didn't ease my anxiety. After a few minutes, I decided to take off and try to get some work done.

Despite my concern about the weeks to come, it was easy to enjoy my last few days in South Carolina. I felt I'd been spoiled there, living and working in such a beautiful, pleasant, and comfortable place. Late Saturday evening came quickly, though, and soon, I was on my way to North Carolina. I had identified Columbia as a stopping point. In my usual fashion, I searched for a place to spend the night, scouting neighborhoods to park my Jeep. It was still early for sleep, so I sat in the car watching people roam the streets. The nightlife was vibrant, and many people were out enjoying themselves. There was plenty of excitement just outside my car window. I struggled to decide whether I should go out and explore or just call it a night and rest. It was impossible to get any work done so late in the night sitting in the front seat of my car, so I decided to go out and walk around. No sooner had I made that decision than I received a text. It was from Sasha, two weeks after she told me she was engaged.

"I lied."

My heart was pounding. Knowing her, I had a sense that this would happen, a gut feeling that she was playing some kind of crazy game to mask her insecurity and instability. Still, I was shocked as I weighed my options. I thought of possible explanations for her text. Did she want an opportunity to apologize for how she had treated me? Did she want to clear her conscience for lying? As soon as the thought entered my mind to drive back to Atlanta, I immediately overruled it. I only saw two options: I could call her back and try to figure out why this happened or I could ignore it. In other words, I could choose to move on.

I sat there, perplexed, staring out the window in a daze, watching people walk by. Every thought, every memory, that came to mind was immediately overshadowed by the cruel game in which I was the victim. I was the object. I thought of my project, the experiences I had, and the people I met. I couldn't think of one stranger I had met on my trip who would treat me as badly as Sasha had. I didn't want to know the meaning behind the text message. I didn't want to be hurt one more time. I didn't want to say something or ask her something and wait for weeks to pass before she replied. It had become clear to me that all our relationship was to her was a game. I was above it.

I looked at the time: Two hours had passed since that text came in. It felt like ten minutes. I decided to grab my sweatshirt and check out the nightlife, just as I had planned.

NORTH CAROLINA

MODEL AND
MODELING AGENT

A nd . . . *I'm no longer in the South,* I thought, while cars whizzed violently by and traffic multiplied as I entered North Carolina. I stopped at a Charlotte YMCA to exercise, which further confirmed my notion of being outside the South. I searched for an open basketball court, but none were available. The courts were packed and people were waiting for their turn to play, as if waiting in line to buy concert tickets. It was clear that I'd have no chance to shoot around. *Basketball is to the East what football is to the South,* I thought. *That should be an analogy question on the SAT.*

I was eager to stay fit and hoping for a miracle: to get a job working as a model in North Carolina. I had called modeling agencies several weeks before, but most of them laughed at me. "Send us your head shot, and if you're a good fit we'll call you in," they had told me.

"I only want to model for a week . . . ."

"It doesn't work like that; it's not up to us. We work with companies that hire our models, so it would be their decision."

Yet again, I was going against the grain. Just as being a rodeo announcer was more fitting than setting up the rodeo, or being a football coach was more appropriate than being a water boy, I had my mind set on being a model instead of some other job in the modeling industry. It was apparent that this wasn't easy to do. When it became clear that I was not going to have a chance to be a model, I settled on becoming an agent.

The plan was to work alongside the three women who run an agency called Directions USA in Greensboro. Directions USA represents models, whom its clients select for brochures, magazines, and television commercials. When I walked into the agency office, I was greeted by posters and photos of beautiful models plastered on every wall. I was also greeted by Pam, one of the agents. "So, why did you choose the modeling industry?" she asked right away.

"Hanes and Wrangler are headquartered here," I replied. "North Carolina's also the furniture capital of the world, and that business needs models for advertising. And Miss North Carolina won this year's Miss America competition."

"You must have done your homework," Pam gleamed, before leading me to the desk where my job was to answer the phone and make confirmation calls for modeling shoots.

After Pam explained the basics, I took a seat to get started calling models. As I made each call, I tried imagining the faces of the models I was talking with. "Are you available on Monday for a shoot from 1:00 to 6:00 p.m. with *Travel and Leisure* magazine? The rate is $1,900 for the day. Make sure to have a clean face, and bring a two-piece swimsuit," I recited. After only a handful of calls, it became clear that every model was available for every shoot I called about. Still, the competition made it difficult to get bookings, and the tough economy made the situation worse. Given this background, I lost faith my first day at the agency that I would get a chance to model. Seeing how hard it was for actual models to get bookings made me doubt anyone would hire me.

So I spent the week making calls, and I learned how to work with composite cards, pictorial resumes clients use to size up models for jobs. Each card includes a head shot, a portfolio of photos from various shoots, and personal stats. Pam wanted to test my eye — my judgment — and asked me to help put together a composite card-set for a particular model. I had to choose pictures from dozens spread out before me, pictures that I thought showed her range and showcased her best. I sat bewildered, sorting through the photos, when Pam interrupted: "Pick up line one; it's for you." *Who could be calling me?* I wondered as I reached for the phone.

When I answered, it was another agency letting me know I'd

been booked for a joint shoot with a model named Sarah! I thought this was a joke, but the agency and photographer had scheduled the shoot in Charlotte the next day. "Do you mind going shirtless?" It was the same question I had been asked in Florida, and I gave them the same answer. I wouldn't find out until later that Pam had reached out to her network to make my modeling dream come true, secretly booking me before I had even arrived in North Carolina. I was committed to my job as an agent, but the opportunity to actually model was icing on the cake. I knew that if I had walked away from the industry when it first turned me down, this door would have never opened for me.

Pam, who had put me up all week, took me out to dinner to celebrate my gig. At the restaurant, I realized how confident and sociable she is. She spoke enthusiastically to two gentlemen at the table next to us. They had recently moved to North Carolina from South Korea. Pam introduced me as her coagent for the week and explained my project to them. When one of the men sprang from his seat, his chair flew back and crashed to the ground. "You're Daniel Seddiqui? You drive a white Jeep, made cheese in Wisconsin, and you're twenty-six years old?"

"Well, twenty-seven now," I laughed nervously.

"Your interview was on the national news in Korea. You're a big celebrity. You have changed my life! I moved here to start over and seek new opportunities," he explained. He ushered me outside to take pictures with me and my Jeep. As we talked, I noticed his hand trembling with nervous excitement. I was overcome with a sense of fulfillment. From the fan mail I had received over the months, I knew my story had inspired people. But this was totally different. Right before me stood someone who had uprooted his life, moved to another country to start over and take the initiative to find new opportunities — inspired by me. My journey had been a risk in my own life, but here was the strongest evidence yet that what I was doing was prompting others to take risks to find happiness too. More rewarding than any booking or money or success I found on this trip was knowing that I had been a positive influence.

Sitting stiffly. The only break I got was when the photographer had to make more room on her camera.

The next day, I drove to the set of my shoot. I was a bit nervous, knowing I would be judged solely on appearance. I had reviewed Sarah's comp card the day before, which made me feel even more intimidated. She was tall, blonde, and beautiful — at least on paper. When I arrived at the site, it was like walking onto a movie set. There were lights, tents, wardrobes, even a trailer, though the trailer was part of the set. "Daniel, you're going to play the role of an unemployed stockbroker that just lost everything, but you still have a hot wife," I was told before being led to the makeup tent to get ready.

Sarah was already there getting made up. "How are you doing?" she asked sweetly. I was surprised by how warm and accessible she seemed. She was too nice to fit the stereotype of the pretty California girls I was used to.

I took the chair beside Sarah to get my face and hair done. As I stood before the mirror, with makeup artists and stylists brushing powder on my face arranging my hair, I felt like a movie star in the middle of a glamorous career.

"How long have you been modeling?" Sarah asked.

"This is my first time . . . and probably my last," I told her. Sarah was confused, and confessed that she had thought I was a real model. That gave me confidence as I walked out onto the set. I was dressed in a seersucker suit, red tie, and fancy white shoes, complementing Sarah in her bright red dress. I took a seat on the set's rusted bench, wondering if it was OK if my clothes got stained from the rust. My jacket hung loosely, so the crew pinched the excess fabric with safety pins in the back to tighten the look. I wanted to act natural, but I was severely uncomfortable. I tried to breathe and be mindful of the camera, thinking back to the interviews I had done and how important it was to gaze into the barrels of the cameras. The crew tried to distract me, but I couldn't ignore the fact that the cameras were mainly focused on me during the shoot. I grabbed a magazine on the set and tried to get into character. Modeling is much tougher than it looks. I was out in the sun, posing for eight hours, having to come up with 3,000 slightly different poses. Patience and creativity were essential. Still, I actually enjoyed modeling and wouldn't have minded going back to it the next day.

After finishing my time at the agency, I spent the weekend in Chapel Hill with some friends from college. So far, I'd had a date in almost every state, and that weekend was no exception. One of my college friends suggested a triple date, and like my co-model, my date's name was Sara. She was beautiful and I was instantly attracted to her. But she was extremely quiet. I couldn't tell if she was interested in me until one of my friends assured me that she was only shy. I had received a generous check from my modeling gig and decided to foot the bill for the triple date, a dramatic departure from my frugal ways over the past thirty-five weeks. I thought my bold gesture would impress Sara, and as far as I could tell, it did, though just for a fleeting moment. She didn't return my calls, and later my friend told me she was trying to avoid getting hurt, since I was a man on the road. Still, as I left North Carolina to drive into West Virginia, the dent in my wallet and the call that never came left a pit in my stomach, and as I approached my next state, that feeling only intensified.

WEST VIRGINIA

COAL MINER

I was headed toward dark clouds when I suddenly entered a narrow tunnel through the mountains. When I emerged, I was in West Virginia, the nation's leader in underground coal production. I had left the glamour of camera crews, makeup crews, spotlights and sets behind and was facing the dark, desolate reality of underground coal mining, a job I knew little about. I had a feeling of dread; there were thunderstorms, it was cold, and I had nowhere to stay and nothing to look forward to. All I had was time to pass that Sunday night.

I knew from the start that in West Virginia, I would work in a coal mine, but finding one to hire me was almost as hard as becoming a border patrol agent in Arizona. Weeks earlier, after making hundreds of calls, I learned I needed a license to work in a mine and that it would take months for the license to be issued. Finally, a week before I arrived, I connected with a company willing to hire me for the week.

The next morning, after a night in the Jeep, I made my way to the mine, a drive that tested the strength and endurance of my car. My route took me through neighborhoods consisting mostly of trailers, used for both homes and churches, to narrow, winding mountain roads bordered by rock walls and railroad tracks reserved exclusively for coal trains. The drive grew more and more desolate until I approached a warning sign advising that only trained drivers should proceed through the pass that lay ahead. I decided to park the Jeep and continue on foot, looking for the offices of Dynamic Energy, the company that had hired me.

After jogging four-miles up a steep slope, I found myself in a rocky landscape with no sign of life. I went back to my Jeep, aware that it was Memorial Day, but I had assumed that coal mining was a

24/7 operation. My cell phone didn't work up there and I was hungry, so I drove back down the hill to look for a town, passing billboards along the way that read, "Coal Keeps the Lights On." Otherwise, the area I passed through was deserted and ghostly. Finally, I came to a McDonald's and a Wal-Mart, where I ate and passed the time aimlessly looking for an Internet signal or cell phone reception. By sunset, I was shopping neighborhoods to park the Jeep and get some sleep. I dreaded waking the next day and starting my search again, especially in the cold thunderstorms that threatened. When morning came, I drove back up the mountain and hiked into the worksite hoping to find actual employees. After trudging around, I found a trailer that served as an office, and met the woman who had hired me. "You made it!" she exclaimed enthusiastically, before continuing. "Unfortunately we were bought out last week." I could feel my eyes widening as I stood there in shock. "You can't work here, but we can show you around . . . ."

"What am I supposed to do the rest of the week?" I asked desperately.

"Well, we can't hire you," she repeated. "I suppose you could drive to Gilbert, that's where they make our clothes."

I was distraught over losing time and eager to come up with a solution. I drove to Gilbert through pouring rain and abusive wind. I was contemplating skipping this state and coming back later, but I thought that would make things worse. When I arrived at the gear shop, I explained my predicament. The shop's owner made some calls for me and left a few messages on my behalf before finally hooking me up with Clayton, who owned several coal mines, including one outside of Charleston.

"What can I do you for?" he asked upon meeting. I explained that I was from California and trying to work in West Virginia. "Are you lost? Did you run away from home?"

"I want to be a coal miner," I said for the umpteenth time that week.

"Is *that* what brings you here to Lil' Switzerland?" he laughed. Clayton was a part-time pastor, full-time businessman, and clearly an influential figure in his community. He generously treated me to lunch, taking the time to teach me about coal mining, show me around the town, and take me to his church.

Clayton also took me to see a beautiful golf course, part of a restoration site for a strip mine in which the mountaintop had been removed to gain access to the coal beneath the surface, an environmentally destructive but common technique in West Virginia. I was planning to work in a deep mine, not a strip mine, but Clayton wanted to make me aware of the environmental benefits of strip mining. "Isn't this a beauty," he enthused. "Now the wildlife can run free with all this open space. They couldn't have roamed around these rocky slopes before."

I kept quiet and remained patient all afternoon, but my foot was twitching with nervous anxiety. It was two full days into the workweek and I hadn't clocked a single minute as a coal miner. So I was relieved when Clayton told me to drive to his mine near Charleston and talk to the foreman.

That night, as I returned to my Jeep, dreading another cramped night, I remembered that an old roommate of mine had grown up in Charleston. I called him and was relieved and grateful when he connected me with his mom, Mrs. Stevenson, who invited me to come stay. The distance to West Virginia's capital was only about forty miles, but the drive took nearly three hours because of the dangerous winding roads and endless thunderstorms. I really appreciated the home-cooked meal that awaited me and sleeping in a bed for the first time in days.

Wednesday morning, Clayton put me in touch with someone at Selah Corp, a mining company that agreed to take me on. When I arrived, I met Danny, the foreman. He was a big guy, like an ex-football player. With him, my West Virginia dream became a reality; we got right down to business.

"Here's a map," Danny explained. "Here's ground level, and this is where we're going, four and a half miles in." Danny brought me the required gear for working underground: a mounted flashlight and a heavy safety suit. Suited up, I felt like a firefighter or an astronaut, but significantly less brave.

I don't know what it was, but something in me suddenly snapped. Something in me begged not to go into the coal mine — but again, my project required it. I knew I couldn't back down and fought to reassure myself that everything would be fine. Still, I imagined all kinds of risks and accidents we could encounter belowground and felt a nagging knot in my stomach.

"Danny, I don't know if I want to do this," I confessed. For the first time in my journey, my fear had risen to the point where I didn't know if I could continue.

"Don't worry, you'll be fine," Danny reassured me. "There's five emergency exits, the mine's been operating eighty years, and we've never had a problem." I was completely distracted as Danny continued to explain mine operations. Realizing this, that my mind had been wandering, made me feel even less suited to descend into the mine. Despite the dread, again I knew that giving up wasn't an option.

I blindly followed Danny onto a battery-powered cart that followed a narrow track down into the mine. Fifty minutes later and four miles in, we approached the worksite. As we climbed out of the cart, Danny told the rest of the crew and me to kill the lights on our helmets. I felt I'd been swallowed into an abyss. The darkness was so thick, it was as though I'd been blindfolded. I could not see, smell, or hear a thing; the only thing I sensed was the crisp air surrounding us. And my only thought was how to get out, which was soon replaced by visions of every accident that could possibly happen to us.

We turned our headlights back on and continued our descent on foot. The path opened to an expansive area resembling a small otherworldly village. Tracks crossed and recrossed in a weblike intersection amid the dozens of men working and operating machinery, riding tractors, tending conveyer belts, shifting coal around and chiseling deeper into it. My anxiety subsided as I realized that every expectation I had from the earth's surface had been shattered. The air felt fresh — and it was, thanks to huge ventilators. I had expected to breathe in lungfuls of dust, but not a speck was illuminated in our

Would you get on that thing and descend four miles into the Earth? I had to imagine I was riding a roller coaster at a theme park.

headlamps. Danny explained that the coal aggregate is too heavy to float; hence, no dust.

After work, I returned home to the Stevensons and checked my e-mail. Over the past few days, threatening messages had trickled in from West Virginians offended by my web site. From my descriptions of the drive and the scenery, locals thought I was giving the state a bad reputation, but I couldn't understand what I had written that was offensive. Here's what appeared on my web site:

> *The roads of West Virginia are so windy, you could drive straight cutting all the corners. If you want to go through a culture shock, drive to the Coal Mountain. There are surprisingly many people living up in the mountains. Either that or it just looks like that because there are endless amounts of trailers along the mountain. Even some of the churches are trailers, and you're only going to find Baptist churches in this state.*

I asked my friend's brother to look it over for me.

"Yeah, I read your site," he said.

"Well, what did you think?"

"If you don't like our state, you should leave," he stated, as he reached for a golf club. "Get the hell out of my house. You're just a spoiled brat from California."

"Wait, what happened?" I asked nervously. "Is your mom here?" Mrs. Stevenson was so kind to me, I couldn't imagine that she would kick me out.

"Don't worry about her. You need to grow up and get a real job, and get the hell out of here!"

As he inched toward me clutching his golf club, I knew I couldn't reason with him and that it wasn't worth fighting back. "OK, I'm leaving. I'm sorry it had to end this way." I grabbed my bags, returned to my Jeep, and sat in it bewildered and plagued by regret — regret that I didn't have the chance to thank Mrs. Stevenson and that I had offended so many locals, though I still didn't understand how. Desperate to avoid another night in my Jeep, I called the reporters who had covered my story, until one offered to let me stay with him.

In my last two days as a coal miner, I worked "ventilation control." In the mines, clean air is a matter of life and death. To direct the airflow to the workers, cement blocks are stacked as high as the braced ceilings to seal off cracks in the mine and ensure that fresh air is routed where needed, that is, where men are working. Essentially, I was stacking the blocks, building a wall for the time being. It was a menial task, but a vital one, and I felt I was in the center of it all.

I went into a kind of Zen meditation building the ventilation wall, reflecting on my experience and that of the workers around me. I understood that miners are nothing like the stereotype: They're normal guys working with pretty basic machines in an extreme environment. The rhythm of the work itself seems to keep fear at bay. So it's easy to lose sight of the dangers that come with the environment; at times I almost forgot I was underground. Nonetheless, at the end of each day, the return to daylight as we ascended from the depths brought a sense of relief. *Whew, I made it,* I thought. That sunlight every day felt like a blessing.

VIRGINIA
MONTICELLO GARDENER

I felt that Virginia would be another homecoming. The year before, I had been a volunteer coach for the University of Virginia, supplementing that work with a part-time job at Bed Bath & Beyond. I had left Virginia abruptly for Georgia, but as I returned more than a year later, I planned to revisit my old haunts and relationships. *Living on one one-dollar sandwich a day, volunteering in the weight room from 4:00 a.m. to 9:00 p.m., biking uphill through the snow: Charlottesville, here I come!* I smirked to myself. But the truth is, though it's a pretty and historical town nestled in the Blue Ridge Mountains and far from major cities, I never thought I'd return to Charlottesville.

I hadn't been in contact with Jacob, my former landlord and roommate, but I didn't think twice about stopping by to surprise him. "Daniel! What are you doing here? Are you still doing your crazy idea?" he asked.

"I'm on number thirty-seven!" I replied proudly.

"That's awesome! What are you doing in this state?"

"Working down the street, at Monticello."

"Do you want to stay here?" Jacob offered. My old room was occupied, but even a couch in the living room was more than I had hoped for. "Make yourself at home! I'll make some dinner."

There were lots of career options in Virginia, a state rich in history. Yet I had been rejected by hundreds of historical sites before I found a position as a gardener at Monticello, the home of Thomas Jefferson. Though I used to live nearby, I had never made a visit.

The next morning, I woke up at Jacob's and after a quick breakfast, drove to my first day of work. The winding mountain road

We look like Grant Wood's American Gothic, *except in this case the farmer is the woman.*

reminded me of commuting in the Rockies, but the elevation was much lower. The grounds were beautiful, with broad lawns that reminded me of Kentucky, manicured trees, and, of course, the estate's famous gardens. I walked along a neat gravel path to meet my coworkers.

Gabriel, an Italian man who managed the greenhouse, greeted me, adding that I was to be his assistant. "Transplant these stems into these tiny pots," he instructed. I flashed back to my days in Iowa working with the soil. I took the sprouts, suffocated them with soil, watered them, and moved them into the greenhouse. Weeks later, they would be planted in the main garden.

The gardeners also had me prepare flower seeds to sell online and in the gift shop. I cut the flowers, shook out the seeds, and packaged them. After a couple of hours at this task, some of the gardeners noticed that I had not collected as many seeds as they expected. I was too embarrassed to admit I had dropped a box of seeds, which had scattered on the lawn. "They are in the flowerbed," I explained, not mentioning that I meant the grass.

Susan, one of the gardeners, asked me to pull weeds around the flowerbeds that surrounded the house. The plants were unfamiliar, so I couldn't tell if I was pulling weeds or the flowers themselves. I was out there for hours, stooped in the summer heat, removing rocks, pulling, trimming, and planting. Later in the day, I was sent to the vegetable garden and fruit orchards. I harvested turnips, cabbage, cauliflower, and the like. The crops, all authentic to Jefferson's actual garden, are given to the employees, so every day, I brought my share of the produce back to Jacob; it was like bringing free groceries home. All my Monticello coworkers seemed to love their jobs — love gardening and helping the environment — but nobody wanted to stay a single minute past three o'clock, when their shift ended. Most days, I tried to stick around to soak up some knowledge, given the short time I would be there.

In my downtime, I visited all my old stomping grounds from fourteen months earlier. I hadn't appreciated it back then, but with the passing of time and wealth of experience I had accumulated, I realized that all the people I knew in Virginia had a role in shaping the person I had become and was becoming through my journey. All my experiences before the journey led me to the journey itself. Newly conscious of this and deeply appreciative, I was eager to revisit the places I used to frequent and people I associated with them. This was like going back to my roots, like visiting an old high school track coach.

I needed a haircut, so I went back to the shop I had gone to the last time I was in the state. On that previous visit, all the customers had been African-American. "Do you guys cut white people's hair?" I had asked ignorantly.

"Shoot, we ain't racist," one guy replied. He sat me down for a trim as everyone looked on curiously. I noticed another customer's manicured hair, wondering if he even really needed a haircut. An hour later, the barber turned me around to face the mirror.

"What the . . . !" I muttered as I stared at my reflection.

"You look like Jon B," one guy said.

"Yeah, you look good," another girl jumped in. And I did, eventually; it took me a while, but I came to like the haircut. Back then, I had waltzed into that barbershop asking for a trim, and when I looked around, I suddenly became aware of the bubble I had been living in. The experience had piqued my curiosity about different cultures and stereotypes and was to help fuel my desire to cross borders and learn about people. Visiting this time around, it was like seeing an old friend instead of breaching my comfort zone. My barber recalled every detail of my visit as he spent another hour lining my hair.

After the trim, I visited Bed Bath & Beyond. As soon as I walked in, the manager recognized me. He seemed excited to see me, in contrast to when I was working for him. "Seddiqui," he said, "I saw you on the news. I was like, 'damn Seddiqui, what is he up to now?'"

My next stop was the grocery store to look for the elderly lady who used to sell me those dollar sandwiches that had been my lifeblood. She had the same reaction as Bob, and I bought another sandwich from her.

Last, I went to the weight room at the University of Virginia during football practice. As soon as I was spotted, the guys came rushing over to see me. The radio was blasting, the athletes were yelling, and it seemed nothing had changed — but me.

MARYLAND

SEAFOOD RESTAURANT COOK

Now I'm really on the East Coast, I thought as I drove into Maryland. The traffic moved faster, the drivers were more aggressive, and there were extra lanes on the highway. I wanted to pull over on the shoulder to snap a photo of the Welcome sign, but that would have required a risky maneuver. As it was, I just hoped my car could handle the rapid pace, especially since the carburetor had started to leak. I had first noticed this problem several weeks earlier in North Carolina, and it was still dripping as I made my way to Baltimore's Inner Harbor.

The Inner Harbor is a beautiful American tourist trap with a high-rise commercial district right on the waterfront. I was about to start working for Phillips Seafood. I had tasted its famous crab cakes at a rest stop and become aware that Phillips is an iconic restaurant in Maryland, just as McDonald's is in the rest of America. The chain even has a concession stand at the University of Maryland's football stadium. It was clear that Phillips, one of America's busiest restaurants, dominates the crab-cake business in Maryland with its famous blue crabs from Chesapeake Bay.

I had called Phillips weeks earlier, hoping to become the restaurant's newest cook. Honey, the marketing director, was thrilled to hire me and put me on display. "You could work right in front of all the passing tourists, while customers watch you cook!" As I headed toward the restaurant that morning, the harbor was enlivened by the sound of ship horns as naval vessels pulled in to dock. They were like a call to work, signifying the start of my thirty-eighth job.

The head chef, Earl, greeted me at the door before opening hours. He handed me a red shirt, black cook hat, and an apron. He also asked me to wear nonslip boots and black pants. By this point in my journey, I had accumulated so many clothes from weeks past, I could outfit myself for any job.

"Let's go over our menu," Earl said as he walked me to the kitchen. There were dozens of dishes, platters, and samplers. As I scanned the wide selection, I realized I wasn't familiar with most of the seafood offered, which isn't surprising given that I'm not very familiar with cooking overall. I never got in the habit of cooking for myself, and having spent the last thirty-seven weeks on the road, I knew the few cooking skills I had would be rusty.

"I never cook at home, so I have no idea what I'm doing," I warned Earl.

"Do you know how to use the fryer?" he asked.

"Not at all."

"It's pretty simple. Just go to the freezer to get whatever's ordered and throw it down." Earl was full of energy and encouragement, and my reluctance retreated, though I was still a bit apprehensive. "Don't worry," Earl assured me, "I'm not going to let you mess up."

James, the restaurant manager and my host for the week, put a billboard outside the restaurant advertising my job there. "Welcome Daniel," it read, describing my project in a few lines. James hoped it would attract customers, and it worked. They streamed in asking if I was that guy — the fifty-jobs guy, the Living-the-Map guy, and so on. They would sneak up on me to take my picture and talk a bit. I had a hard time carrying on conversations, though, because I was consumed with memorizing orders, preparing plates, and trying to avoid burning the seafood in the fryer.

Cooking in the restaurant was not easy. I was constantly burning myself as bubbling grease erupted from the pans and splashed onto the skin of my hands. With each incident, I risked dropping the food and having to start the order over again. I couldn't get the hang of it. I watched my coworkers beside me calmly and methodically prepare the food and noticed the scars on their hands from their own oil burns. "Order number seven," Earl called out over the microphone. I was exhausted, but couldn't take a break to regroup. The floor was covered with grease, and with every step was hazardous. My back started to ache from hovering over the food. I couldn't believe how this taxing, fast-paced, high-pressure job didn't seem to faze the other cooks. Most of my coworkers had joined the food industry as soon as they were able to work, and what to me was painful and daunting was natural and easy for them.

"How's everything going here?" James asked.

"Here I thought I was going to eat well this week," I teased.

"My wife, Jen, and I will take you down to Annapolis tonight for some real hard-shell crab."

Sure enough, we went down to the docks that evening and ordered all-you-can-eat crab. The waitress brought us a tray of a dozen

Juggling eight fryers at a time. At this point, I was hoping customers weren't that hungry or wouldn't come at all.

hard-shells. Jen coached me on how to open them. After cracking some claws for little meat, I was perplexed. "This isn't worth the effort," I announced. "You just have to get used to it! We've been doing it since childhood," James replied.

I felt like a true local that week, taking the train to work from James's apartment already dressed for my shift. Sometimes, Jen would drive James and me to work, and it was terrifying to be in the car with an East Coast driver. I wasn't sure I'd survive the honking, road rage, weaving through lanes, sudden breaking and accelerating. From the backseat of the car, I tightened my seat belt and held on for dear life. I was relieved there was public transit.

On my last morning, as the doors of the restaurant were about to open to customers, I turned to Earl and confessed, "I don't think I can do this." Flashbacks from the week haunted me, and looking out the window, I knew the worst was about to come. It was like Oregon and West Virginia all over again: I felt I could not go on. The paralysis I felt as I looked out on a line of three hundred school kids waiting to come in was similar to the exhaustion of logging and the fear of descending into a mine. Otherwise, it was a perfect day, bright and cloudless, and thousands of people were touring the harbor. I couldn't face more stress and exhaustion from nonstop food orders, managing eight fryers, incessant burns, constantly slipping on the greasy floor. My shift was just beginning, but I felt I couldn't face even one hour of the pressure.

"You'll be all right. We've got a team," Earl encouraged me.

I rallied, if barely. I had to struggle all day just to read the food tickets with their microscopic print. I was frustrated and ended up throwing down all the frozen food in the fryers, hoping it would match the customers' orders. When my shift ended, I walked into the main kitchen. It was hot, steamy, and crowded, with servers standing by impatiently waiting for their customer's orders. Chefs prepared food from scratch, in contrast to me, frying frozen seafood in grease. I couldn't handle being in the main kitchen for more than ten minutes. *Is cooking the toughest job in America?* I wondered. I knew it was up then and there, and I was ready to throw my apron into the laundry bin, kick off my boots, and drive up to Delaware, our nation's first state.

DELAWARE

INCORPORATION SPECIALIST

Delaware is in a peculiar location — it feels like a suburb of both Philadelphia and Baltimore; yet it's just a stone's throw away from New Jersey. In the business world, however, it's the famed capital of incorporation. More than half of all Fortune

500 companies are incorporated in the state of Delaware, so my career choice wasn't difficult. Finding an employer to actually pay me, however, required a bit more work. I thought I had found an employer, but I had to withdraw because the company in question waited until the last minute to mention that it could not compensate me. So I made more calls, including one to Corporations Companies, Inc., a.k.a. CorpCo. Christy Snow, CorpCo's manager, was very receptive, in part, because she had been looking for help. "I interviewed a recent college grad last week, and he walked away because he thought he was above this sort of work," she vented, as I noticed her thick, southern accent.

"Are you from Alabama?" I asked.

"Yes! How did you know?"

"I've been around," I laughed, mentioning that I worked as a high school football coach in her home state.

"If you're going for stereotypical jobs, that would be it!" she agreed.

I felt an immediate connection with Christy, and realized a trend—that I had been feeling that way in almost every state, with almost every individual. Having experienced so much of America and its culture, I felt like a kindred spirit with lots of Americans. This was one of the goals of my project, to understand one another. It was rewarding to connect naturally with others, even as a sort of side effect of working in each state. It was as if, having something in common with everyone, I could understand people better and know what they go through at work and in their daily lives, whatever the cultural differences.

I met Christy at the hotel she had booked for me, within walking distance of the office. She greeted me with a gift package filled with brochures, food and candy, notebooks, and a beautiful picture book of Delaware. After I checked into my room, Christy took me out to eat.

We went to New Castle, where Christy showed me around and told me about the history of the area. She told me about CorpCo over a Bobbie sandwich, consisting of turkey, cranberry sauce,

Small office with a mighty force. From left to right: Christy, Eric, the owner, me, Eric's daughter Samantha, and Allison.

and stuffing. It's basically a Thanksgiving meal between bread. "We're a small office, with four employees, but we're a mighty force," Christy explained. "I'm thinking about the tasks you could do this week. You could work with me, preparing and filing documents, learning how we interact with our clientele. You could also work with our marketing manager and help her put together some things for our web site." Christy wanted to make my week as exciting as possible, since desk work could get dull compared with what I'd been through.

After the fast-paced limelight of Phillips Seafood the previous week, it was an adjustment to sit in front of a computer. "Aren't you glad you can relax in an office this week?" Christy asked, as though she were reading my mind. She was right: I really needed to take it easy.

Companies prefer to incorporate in Delaware, compared with other states, because it's considered business-friendly. It offers tax breaks for corporations and provides a special court system. As a rule, companies must incorporate where they run their business, and Delaware is no exception. So, to incorporate in Delaware without actually locating their headquarters there, they need a local registered agent. That's where companies like CorpCo come in.

Most of the work I did that week was tedious: filling out documents, filing, and basic office tasks. I registered Living the Map and completed paperwork to reserve the name. It was a rewarding task, since I knew from day one that I wanted to do this while I was in Delaware. But doing so also hit home, because I was aware that my idea was *officially* official; what was once a concept had become a legal entity. As I made my way to Pennsylvania, driving by endless mansions with lacrosse goals in the front yards instead of soccer goals or basketball hoops, I couldn't wait to reach Amish Country.

NEW YORK

PENNSYLVANIA

Lancaster County ......

Adapting to New and Different Cultures

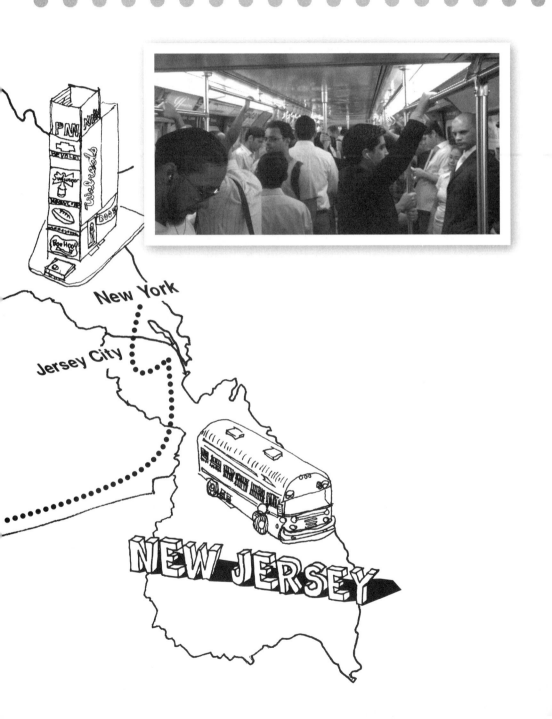

New York

Jersey City

NEW JERSEY

PENNSYLVANIA

AMISH WOODWORKER

*A*m I in Amish Country yet? I wondered as I drove through the rolling hills of Lancaster County. *I couldn't be; there was a gas station back there.* On the pavement of the two-lane highway, there were white circles every twenty meters; I later learned that these are there to warn cars to keep a two-circle distance from one another to prevent tailgating. As I drove around a turn, I spotted a horse and buggy trotting along on the shoulder of the highway. *No way; this is so unreal*, I thought to myself. But there they were, a little girl and her father riding in their own lane next to the heavy car traffic. If not for the large reflector on the back of the black boxy buggy, I might have overlooked it as it was obscured in the shade of the trees. So the reflectors are important modern additions. I drove slowly and carefully as I approached from behind. I could hear the horses' hooves pounding the pavement and was eager to catch my first glimpse of the Amish.

When I finally arrived, I searched for a place to eat and found a "Pennsylvania Dutch" restaurant. I didn't recognize any dish on the menu. I ended up eating chicken croquettes, Amish breaded chicken. It was so good, I wanted every other dish I'd never heard of. From the window of the booth I sat in, I saw a line of horses and buggies following one another to a park across the street. I decided to walk over and see what the occasion was.

When I got there, I found a baseball game in progress, Amish kids against the English kids, "English" referring to non-Amish people.

I didn't know they integrate and play sports with the English, I mused. *Heck, I didn't even know they played sports.* All I really know about Amish culture was very basic — plain dress, beards on men, no cars, no power equipment, no TV or telephones — so I was curious to have a look for myself. Sure enough, in the park, there were teenaged girls wearing long dresses and bonnets, but they were snapping photos of the baseball game with digital camera. I walked up to a group of four girls who were smoking cigarettes, another surprise, and asked if everything I'd heard was false. "Yeah, we use electronics," one girl replied, before turning away. They were quick to brush me off, but not before I noticed they were speaking a different language among themselves. I had never been more confused in my life.

Lancaster County, Pennsylvania, is the home of 20,000 Amish and the first and most concentrated Amish settlement in the United States. Despite being English, I miraculously lined up a job in an Amish-owned business, as a woodworker at Wolf Rock Furniture. It had been nearly impossible to arrange this. Since I assumed my prospective employer had no telephone, I couldn't call the company directly, as I normally did; nor could I research Amish companies online or e-mail them. Instead, I contacted furniture outlets in the area. "Do you build Amish furniture?" I'd asked.

"We don't build here, but we do get our furniture from them," was a common response.

"Do you know any Amish I could work with?"

"I can check and find out."

I made dozens of such calls and didn't hear back for months. I called just about every furniture store in the county, and not once got a hold of an Amish person directly. When I finally found an outlet in New Hampshire and asked if anyone there knew Amish woodworkers in Pennsylvania, I was connected to Sam, the owner of Wolf Rock Furniture. I didn't actually speak with him until I arrived in Week Forty.

I followed the directions to his workplace along busy Highway 30 and ended up in an empty parking lot. *Is this an Amish holiday or something?* I was baffled. I didn't see a single car, or buggy for that matter. After walking around aimlessly, I spotted an open garage door on the side of the building. I walked in to the sound of machines cutting wood.

"Do you know where I can find Sam?" I asked one of the workers. He wore clothes that looked authentic and homemade, and had a bowl-shaped haircut.

"In the office, down the hall," the man replied, pointing.

In the office, I saw Sam sitting at a desk with papers spread in front of him. All his papers were handwritten, and he was on a company phone, similar to the one I saw the previous week in Delaware. I realized I'd made a stupid mistake by having a mediator set up the job when I could have called Sam myself. I waited outside until he got off the phone. When he came out to greet me, I noticed how tall and thin he was, though his arms looked like those of a weight lifter. He had the same bowl haircut and clothing as the worker in the shop, and a nicely trimmed beard lining his jaw. "I'm going to take you up to work with the guys," he said kindly. He was extremely friendly, and we exchanged pleasantries about each other's background and his work.

Upstairs, three men were sanding chairs. "Join in!" Sam encouraged me after introducing the others. It felt as if I were representing the English and that I needed to demonstrate a work ethic that would compete with that of the Amish. I wanted to prove myself, but regardless, my new coworkers stared at me with confused expressions, wondering who I was and why I was there. Sam explained, but they remained a bit reserved. My presence seemed to create tension, interrupted only by the sound of sandpaper smoothing out rough spots in the wood. Finally, Jeb, one of the workers, broke the silence.

"So what kinds of jobs have you done?" he asked.

As I recited my resume to them, I realized that nothing I had been through really mattered. Here, it was like I was starting over. "Have you guys been out of the area before?" I asked shyly.

"I went to New York City once. I hated it," Jeb said.

"How did you get there?"

"Train. We usually take the train if we go somewhere that the horses can't."

"You sound like you have an Irish accent . . ."

"We do? That must be Pennsylvania Dutch. That's our language," Jeb told me. I was unaware that they had their own language, but their ancestry is Swiss-German; hence "Pennsylvania Dutch," a corruption of *Deutsche*, the German word for the German language and people.

Within minutes, I started to feel more comfortable. We smiled and joked like old friends. Suddenly, the men dropped their work and went downstairs to have breakfast together. I followed as though this were routine for me, too. As we sat at the table together, the workers reached for each other's hands and prayed before eating. "This is milk from our farm with some graham crackers," one of the workers explained. Sam noticed I wasn't eating, and offered me some food.

"My wife made this, knowing you were coming," he said.

"Oh wow, that was nice. Where can I get those suspenders?" I asked curiously. Just as I had suited up for rodeo work in South Dakota, in Amish Country, I really wanted to fit in too. I started the very next day, when I went to work with a beard trimmed like Sam's.

That week, I stayed with Aaron, a coworker. He's Mennonite, which I think of as like the Amish, but more receptive to technology. Their religious beliefs are similar, but Mennonites ride bikes, drive cars, watch TV, and use electronics. Aaron was happy to share his life with me. He cooked dinner as he listened to Christian music. He owns a car, but rarely used it, preferring to ride his bike the five miles to work every day.

Each morning, I woke up to the sound of horses trotting outside my window. At the crack of dawn, I showed up at the shop wearing black pants, a plain white T-shirt, and a trimmed Amish beard.

"Are you married?" Sam asked when he first noticed my beard.

"No, why?"

"The beard is grown when you're married."

"Well, I guess no dates this week," I joked as Sam stood bewildered.

"My wife wants to have you over for dinner. Then we can go get you an Amish hat."

As we worked, we wore masks to avoid fumes from the paint sprayer, one of a number of power tools in use. I was curious why my Amish colleagues were using electricity. "Some shops use hydraulics, but we have high demand and need quick turnover," Sam explained. I couldn't wait to go to his house and learn more about how the Amish, or at least some of the Amish, have adapted and modernized. When the shift ended at 4:30, Sam asked me to drive him home. He explained that his crew usually gets picked up and taken home in a taxi van. "We don't drive, but we do get rides," he continued. As I drove Sam through the beautiful rolling farmland, dotted with large homes, I saw little kids working in the yards. I had never seen such young children washing houses and pushing lawn mowers.

"I hope you like steak!" Sam's wife said, as she set the table with salad, potatoes, and shoofly pie, an Amish dessert made with brown sugar and cinnamon. While dinner was cooking, I went outside to play basketball with my hosts' four young kids. After playing outside for a while, I returned to the kitchen to wash up for dinner.

"Do you need any help?" I asked. The sun had set and the house was getting dark. Sam was rolling some kind of light around on the kitchen floor. The light fixture was unlike any I'd seen before. It was perched on top of a pole affixed to a small propane tank resting on a board with rollers underneath it, like a small wooden skateboard. It was basically a rolling floor lamp with a propane tank at its base. I had assumed that the Amish would light candles to see in the dark, but I was wrong; instead, they have mobile propane-fueled lamps, which helped explain the propane tank next to the basketball hoop; it was so big, it got in the way of our game.

"We'll go out on the buggy to buy you an Amish hat," Sam said after dinner. And so we did; the entire family and me made for seven passengers in the buggy. As the horse pulled us at top speed, it was scary riding in the open spring wagon. With every bump in the road, I feared I would fly right out. We passed local resi-

Bailing hay with a fourteen-year old Amish boy. He came to work after school but once he's fifteen, he'll be working full time. His work ethic was astonishing.

dents in their yards, children running into the street barefoot, and some riding manual scooters. As we passed through neighborhoods shared by Amish and English families, you could easily pick out the Amish houses because they were the ones with laundry hanging out to dry.

Toward the end of the week, Sam suggested I work with his brother-in-law, Ike, on his farm. Ike came down his long dirt driveway to greet me, riding on a bailing machine pulled by six horses. "I hope you're not filming," he said nervously, after spotting my camera. I was embarrassed, not realizing that he was a conformed Amish — that is, extremely traditional — and didn't like or support the use of any electronics, including my camera.

As we bailed hay and stacked it to fit on the wagon, a fourteen-year-old boy worked beside me, intermittently commiserating about my camera. "Don't worry, I use a camera sometimes. I go watch TV at my brother's house. A gang of us do."

"You have one more year left at school, right?"

"Yeah, we're done at fifteen. Then it's full-time work after that."

We took a break from the heat and gulped peppermint tea; it's like Gatorade to the Amish, a cold drink meant to hydrate, except it tastes more like toothpaste. As I soaked up the environment around me, I reflected on how impressive Amish culture is. It is supported by a well-structured community of people who are good-hearted and family oriented. My week among the Amish was so peaceful. Looking back, there were so many jobs and states I felt I could be happy in. For a moment, I thought of becoming Amish, but I knew I would need my car to get to my next state, New Jersey.

NEW JERSEY
BOYS AND GIRLS
CLUB COUNSELOR

Crossing over yet another state line, the difference this time was that I didn't have a job lined up. I had tried finding work in psychiatry, therapy, even social work. As usual, I wanted a job that was characteristic, something that represented the culture and economy of the state. I had asked my parents for advice, since they are from New Jersey, but neither could think of much. "You could work in a diner," my mom suggested, but somehow I thought I could do better.

After enjoying the afternoon in Philadelphia, I motored over the bridge to the second most dangerous city in America: Camden, New Jersey. Police cars were everywhere, on every block, which consisted mostly of run-down brick buildings and barbed-wire fences blocking vacant lots and parking areas. It was a threatening environment and I felt anxious, but I also had an inspiration: *I should work in the inner city.*

I continued my drive toward Atlantic City on Saturday night. Walking across the boardwalk and taking in the activity around me, I started to feel a bit desperate. *Maybe I should work at a hotel, since I missed out in Las Vegas.* So I went inside of one of the giant hotel/casino complexes and asked to speak to a manager. As we talked, though, I realized I didn't feel right about this direction. There are tourist traps in every state, but they're not usually representative of the state's culture. If anything, New Jersey is known for turnpikes; even being a toll collector on the turnpike was more fitting than working in a hotel.

Sunday morning, I woke up from another night in the back of the Jeep and headed north to Jersey City. I was on my way to meet my dad's cousin, Syed, who'd been expecting my visit when I came through his state. As I drove through the cities of New Brunswick and Newark, the thought of working in the inner city kept weighing on my mind. Driving through the Garden State, I was constantly looking for some green space, but all I saw were buildings, factories, and bare cement covering the earth.

Before long, I called Syed. "I'm almost to your apartment; I'm just looking for parking, but I have to detour around this Latino parade," I told him. I finally found a spot over a mile away, in front of a car repair shop. My car had been leaking for weeks, and I had finally saved enough money to get it fixed. As I walked around the corner to head to Syed's, the sun beamed down on a huge brick building: The Boys & Girls Club. *That's it,* I thought. *Inner city — working with kids!*

First thing on Monday morning, I marched into the building to look for the program director. "You'll need to see Gary," the receptionist told me. Squeezing through crowds of children and their parents, who were dropping them off, I couldn't help but notice that everyone was African American or Latino. *What a difference from last week,* I thought, remembering my Amish counterparts as I stumbled upon Gary's office.

"Hi Gary, I'm looking to work as a child counselor this week," I told him.

Practice, practice, practice. Very talented young girls. I wanted to dance too, but I was too shy to show off my moves.

"Well, just go back down and fill out an application."

"Um, I'm going to have to bypass that right now."

I explained my project, and Gary was hesitant, especially since I didn't have a background check. He reminded me of Principal Levett in Alabama, playing hard to get.

"Come back during our afternoon session, when we return from our field trip, and I'll have the day to think about it," he told me.

I walked back to Syed's apartment. "I got the job," I announced. I wasn't 100 percent sure, but I had been through this before and I had Gary right where I wanted him. I took the rest of the day to find a job for my next state, New York, and schedule meetings with publishers who had contacted me during my journey about writing a book. In the afternoon, I returned to the Boys & Girls Club to follow up with Gary. At our meeting, he nonchalantly told me he'd see me tomorrow. I couldn't wait for my first day.

I showed up to work feeling out of place. The kids were all from the same neighborhoods and had grown up together. The same was true of the counselors. As I walked in — a tall, pale, random guy, somewhat aloof — I stuck out like a sore thumb. That is, until the magnificent game of basketball brought us together.

They all knew how to play, and so did I, having played for years. But I had an advantage because I was a foot taller than the rest. I was like Lebron James on the court, and I sensed that this was gaining their respect. The game brought some competitive tension, but also a lot of team bonding. It set the right tone for the rest of the week.

As a counselor, I was responsible for a group of kids — I had to control them, make sure they behaved, and motivate them to participate in group activities. Some were easy to motivate, channeling their energy toward something positive, like dance. Dance was a required class, as were career counseling, art, gym, life skills, and computer training. I was excited to get involved in the careers course. I talked to my kids about finding jobs and answered their questions about figuring out the future. I realized that many kids viewed me as a role model. "You're an inspiration, Mr. Daniel. I look up to you more than Obama," one kid told me. Many of these children had never left their hometown and were not very aware of other cultures or of employment possibilities beyond low-paying retail jobs. Many had parents who worked three jobs just to keep afloat and greatly appreciated and depended on the Boys & Girls Club, which costs just twelve dollars per year.

In addition to career counseling, I took my kids on field trips. We would eat breakfast together in the cafeteria before heading out on trips to parks, museums, the Jersey Shore, and the like. As I started to spend more time with the kids, I realized they were starved for attention. They clung to me constantly. "Mr. Daniel, can I sit next to you on the bus?" one girl asked.

"Maybe on the way back from the museum," I answered diplomatically.

When not hovering near me, the kids were touching one another — and by touching, I mean all sorts of contact, including hitting. I could get them to stop by yelling at them, but never for more than five minutes. I was constantly separating kids from one other and taking personal possessions away after they used them to pummel other kids. Sometimes, music in their headphones would keep them busy, but typically, it was so loud, it drew more attention to them.

The bus rides seemed to last forever, in part because there were usually three buses and we could only proceed as fast as the slowest bus, and in part because the traffic was clogged nearly everywhere we went, especially on field trips to nearby New York City. The kids would get cranky from all the delays and from hunger; sometimes we couldn't have lunch until three o'clock. "Just take a nap," I would advise, hoping they would at least calm down.

"Can I borrow money, Mr. Daniel?" one kid asked. He didn't have money for lunch and would have to wait until the arranged snack was distributed. In the beginning, I actually gave a few dollars without a second thought, but as others stood by and watched, I realized the mistake I had made. Before long, the rest of the kids were asking for money, too.

Regardless, in the end, I loved the job; in fact, it didn't seem like a job. It was too much fun. I spent the days playing sports with the kids, talking to them about life and work, and trying to encourage them. I knew I would miss them. They were often boisterous, and sometimes out of control, but they were good kids who only needed to develop a sense of self-worth to avoid heading down a dangerous path.

To get to my next job, all I had to do was go through the tunnel to Manhattan. "Come see us next week, Mr. Daniel," the kids urged as I said goodbye. I picked up my car from the repair shop and started driving to my next destination. Within minutes, I hit a pothole. *I'm sorry I had to drive you in New Jersey; I'm sorry every pothole is taking a toll on your suspension*, I thought as I reflected on all the Jeep had been through. *Speaking of tolls, I'm surprised it costs money to drive on these roads. But don't worry — I'll be taking the train all next week.*

NEW YORK

INTERNET MARKETING
SPECIALIST

On Monday morning, I boarded the PATH train in New Jersey to the Big Apple. One of the athletes I coached in Virginia had introduced me to the Hinton family, and they were hosting me for my week in New York. I wouldn't see much of them, though, since they worked from sunrise till late at night, as did I. I had gone from wearing shorts and a T-shirt working with kids to dressing up in a suit and tie working in midtown Manhattan.

I approached the morning commute at my usual pace, boarding the train leisurely and acknowledging those next to me. I couldn't help but notice, though, that everyone else was in a single-minded rush. People jammed themselves aboard the train without giving others a chance to get off. *Why don't they just wake up earlier and give themselves more time?* I wondered, thinking it could reduce their stress. Personally, I was making good time—I arrived to work an hour early. As I waited, I paced the halls before meeting my new boss at Blueliner Marketing.

I had looked forward to working as a stockbroker in New York, thinking it was the most typical job for the state. Yet even with my networks and my educational background in economics, I could not land a position. Like General Motors, companies could not justify hiring me when they had laid off thousands of employees. So once again, I drew inspiration from my surroundings. Walking through Times Square the weekend before I started, the advertisements, billboards, lights, and signage had been overwhelming. I knew then that marketing would be the most fitting alternative to finance.

Her high heels echoing through the halls, Dali Singh approached me as I stood at the entrance to Blueliner's offices. "Hey Daniel, you're really early," she said.

"Yeah, I wasn't sure how long it would take to get here. But I'm always early, for everything."

"Well, let me get you set on your computer. Do you want coffee? I'm going downstairs to Starbucks."

"No thanks; I don't drink coffee."

Dali marched off as I booted up the computer. Though I was back in an office environment, not my favorite kind of place, I was excited about the assignment she had delegated to me. Dali wanted me to create a flash image for the homepage of a client's web site. The client was a language translation firm and its site was bland. The company wanted more online traffic, so one component of the solution was simply to make its site more interesting; hence, the need for a flash image on the homepage.

"You're such a marketing expert, this job should be real fitting," Dali encouraged me.

"I have us booked to go live on Fox Business," I mentioned casually.

"Wait, are you serious? I've never been on television before!" Dali was shocked. "You're such an A-lister." Sure enough, later that week we went to the studio for the interview. Fox asked Dali about her motivation for hiring me and what I had learned. She replied that she didn't flinch from hiring me because it was obvious that I have an entrepreneurial spirit and think outside the box. The media in New York even added a parallel story about, as they put it, my search for 50 *Dates* in 50 States. "My parents told me that I better find a wife on this journey," I joked.

My entrepreneurial spirit, however, wasn't pulled toward social media. I had participated in over six hundred media interviews by the time I hit New York, but I still wasn't familiar with how to best use social-networking sites like Facebook and Twitter to my advantage. "You've got to use Twitter; people would love to follow you step by step," Dali urged. I thought the idea was weird; I couldn't grasp people being interesting in following someone's every move. But if it would help, I was all for it. "When you go to your meetings with book publishers, they would love to see that you already have a following," she continued.

Since I had lots of meetings lined up with publishers that week, my parents decided to surprise me with a visit. Their sole purpose was to support me and help me land a book deal. "Since you've really made it this far, you've got to make something more of it," my dad encouraged. "Don't leave this city until you have something signed. You'll never get this time back," my dad warned.

They wanted to come to the meetings with me, but I insisted they stay behind. Before my first meeting, though, I did join them for lunch. We went to a nearby sandwich shop and waited in line for forty minutes before ordering. We waited another twenty minutes for a table to open up. I realized how much this explains city life: People are so edgy and irritable because they are always in a rush. They always want to get to the front of the line, beat the traffic. Everything is urgent and this generates constant worry. No one ever wants to wait for anything. Hurry up! Move on! Outta my way!

That afternoon, I got a crash course in the publishing industry. I always figured that if a publisher was interested, then the meeting would be a straightforward session to go over options and sign a contract. I was wrong; the publisher had no contract to offer me. Instead, I was expected to present my project as if no one at the publishing company had ever heard of it. Afterward, the editors and marketing people assured me that they were interested in my story, but needed to see an actual book proposal. "We need an outline of the book," they insisted. I was completely confused. Worse, I left these meetings with publishers feeling more and more burdened by the work piling up on my already full plate.

As the week progressed, I felt a growing sense of urgency, as if there was something more I was supposed to do. Or maybe this was just the effect of working in New York. Maybe I had become a New Yorker. I constantly worried that I was forgetting something. My mind raced constantly from the ceaseless noise, movement, and

A short presentation with a short suit jacket. I hadn't packed a suit for the journey and never needed one until this job.

stimulation everywhere — from the office to restaurants, on the street, in the subway. I had never heard so much cursing in public. People spoke with total disregard for those around them, as though no one else existed. Unlike Mississippi, where it would be awkward to avoid saying hello to a passing stranger, in New York people barely make eye contact. I couldn't imagine saying hello to a random stranger on the sidewalk or the train. There were just too many people and so little time to care.

At the end of the week, I had to present my work to colleagues at Blueliner for approval before it could be shown to the client. Since the client was a translation firm, I created a flash series showing different world monuments. The visuals were accompanied by a voiceover of someone saying "welcome" in different languages. I felt as if I were giving a final presentation at school. I needed to look professional, so I borrowed a suit jacket from a coworker. The jacket was too small, the sleeves barely reached my wrists, reminding me of the borrowed suit jacket I had worn as a model in North Carolina.

As I stood before my coworkers in a small conference room, local news crews filmed my PowerPoint presentation. I had grown accustomed to being in front of cameras and audiences, but this time, I was nervous, and for a simple reason: My colleague Tara was watching. I was hoping to ask her on a date before the week ended. I had asked Dali about Tara, and she urged me to go for it. Sure enough, Tara said yes, and we went out that very night. As far as my presentation was concerned, Dali told me later, the client bought the idea.

MAINE

NEW
HAMPSHIRE
Concord

MASSACHUSETTS

CONNECTICUT

10 Hitting Curveballs

RHODE ISLAND

AMBASSADOR
OF TOURISM

Y ou've gotta come to Newport by Sunday morning," Tim
urged. It was Saturday night, and I was standing in Times
Square on my second date with Tara. I wanted to stay
through the weekend and spend more time with her. There seemed
to be some potential, and I found myself wondering if she would
become my girlfriend.

"Looks like I have to go," I told her. "But I'll come back."

Tim Walsh, Ambassador of Tourism for the city of Newport, had
e-mailed me months earlier about working in the tourist industry
at the Visitors Bureau. He didn't specify the exact job I'd be doing,
but it didn't matter — after reading his e-mail, I was convinced he
was offering me a job in the right industry for the state of Rhode
Island. Tim had contacted me while I was still trying to figure out
what kind of work best characterized the Ocean State. My research
and the advice I'd solicited from local residents had not been suf-
ficient, and Tim proved to be persuasive.

"Great interview on NPR. You should work for us when you come
through Rhode Island. Which month will you be here?" Tim wrote.
He even offered to arrange for me to stay with a local family for the
week. I'd never before relied on a stranger's input to help me choose
a job, but Tim sold me on his proposal, to work during the "Blackships Festival" in July, when, he pointed out, Newport is "the sailing
capital of the world."

Taiko drummers at the Blackship Festival.

As I crossed the border from Connecticut into our country's smallest state, I was curious about what I'd find and how I would fit in. I drove over a number of impressive bridges, long and tall, spanning waters crowded with sailboats. I arrived in Newport to the sound of Taiko drumming from nearby baseball fields. The noise infused me with energy, which I needed after the taxing drive.

"You're Daniel, right?" Tim asked when I arrived. He was full of energy, talking a mile a minute — when I was only going a mile an hour. "Get dressed and start drumming!" he ordered.

I tied a Japanese headband around my head, put on a coat with Japanese stitching, and jumped right in. I wasn't fond of drumming and knew I wasn't very talented. Still, I had to perform for the tourists, who were packed in the bleachers looking on. I couldn't keep pace with the other drummers; I was worn out from New York City, mentally and physically. I didn't think I would have a chance to fully recover.

"We're going to take you to the sumo wrestling exhibition," Tim said when the drumming stopped. Once again, I wondered what lay ahead. When we arrived at the exhibition, a girl handed me a sumo diaper to wear.

"Take off your shirt and pants," she instructed. I reluctantly stripped down to put on the diaper. It was the last thing I wanted to do, but I felt like I had no choice. *I guess this is what the Blackships Festival is all about*, I thought.

I walked in front of the crowd, which had gathered in a courtyard to watch, and was greeted by three men, each weighing between five hundred and eight hundred pounds. I wasn't sure what was about to happen, but I wasn't in the mood to be picked up and tossed around, or sandwiched between two sweaty men. My neck ached from the drive, and I needed rest. Within minutes, two of the men did their routine, even lifting me off the ground by squeezing me with their stomachs. It was unpleasant — gross even — and the heat made it worse.

Hours passed until before I was introduced to Nasia, the daughter of Brenda Bachman, my host for the week. Brenda and Nasia, I learned, hosted visitors throughout the year. They were friendly, generous, and hospitable. Nasia brought me back to their house so I could, at long last, settle in. I noticed a spa in the backyard and did not hesitate to ask if I could soak there until dinner.

"What do you want for dinner?" Brenda asked thoughtfully.

"Anything," I replied in my exhaustion.

"We'll bring you some Rhode Island Lobster."

As I sat in the spa, I felt like a loser. I was weak and tired, and felt totally out of it, while everyone around me was pleasant and uplifting. It was draining just to think about getting through the next and final seven states while also keeping up with my web sites, the media, and composing a book proposal. *I'll make the best of this week*, I thought, *starting tomorrow.*

So I took the week day-by-day. The variety of work was daunting. Tim had a slew of roles for me to play. The first was Gully.

"Do you want to be the mascot for our local baseball team?" Tim asked. I didn't feel like I had much choice, but being a mascot was something I had always wanted to try. I put on a large sweaty seagull costume. I could barely breathe through the heavy mask or see through the netted eye holes. The head of the costume was too big for me and kept slipping down, further obstructing my vision. At times, I had to take my chances and go blindly into the crowd.

With the crowd cheering "Gully!" as the baseball game went on, I grew excited. The music was blaring, and I was dancing like a wild bird. No one could see who I was, so I took advantage of the anonymity by acting like a fool. I climbed the bleachers, flapped my wings, and shook my rear. Kids loved it, running up to me to ask for Gully's autograph; I couldn't write very clearly, but I made an effort to sign whatever they brought me.

"Do you want to be an actor at the Astors' Mansion?" Tim asked later in the week. Again, I didn't feel I had much of a choice and agreed to what he had planned. When we got there, I realized I didn't know much about Newport and its history. We drove by one historic mansion after another, each set in beautiful grounds and expansive gardens right on the water. I hadn't seen anything like it in all my travels.

When we arrived at the Astors' palatial house, I put on a tuxedo to fit in with other actors from the University of Rhode Island. We were dressed to portray members of the Astor family and staff. I wasn't sure of my role, so when the tourists came in, I tried to improvise, answering their questions with my best British accent.

"Who are you supposed to be?" One tourist asked, while I stood in the kitchen.

"Oh, I'm the brother-in-law of Mr. Astor," I replied with my flawless accent.

"No, you're the neighbor," one of the actors corrected me.

"Oh, never mind, I'm the neighbor," I told the tourist.

"What are you doing in the kitchen?" he asked.

"I'm not sure," I replied, walking away. When it came to dancing the waltz in the ballroom, however, acting and accents couldn't help: I couldn't cover up my inability to waltz. My next location was Belcourt Castle, known to be a haunted mansion. It was on the show *Ghost Hunters*, and I remembered some of the stories I'd heard about its resident ghosts. I felt uncomfortable working there, thinking back to what I'd heard. That didn't stop me, however, from having fun when the tourists passed through. There is one well-known myth of a ghost who trips people. Whenever tourists passed by me, I would pretend to trip to see if I could scare anyone. But before long, I found an excuse to leave. I told colleagues that I had to be at another venue, and they naively let me go.

By the end of the week, I felt like a local. I tried all the native dishes, like Del's lemonade, clam chowder, coffee milk, and lobster rolls. I had worked at the Newport Vineyards, ushered at Michael McDonald's concert on the waterfront, and served on the sailing crew for boat tours. All of this was in preparation for a stint at the Visitors Center on the weekend when thousands of tourists were expected in the city. By the time I got there, I was well-oriented and could give tourists accurate directions and recommendations based on my own experience. I met hundreds of new people every hour and told all of them that I was Newport's newest employee.

"I'm free for a couple of hours; what should I do here?" an elderly man asked me.

"Walk the harbor and enjoy the beautiful scenery," I suggested. Most of the time, the best things to do are free.

CONNECTICUT

INSURANCE BROKER

It was while I was in New Jersey that my job for Connecticut solidified. I called insurance broker after insurance broker, and all of them said the same thing: We're not hiring, so stop calling us. I had just about lost hope of working for an insurance company in "the Insurance Capital of the World" until I got an e-mail from Jerry at Amity Insurance.

"I got your message, looked at your site, and remembered seeing you on MSNBC as the 'Most Employed Person in America.' I like what you've been doing, as I am someone who has always loved taking risks. I'm going to have to run this by my partners," he wrote.

Reading Jerry's e-mail and waiting for his response made me think about how far I'd come. Less than a year earlier, I was considered a loser — a disgrace to my university, a lazy man lacking enthusiasm. Though people had told me I was all of these things, in my heart, I never felt that way; still, it was a drastic change from being unemployed to becoming the "Most Employed Person in America." I wondered what my parents thought when they caught sight of that article.

Jerry successfully convinced his partners to take a chance on me. "They're extremely conservative and I had to fight them on this. I believe in your message and your unconventional way of thinking. I've always wanted to do something out of the norm in my own life. When you come here, you can stay with us and set a good example for my two college daughters," Jerry wrote me. Relieved, I drove to Orange, Connecticut, just outside New Haven. I was surprised that in such a densely populated state with heavy traffic, the highway was surrounded by forests and beautiful green landscapes. They reminded me of the South.

When I arrived at Jerry's house, his three kids, who were busy working on their laptops, glanced up at me to say hello. "Hope you don't mind we're having meatloaf tonight," his wife said.

"Sounds great, but I hope you don't mind me going out for a run first," I asked, eager to stretch my legs.

"Can you give my son some pointers? I'm trying to get him in shape."

Jerry and his family had moved to Connecticut from Israel and kept up with Jewish traditions. Likewise, they were eager to help me adjust to my new environment.

"You look exhausted," Jerry observed after dinner in a heavy Long Island accent. "Go on upstairs and get some rest. Do you want to carpool with me tomorrow?" Before I could answer, he jumped into

The partners crowding around my temporary desk.

a series of follow-up questions. "Do you want to go out for lunch? Do you want to see the town after work?" He wanted to make sure that my time in Connecticut met the standard of the states where I had already worked. It was as if he thought each state had to meet certain requirements to be worthwhile.

"Just do what you normally do," I told him.

"Do you want to come down to our basement and jam with me and my son?" he asked.

"I'll come down, but I'm not that instrumental."

The next day, we carpooled into his newly renovated office building, where I met Jerry's three partners. Though I knew they were skeptical, they seemed pleased to meet me. Jerry showed me to my own office, handing me his company's brochure and background information. I was to compose thank you letters to newly signed clients.

"Before I get started on this, can we talk about what you do and your position?" I asked.

"I'm a broker, working with many insurance agencies, trying to find the best rates for our clients. We get a percentage of that rate because of referral. It doesn't cost our clients or anyone to use an insurance broker to help them find practical rates," he explained.

Jerry returned to his office and spoke on the phone with clients, most of whom he probably never meets in person. I could tell he cares and is committed to assuring them the best rates. At times it seemed Jerry agonized more about the cost of the policies than his clients did. "I hate saying this, but God forbid that you get in a nasty car wreck; you're not going to be fully covered." Jerry had a habit of saying "God forbid" about all his insurance scenarios.

The poor job market had caused people to drop insurance on many of their possessions in order to save money. I learned that millions of Americans are uninsured, which was both surprising and alarming. It was interesting to hear Jerry's clients' most personal information: their credit scores, salaries, and accident histories. As I worked with them, I couldn't help but be reminded that these were issues I needed to pay attention to myself.

That week, Jerry took me out to snap photos of client properties for submission to the insurance companies. "Why are we doing this? What's it for?" I asked.

"Preferred home credit for home owners to get their premium lower. Looking for pride of ownership," he explained.

Later in the week, Jerry suggested going out to dinner. His daughter and I waited out by the car for Jerry to lock up the house. When he wanted to close the garage door, he pushed the automatic button before running to duck under the door before it closed.

"Aah!" he yelled, as I turned around to find him stumbling and falling to the floor. While running out of the garage, he had tripped in the dark and broken his ankle. Though he cried out in agony, Jerry told us not to panic. Despite his assurances, however, he was sweating bullets and getting dizzy.

"Let us take you to the hospital," I said.

"No, I'll be fine," Jerry replied. We knew he wasn't fine, but he was a tough man.

"Get in the car; we're taking you to the hospital," his daughter insisted.

"I hope you have insurance!" I joked.

"Yes, can you bring my insurance card?" he replied intently.

For the rest of the week, Jerry was in a cast and walked on crutches. "Were you trying to show me the importance of carrying insurance?" I asked lightheartedly.

"Well, I was afraid your week wasn't going to be that exciting," Jerry joked, before reiterating how many people in the country are uninsured. "People live at risk every day, and that risk ruins their lives."

By the weekend, Jerry's partners had changed their mind about me. "I thought this was a gimmick, but it was genuine and you've asked many important questions, really wanting to understand the career," they told me. They even wanted to take me golfing, but I had planned on returning to New York City that weekend for Tara's birthday party.

Tara hadn't been in touch with me since I left New York. I tried calling her, e-mailing her; I even sent her a postcard from Rhode Island, but she never followed up, except to say she had been busy. I was already doubtful, but with an invitation from Tara and with Dali's encouragement, I decided to return to New York and see what was up. I left my car at Jerry's and took the train into the city. I spent the evening exploring the other boroughs of New York, before arriving late at Tara's apartment.

When I got there, Tara was excited to see me and gave me a great welcome, but I realized she was drunk. As we talked, I felt that this side of her was different from the person I came to know the last time I was there. I thought Tara was sweet and quiet, but at her party, she seemed provocative and obnoxious. She wasn't the sort of person I pictured myself with. After having ignored me for weeks, I wasn't interested in a game of chasing her. I had enough of the chasing game with Sasha. Without a second thought, I decided it wasn't worth it and returned to Connecticut that night, ready to move on to Massachusetts.

MASSACHUSETTS

BASEBALL SCOUT

I was shooting for the big leagues, but the Boston Red Sox shot me down. My aim was to become a professional baseball player for the week, but like modeling, however, breaking into the role of a professional athlete is far from straightforward. It didn't hurt to try, especially since I had an alternative. I was signed on as a baseball scout for the Brockton Rox, a team in an independent league in the Boston suburbs.

This time, it wasn't persistent effort that secured the position for me. Instead, it was a stroke of fate and networking in the New York City subway. Three weeks prior, I noticed a man sporting a USC T-shirt, and I couldn't help but mention that USC was my alma mater. After I explained my journey, he said he was eager to help, and he put me in touch with the owner of the Brockton Rox. Despite the awkward nature of confronting a stranger on the subway, the networking paid off when I reached Massachusetts.

I had heard enough about Boston drivers to know that I should head in slowly and cautiously to avoid the mayhem. It was a short drive, but more taxing than any to date. After merging into a web of traffic, I decided to call it a night and found a parking lot to rest until the next day. *I'm glad I covered the West Coast first,* I thought, as the East Coast drives would have worn me out from the beginning.

In the morning, I headed straight to the stadium to meet with Jack, co-owner and president of the team — and my host for the week. "Heya, Danny" he called to me with a sharp Boston accent. He sounded like JFK.

"Beautiful stadium! Thanks so much for inviting me," I said.

Jack showed me around the ballpark, and afterward around the city. He told me about Brockton's history — it's the hometown of Rocky Marciano, the great Italian-American boxer — and the role of baseball in the locals' lives. "This community has really come together. There's a lot of diehards and pride for this team." Jack also mentioned he was the former mayor of Brockton.

"I'm working for a local celebrity!" I teased him.

"You're also working for Bill Murray. He's part owner of the team. He'll come by later this week," Jack told me.

That week, I met with Coach Chris and the team's scout, Kevin, in the locker room. "So, you want to help us scout this week?" Coach Chris asked.

"You bet I do!"

"We should've had you sign a contract to play one inning," Coach Chris joked.

"You came during the best week — we have a home game every day this week. We'll have you chart tonight," Kevin told me. I wasn't certain what that meant, but I knew it had to do with tracking batter statistics. As I tried to review the information I'd been given and engage myself in charting, two things distracted me to no end. First, I didn't like baseball; I didn't enjoy the sport, especially watching it. I hoped the week would change my perspective of the game, since I'd be a part of the sport instead of a mere spectator. Second, everyone around me was constantly spitting. For hours at a time, players and coaches were chewing tobacco, gum, sunflower seeds, and they constantly needed to spit, spit, spit. With every step, I looked before I leapt to avoid landing in a puddle of saliva.

The spitting didn't stop as I got to work scouting players of the opposing teams, and I came to realize that being a scout is the most underrated position in sports. Without a good scout, it's impossible to put together a good team. "You need to look for the five tools of a player: hitting, hitting hard, throwing, fielding their position, and running," Kevin advised. "More so, what's their competitive nature? Are they a responsible individual? Do they get along with the team? Do they follow instructions?" he continued.

Early afternoon batting practice before an evening game.

After a few nights, I was given the chance to throw the game's first pitch. I had never thrown from a professional mound, but was eager to prove I could play the game. "Clock the speed!" I told the coach. As I approached the mound, I started to get nervous. I was going to give it everything I had; I tried to channel my nerves into confidence as I observed the crowd in the stands and did the wind-up to the pitch. Just when I was about to release, I paused. *What if it throws out of control?* I wondered. *I'm really going to embarrass myself if it does.* I decided to take some heat off the throw, to be more accurate. I threw the ball directly ahead, clocking seventy miles per hour. As the crowd cheered and I jogged off, the catcher approached me.

"Crap! That was a good throw! I saw you hesitate though," he shouted before quickly taking his position behind the plate. Within minutes, Coach Chris came up to me.

"You're our first-base coach tonight. Put on a uniform."

I was excited to get the uniform on and be a real part of the team. I stood out there behind first base, advising players when to run and when to stay, though I'm sure they already knew this better than I did. After four innings without a score, Coach Chris came back.

"OK, you're done," he stated harshly.

"It's not my fault we haven't scored," I defended myself, hoping to stay involved in the game.

"Well, you must be bad luck," Coach Chris reasoned. At that moment, I realized just how superstitious athletes and teams are. Still, I thought that Coach Chris was being ridiculous. As I took my seat, I selfishly hoped we wouldn't score the rest of the game to prove him wrong — but we did. After the game, the whole team — coaches, scouts, and players — came together for a conference. But first, the coaches had a private meeting with the scouts.

"We've got to get better players on this team," Coach Chris said anxiously. "I need just one guy — one guy that will shove it up their asses. Can you get me that guy?"

Throughout the week, Kevin and I had been scouting opposing teams from our box seats. "There's not really anyone that stands out in this league," Kevin told him honestly. "We're going to wait until someone gets cut from the Big Leagues."

"We don't have time for that. We have forty-two days left of the season to win the championship!" Coach Chris's voice intensified as he went on. "Call all the players into the clubhouse!" he demanded. Twenty-five players paraded in and huddled around to hear Coach Chris's spiel.

"Forty-two days left guys!" he began. "Forty-two days until that field is taken away from you. I see tired people out there, but there's a time when the mind has got to take over. I've got to be honest with you guys: The chances of any of you making the Big Leagues is zero, but the chances of you marking your place in history by winning a championship is very high. This isn't a college rah-rah speech; this is that your dinner is going to be taken away from you in forty-two days!"

After that, the team won the rest of its games. It was either Coach Chris's threatening huddle, or maybe they were trying to show off while Bill Murray was in town. I got to sit with him during one of the last games of the week, eating fried dough until Jack summoned me to meet the team's cheerleaders.

"Danny, I'm going to introduce you to some of our cheerleaders, the Roxies," Jack said enthusiastically. We walked up to a dozen Roxies as Jack asked me, "Which one do you want to go out with?" I knew Jack was a go-getter, but he was embarrassing me. "Take this guy out!" he shouted to the girls.

I had asked one if she wanted to explore Boston with me that weekend, but she wasn't free. That Saturday, I decided to take the train into the city myself, and I spent that entire August day exploring America's "Walking City." I tried to cover most of it, even crossing the bridge into Cambridge and scoping out Harvard. As I walked back through Faneuil Hall, I tried to jog my memory: *I've got to know others in this city*, I thought to myself. Suddenly, I remembered: *I know a girl named Kristen.*

We had been in touch for years through a mutual friend, and though we'd never met in person, we had talked on and off. Since first speaking to her, I had became curious about Kristen. She was always outgoing and pleasant when we spoke, and I knew she was beautiful. Kristen knew all about my project, and months ago, had urged me to let her know when I got to her home state. That night, when I returned to Brockton, I sent her an e-mail asking her to call.

Later that evening, she did. "Hey, you're here!" she said with excitement.

"I'm leaving tomorrow for New Hampshire. Do you want to meet up before I leave?"

"I wish I could," she said regretfully. "I'm at home with my parents this weekend in southern Mass. I'm moving next week, so they're throwing me a going away party tomorrow." I didn't want to miss the chance to meet, so I offered to drive down to her parents' house and bring Kristen a ride back to Boston the next day. She agreed, and invited me to the party, though not without some hesitation since we had not actually met. Regardless, I jumped at the chance to see her.

"Great, I'll be there. Text me the address."

I didn't get her text message after we hung up. As much as I wanted to call her back and ask why she didn't follow through, I decided to let it go. *If it's meant to be, it's meant to be*, I thought as I fell asleep.

In the middle of the night, I was awakened by Kristen's text with her address. I was relieved, and I was so anxious to meet her that I couldn't fall back asleep.

The following day, I drove to her house as planned. As I walked over from my car, I spotted Kristen just as she saw me. Upon meeting, I was utterly distracted by her persona. I sensed something different about her. At that moment, I was convinced that I wanted to be with only her.

Kristen walked me into the party, and I was excited to get to sit down and talk with her. But when I did, she walked away; within minutes, I followed, but she only moved away from me again. *She's playing hard to get*, I thought. *This is something I'm used to*. I decided to be patient rather than chase her around the party. I knew I would have time alone with her later and invited her to tour Boston with me that evening.

I was happy to have a companion as I explored the city. I wanted to check out Boston College, and as we walked through the campus, I didn't prevent my hand from gravitating toward hers. When we got back to my car, I tried to brainstorm where we could go next. "How about Fenway Park? Are you hungry; do you want to have dinner?" I asked anxiously.

"It's getting late," Kristen said.

"I really like spending time with you," I confessed, before she smiled back at me.

"If you want to drive by Fenway, I know a great restaurant nearby," she suggested. As we drove to the ballpark, I knew I'd hit a home run meeting Kristen. And I knew for sure I'd be back to see her.

NEW HAMPSHIRE

POLITICAL PARTY
WORKER

The New Hampshire Democratic Party had reached out to me weeks ago to see if I would join its staff. "Politics is what New Hampshire is famous for — home of the first-in-the-nation primary!" Alexa, a staffer, had written me. Without hesitation, I replied, gratefully accepting the position.

"You're coming during a great week," she assured me when I called to confirm. *Nothing new there,* I thought; lots of my employers had said exactly the same thing. By chance, I had had dozens of great weeks throughout my journey. "President Obama is coming to New Hampshire to give a health-care talk!" she continued. There may have been nothing new in terms of my timing, but this was a ridiculous coincidence. *What's the chance I'd be working for the Democratic Party the same week the president visits?* I thought. Weeks earlier, family and friends had urged me to write a letter to the president about my project. To my parents, it was especially important; they thought the journey would be more extraordinary if the president supported me. To me, it was more than that — through the president, I could communicate the real message of my journey. If he used me as an example to others, perhaps more people would be inspired in their own job searches and to learn more about their fellow Americans. I wrote the letter, but how could I get it in the president's hand?

I showed up to the office, where anxious, overwhelmed staff members prepared for the big event. "Grab some markers and create some picket signs," my coworker Wyatt told me.

"What should I write?"

"Anything that supports health-care reform."

I had not followed politics very closely during my travels and wasn't sure what this was all about. I searched the Internet to read about the health-care policy before sitting down with some markers, generating slogans and creating "Obama Cares" posters for the rally. Between poster-making sessions, I printed copies of my letter to the president, leaving no doubt in my mind that I would get it into his hands.

The day of the event, I was as prepared as I'd ever be. I left the house eager to get the day started. Wyatt had introduced me to my hosts, Donna and Mark, teachers who often host guests during political events. They had filled their home with framed pictures of themselves with former presidents, as though they were longtime friends of the family. "If you're ever going to meet a political figure, this is the place," Donna encouraged me. They gave me hope, but I knew it would take more.

As I hopped into Wyatt's car to drive to the event, I pressed my mission. "Did you get my ticket for the town hall meeting?" I asked urgently.

"Sorry, I couldn't get you one."

"OK, this isn't going to be easy at all," I thought aloud. "Is there a chance I can get one there?"

"I'm looking for a ticket myself," Wyatt replied.

Great, now I have to compete for a ticket, I thought.

We arrived at the event just as rain started pouring down. We joined a crowd of supporters and passed out the simple posters I'd made to those who were empty-handed. The crowd started chanting: "We want health care! When do we want it? Now!" As the rain fell, my clothes got soaked and I noticed my letters to the president getting wet. I tried to protect them, shoving them beneath my jacket, which started to discolor from the rain. *It's only 7:00 a.m. and my day is ruined*, I thought.

As Democrats chanted "Obama Cares" on one side of the street, Republicans fought back "No-Bama" from the other side. I approached my coworkers, strangers, and those in the crowd still on

Angry protesters. One even brought a gun to the protest, but "live free or die," right?

the hunt for tickets. One of my coworkers, Dave, whistled to me to come over.

"Hey, I got you a ticket, but don't tell anyone. This was supposed to be for someone else, and they're not here yet."

"Thank you!" I repeated gratefully. I stood in line with political figures, eager to get to my seat.

After handing a dozen letters to people I thought had a better chance of getting up close, I decided to make my way into the venue. I went to the front of the line as though I worked at the high school, following actual employees. My strategy worked; I was the first to sit down, with a first-choice seat: front row, center. *Maybe I could go on stage*, I kidded myself. *OK, I'm here now, and close; that's the first step.* I watched Secret Service agents pacing the stage. I had more copies of my letter to pass around, so I approached one while I waited for the event to start.

"Could you hand this to the President?" I asked.

"Sure, no problem," he replied.

What if he doesn't do it? I thought, searching for someone else I could ask.

When people started to fill the bleachers, I noticed that all the politicians were sitting to the right of the stage. *Maybe I should go there . . . . The President will greet them*, I thought tactically. I left my jacket on my chair and walked to the other section to network with the governors of New Hampshire and Maine. I scored a seat next to them and handed each a copy of my letter, just in case. Now, I had one letter left.

President Obama came out and greeted the room, addressing the politicians in my seating area and announcing his plans for health care. As he searched the crowd for questions, he called on the gentleman sitting beside me. My heart palpitated with anticipation. After a standing ovation, President Obama shook hands before being led out by his security detail. People tried to hand him things, but his guards wouldn't allow it. As he came my way, I tried snapping photos, which was hard with so many crowding him. I was the last guy in line, and it came down to me.

"I promised myself I'd meet you today and hand you this letter," I said as he walked by.

"You did it!" he replied as he grabbed my letter and placed it in his jacket. Part of the letter read:

In many of your inspiring speeches, you remind us that the "American Dream" is not dead and America's renewal is dependent on the continuing ingenuity, hard work, and determination of its people. I am proud to serve as an example of your message.

I reconvened with my coworkers, triumphant and pleased with myself. "How did you avoid getting tackled by security, handing him that letter?" Dave asked.

"I don't know, but he has it."

"Well, let's head back to Concord," Dave said.

The experience was a thrill. *I hope he reads it*, I thought. I went back to the office and spent the afternoon making calls to volunteer Democrats and texting Kristen. We were eager to spend more time together, so that afternoon I drove back to Boston to see her. We spent the evening strolling leisurely along Boston Harbor, hold-

President Obama pocketing my letter as he gives one last glance at the crowd.

ing hands and stopping at every park bench. Kristen invited me to another going-away party that weekend with her friends. I couldn't wait to get back and see her again.

For my final days in New Hampshire, I wrote letters to clear up myths and rumors about health-care reform. I wrote for the office's blog and newsletter and sent letters to the local newspaper. At the end of the week, I drove back to Boston to see Kristen and attend her party.

I took my time getting there, hoping that she would miss me and give me a warm welcome. My strategy worked. When I arrived, her eyes lit up and she was excited to see me; it seemed as if no one else mattered. As I was socializing with her friends, I kept glancing over at Kristen, waiting for the opportunity to talk to her more. Suddenly, one of her friends approached her; he seemed drunk, and when he grabbed her flirtatiously, my heart sank.

I had been chatting with one of Kristen's friends, but apparently my face sank as much as my heart. "Are you OK?" he asked, noting my expression.

"No, I'm not," I said before walking directly past Kristen, out the door of her apartment. I was heated and confused, and I decided the best thing to do was leave. With every step I took down her walk-up, I was praying she would follow. After two flights of stairs, I heard her call my name.

"Daniel!" she shouted, as she flew down the stairs after me. We met and walked out of the apartment building together.

"Are you mad at me?" she asked, confused.

"Well, to be honest, I just don't like being in this sort of environment."

"I'm sorry; trust me, I don't like house parties either," Kristen apologized. At that moment, I knew she really cared about me. "Let's just hang out here and get some air," she suggested.

As we stood outside enjoying the summer breeze, I couldn't hold back. "Are we going to be together?" I asked. I didn't want to go through more questions; I didn't want to keep playing a big game. I knew I wanted to be with her.

"What do you mean?"

"Are we going to be in a relationship?"

Her eyes widened with reluctance. "I don't know . . . . This is happening really fast . . . ."

I knew I didn't want to leave it up to chance. "I can't just wait and see what happens," I explained. With me traveling and Kristen moving, I knew that our relationship would only work if we committed to making it work.

Kristen understood. "OK, let's be together," she agreed. "I want to make it work."

After everything I'd been through and after finally having found Kristen, I was sad to leave for Maine. But I had no doubts that I'd see her again.

MAINE

LOBSTERMAN

I approached Maine anticipating a breakdown, but I don't mean my car. As I saw the Welcome sign get closer, I pulled over on the shoulder of the highway. I took a deep breath. *This is it. Last stop,* I thought. As the traffic whizzed by, I was motionless and silent. Memories of the past year blinked before me like flash images. *After 28,000 miles, driving around the whole country, this is the last state I have to drive to,* I said out loud. I noticed I had developed an accent, though I couldn't nail where it was from. I didn't know what I would do with the Jeep, but I had one final week to figure it out. I couldn't believe we made it this far: no accidents, no tickets. *Come on Jeep, one more job!* That vehicle was the best investment I ever made.

Driving up the coast of Maine, the towns were crowded with lobster restaurants, recalling syrup stands on the roads of Vermont. I passed someone in a red lobster costume on the sidewalk trying to attract business to a restaurant. *I couldn't have picked a better career for this state,* I thought. *Lobster is the culture and economy of Maine.*

When I tried to set up my position on a lobster boat, I had no idea whom to contact or how. I tried lobster restaurants and grocery stores, asking, "Where do you get your lobster from?" and "Could you put me in contact with the lobstermen that supply your store?" No one was willing to help me.

After searching on Google, I was ready to settle for a lobster-trap company. Ralph Dean of Branch Brook Lobster Trap Company answered my call.

"Sir, I was wondering if you know anybody who goes lobstering? If not, could I work for you?" I asked desperately. He immediately assured me that I should have no worries when coming to Maine.

"I know a couple of crews that go out in the morning. Give me a week and I'll track them down for you," Ralph replied. All my faith was riding on Ralph. I didn't consider looking further or establishing a backup. Either it was faith alone or I was dead exhausted looking for my forty-seventh job.

Luckily, my faith in Ralph was well placed. I made my way to his house in Thomaston. His long gravel driveway opened onto a large wooden home decorated with a little lighthouse and surrounded by stacked firewood. I emerged from my car and was greeted by three huge barking dogs that reminded me of the horses in Kentucky. I looked around and was momentarily confused, wondering if I was in the right place. But then Ralph's wife appeared and introduced herself.

"Come on in, Ralph will be ready shawtly. I'm Loretta," she said plainly, her accent a mix between Canadian and Bostonian.

She led me to the kitchen, where I met Ralph. "You must be exhausted," he noted. "Are you sure you want to go out tomorrow morning?"

The truth is I would have done anything to get out of work. I knew the ocean didn't agree with me and I dreaded the dismal experience of rising and falling in a boat pummeled by waves. Still, I knew that not going wasn't an option.

"Yes, I have to. That's why I came all this way," I told him.

"Well, you're going to go out with Keith Miller. My son-in-law will pick you up around 3:45 a.m. tomorrow morning."

"I should probably get to sleep then."

"Do you want to have dinner first? If not, Loretta will be up making you breakfast tomorrow."

"At 3:00 a.m.?" I was shocked.

"Yep; she'll be there to send you off to work," Ralph assured me.

I went straight to my attic bedroom, where I tossed and turned in bed all night. The humidity was trapped in the room like smog on a highway. The sheets were sticky and the fans blew hot air over me. I tried calling Kristen, but my cell phone reception was weak. Though it seemed impossible, I must have fallen asleep, because when it was time to get up, I awoke to the sound of Loretta working in the kitchen.

"Good morning," I said.

"Good mawning. I have yor bweakfast and packed you a lunch box for this afternewn," she told me. I couldn't believe her kindness, seeing me off to work in the early morning hours and getting my food ready. "Steven, my son-in-law, will be heur shawtly," she continued. I hastily finished my meal and ran upstairs to dress, searching for clothes I didn't mind getting dirty.

I waited outside so Loretta could go back to sleep. As I paced back and forth on the driveway, I was overcome by intimidation about the job. I wasn't sure how long we would be out on the water, and I knew I needed to be adaptable and go with the flow. I saw headlights peeking over the hill and sighed with the realization that it would be a rough day.

I stepped into the truck and met Steven. The experience reminded me of Oregon: The early morning, pickup truck, and rush of others headed to work was reminiscent of my logging days.

"We're late," Steven said. We cruised at the speed limit, but were run off the road by other late lobstermen. Their careless driving was scary.

"Early bird gets the worm, huh?" I mentioned.

"Well, the sooner you're out there, the more traps you have time to pull."

When we arrived at the dock, fishermen were already out in the water. "Let's get the bait on the boat," Steven instructed. As we approached, a horrific smell penetrated the air and I thought I would vomit. I shoveled the bait and transferred it between bins. Meanwhile, I could feel mosquitoes attacking my body. I wore shorts and a T-shirt in anticipation of the heat; I had no idea that I would get bitten the whole time. Mosquitoes sucked my blood as I shoveled bait that made my stomach cringe, and I felt as if I had stumbled into hell. That's when I met Keith.

"Don't worry," Keith consoled me. "The mosquitoes won't follow us on the Atlantic."

"What about the smell of the bait?"

"Oh, the salted herring. That will be with us the entire day."

We brought a couple thousand pounds of bait onto the boat before heading off. The boats were smaller than I expected, usually carrying a crew of just two men. So things were a bit crowded with a third person aboard. I had envisioned lobstering being something like *Deadliest Catch*. Such thoughts dissipated as the sun came up, revealing a beautiful morning. "Daniel, you came on a great day. The waters are extremely calm," Keith said, before continuing with a warning: "But we're about to hit an intense fog."

As we motored on, the cool breeze relieved my mosquito bites. But within moments, we rolled into the fog. My sense of direction was immediately thrown. "What if we hit another boat, going this fast?" I asked with concern.

"We have radar. We'll get out of this rough patch soon."

What if the radar doesn't work? I couldn't help but worry. Soon enough, however, we approached our first traps.

"How do you know which ones are yours?" I asked.

"By the color of the buoy," Keith taught me. "We've got hundreds out here, pulling them up every three days." We pulled up our first trap, a big cage containing six lobsters and old bait. Steven took a look at the lobsters, keeping one and throwing the rest back.

"Why did you throw five of them back?" I asked.

"They were breeders and some were too small," Steven said, while handing me the one remaining lobster. With Keith's instruction, I grabbed rubber bands to tie up the lobster's claws and threw her into the water tank on board.

As the pace started to get faster, mine started to slow down. The smell of bait, the saltwater, and the swirling fog were getting to me. And the diesel exhaust from the boat was making me lightheaded.

"Not feeling well?" Keith asked. "Here, let me turn on some music," he suggested, thinking it might distract me. For yet one more time on my trip, the sound of tangling guitars and old country music filled my ears. I tried to keep working, but I couldn't focus. I just wanted to fall overboard.

Steven measuring and marking the lobster, while balancing two traps on the side of the boat. AMAZINGLY fast paced.

"Sit in the middle of the boat," Steven recommended. "There's less rocking there."

I got weak as I walked to the back of the boat, embarrassed. *I can't believe this*, I thought. *It's been only forty minutes and I'm seasick.* But it got worse: I vomited twelve times.

"When are we going back?" I asked, distraught.

"We still have seven hours out here."

I felt like I was going to die. I went to the front of the boat and slept on the window shield. I couldn't wait until the workday was over. When we got back to the "Maine-land," I felt like I was coming out of the coal mine and seeing daylight for the first time.

"How was your first day?" Ralph asked, eagerly when I got back to his house.

"I don't deserve to eat lobster," I replied.

"Seasick, huh? Nothing is worse than that, but get some rest. We'll give you these wristbands that will help you for tomorrow."

Before heading back to the attic, I checked my e-mail. I had received a message from USC inviting me to speak in front of the school's freshman class. "We have chosen you as our celebrity guest speaker. Where will you be this Friday?" the organizers asked, offering to fly me to Los Angeles en route to my next stop, Alaska. So I arranged to be in Los Angeles by Thursday night.

That meant only three more days of lobstering. I went out the next morning, prepared for the worst. My jitters were more intense than the day before, because I knew what I was up against. I got back on the boat and was again swarmed by mosquitoes. The same smell of bait and diesel exhaust infused my lungs. And the same outcome resulted. I vomited again, but this time, it took two hours instead of the forty minutes to reach that milestone.

The next day, I tried again; I didn't vomit, but I was woozy. "Man, you never give up," Keith noticed. "My wife came on once, like, twenty-five years ago, and she never came again."

"I think I'm going to build lobster traps in Ralph's warehouse tomorrow," I mentioned.

"Yeah, you've had enough," Keith agreed.

My last day in Maine, as I was building traps with Ralph's daughter, I couldn't help but think: *Finally, a job that beat me; a job I couldn't fulfill.* As my competitive nature got to me, I felt like a loser. On my last evening, Keith came over to Ralph's house with thirty lobsters — lobsters I didn't help catch. I still consumed eight of them; they were much easier to eat than crab.

That night, I rushed down to Massachusetts. I returned to Brockton and parked my car at Jack's house. My Jeep would stay there through the end of my journey, as I wrapped up the remaining states on the West Coast. From Jack's, I took the train to Boston and flew that night to Los Angeles.

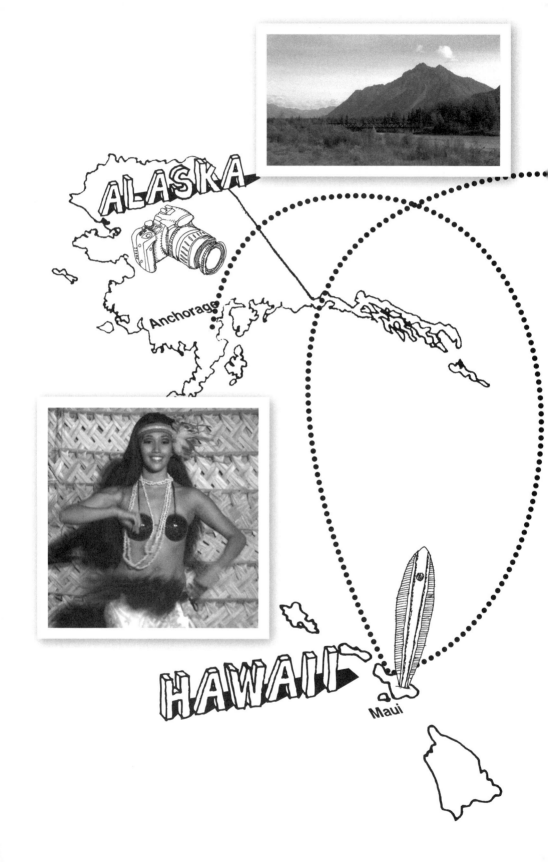

ALASKA

COMMERCIAL
PHOTOGRAPHER

Waiting in a terminal at Seattle-Tacoma International Airport, I watched eager passengers standing in line to board my plane to Anchorage. Most were elderly white-haired men carrying fishing poles onto the plane. This reminded me of passengers boarding my flight to Vermont with their skis. Just before boarding myself, I made the last call on my list of photographers in Alaska, hoping one would pull through with a job offer by the time I landed in Anchorage.

As with New Jersey, I was headed to Alaska without a job already lined up. But unlike New Jersey, my flights were booked and I only had one shot, one week, with no backups. At this point, I was utterly exhausted from the forty-some-odd weeks before. I wasn't in the mood to make endless calls or to sell my project again. This time I was going to cross my fingers and hope for the best.

In Anchorage, I got off the plane and walked through the terminal, pausing beside a stuffed fifteen-foot grizzly bear. I anxiously dialed in to my voicemail. "Hi Daniel, this is Clark Mishler. I just got your message. Let me know when your plane lands and I'll come pick you up." Clark is a successful and very well-known *National Geographic* photographer. All my worries about finding a job, finding a place to stay, and even about having to relocate within the state, immediately dissolved. I called him right back to tell him I had arrived. I didn't want to admit how desperate I'd been, but I knew he was my savior. I had depended on fate in Alaska, and my good fortune surpassed my hopes. My week could not have gotten off to better start.

It was fairly late in the evening, but the sun was still high. I wondered if it was nearing the season when the sun doesn't set. I walked through the airport and met Clark curbside. Riding back to his loft, I admired the skyline, a bit surprised by how developed the city is.

"How many people live here?" I asked Clark.

"It holds almost half of our state's population, around 300K," he replied.

I knew that Alaska is one-fifth the size of the lower forty-eight, and it turned out to be one of the more beautiful and peaceful places I visited. It seemed like we were the only car on the road, an impression that reminded me of driving through Montana.

"That's a Russian Orthodox church," I pointed out.

"There's a lot of Russian influence here," Clark told me.

"Hey, Northern Lights Boulevard!" I was excited to observe so many new things, knowing that not many Americans make the trip to Alaska. Likewise, not many Alaskans make the trip to the lower forty-eight. In its seclusion, I started to realize how independent this state is compared with the others in the nation.

When we arrived at Clark's house, the dinner table had been set by his wife, Mitzy. "I hope you like king salmon," she said. I wasn't sure if I would. I wasn't even sure what king salmon looked like despite having been a marine biologist.

"This is really amazing!" I marveled. "It sort of tastes like a cheeseburger!"

"That's not really a compliment," Clark laughed. I didn't realize what a costly piece of fish it was — my mistake for comparing it with a two-dollar burger.

The next day, we rose bright and early. I sat in the kitchen with Clark, reading the newspaper (which pictured a bear on the front sports page). Over breakfast, I started with my questions.

"Do you take photos for the newspaper sometimes?"

"Yes, sometimes they look into my stock photos," he said, before getting down to business. "I'm going to teach you the basics of photography. First off, I never leave home without my camera. You never know when there's a great opportunity for a photo."

I was familiar with his philosophy; I had carried my video camera with me for nearly a year, especially after nearly losing it in Colorado. Since then, I always had my hand on my camera, no matter where I went.

"I never use the flash," Clark continued. "The flash ruins pictures; it will give you light exposure or illumination, but very bland and boring. Backlight, backlight, backlight, is what I use in every picture. The light should always be behind the subject." Clark paused and positioned my body to face away from the sun. "See, it's more interesting this way."

That week, I took his lessons with me as we went into the field to snap photos. Clark took me to the annual Alaska State Fair, forty miles from Anchorage. On the drive, it felt as if we had escaped the city immediately and found ourselves in the wilderness. "Moose crossing" signs lined the road, which ran along mountains and rivers.

The state fair granted me a badge allowing me to shoot as an official photographer. "This will enable you to go anywhere and everywhere," Clark told me. As we walked through the fair, Clark approached strangers and chatted with them. I realized how social he was and wondered if this had something to do with Alaskan culture or the nature of being a photographer. Perhaps to get good photos, you need to be able to direct people to work with you the way you want. Clark carried photo-release forms with him everywhere all the time, so he was always prepared to get his shot.

At the fair we took pictures of animals, roller coasters, people eating and enjoying themselves, and even a scarecrow costume contest. "When you're taking pictures of people or animals, make sure you focus on the closest eye of the subject," Clark instructed. He held his fist up in front of him, capturing the light reflection of the sun. *Maybe I should have done this job first, before I snapped 9,000 photos in the other forty-seven states,* I thought.

Photographer Clark Mishler's photograph of another photographer.

In his studio later that week, Clark decided to take on an ambitious project on my behalf. "Let's look at all your pictures from the lower forty-eight and make a published book for you, of photos from your trip." He glanced through my photos rapidly, knowing exactly what to look for.

"Some of these are good. I wish I could've taken them," he noted. I realized which photos he was looking for—pictures with great expression and symbolism. Of all my photos, Clark chose 350 worth printing. "This is how my clients work with me," he told me. "I take hundreds of the same shot, and they pick one to buy."

At the end of the week, before I flew to Hawaii, I was invited to speak at the University of Alaska. After my talk, Clark and Mitzy took me to the airport. As we said our goodbyes, Clark left me with a final thought to take with me as I completed my project.

"I don't want you to think this is the only thing you're going to be known for or the biggest thing you'll ever accomplish" Clark told me, "because it's not. You're going to look back on this experience years from now, and it's not going to define you."

I had found Clark to be a wise, prudent man, so I didn't take his words lightly. I knew what he was getting at — that I couldn't limit myself to this project or to any one thing I accomplish, that there's more to life, more to the future. As I prepared to board my flight to Honolulu, I knew his advice was something I'd never leave behind.

HAWAII

SURFING INSTRUCTOR

For forty-eight weeks, one question was constant: "What are you going to do in Hawaii?"

"Surfing instructor," I'd reply with a smirk, prompting the usual follow-up question. "Have you surfed before?"

"I've never touched a board in my life." I arrived in Honolulu hoping for a ferry crossing to Maui, where I was set to be a surfing instructor for Maui Wave Riders. Instead, I was forced to fly on a small interisland airline. All flights were booked until the next day, except for a few first-class seats. Since my hosts and employers, the Castletons, were already waiting at the terminal in Maui, I decided to fly first class, a luxury I never afforded myself over the preceding year.

At the Maui airport, I felt as if I were living a dream. I was greeted by the sound of a strumming ukulele as Alicia Castleton jumped out of the car to give me a hug and place a lei of flowers and sea-shells around my neck. Her husband, Tommy, had been through a lot, as he explained, though he was only in his early forties. He had been kidnapped, suffered horrific surfing accidents, and even gone through a near-death experience when he crashed into a palm tree at night on one of the island's winding roads. Hiring me for a week was the least of his worries.

"I came a couple days early, since I need to learn how to surf before I can teach it," I told him.

"We've got great instructors at the school. They're great guys," Tommy said.

The next morning at five o'clock, Tommy knocked on the door of my bamboo cottage to see if I was awake. I had been awake, lying in the dark since 3:00 a.m. due to the time difference. I turned on my pineapple-shaped lamp and got ready to head out. "Let's go hit the surf," Tommy said. And with that, we prepared for the day.

While we were watching the weather report, Tommy handed me a bottle of sunscreen, board shorts, and a visor. The smell of sunscreen reminded me of the unforgiving Atlantic, only two weeks earlier in Maine. We made our way to the surfing school, where I met the other instructors, all of whom were either Hawaiians or came from other islands in the Pacific and were accompanying themselves with ukuleles as they sang.

"Get yourself a pair of booties and a rash guard," Tommy said. I thought the shirt was to protect me from the sun; little did I know, it was to protect my chest from bleeding after rubbing harshly against the board that day.

Two teenage girls from California and a newlywed couple from Michigan joined me for a land lesson. "Grab your boards, guys!" the instructor, Ikaika, said. I didn't know the difference between boards, but soon learned that size was everything: The bigger the board, the easier it is to maintain balance. I grabbed the largest board, a whale-sized twelve-footer, as did the other students.

"You want to stand in the middle of the board to keep balance," Ikaika explained, as I filmed his instruction. I wanted to be able to refer back to it since I'd have to give the same lesson the next day. "Make sure you're standing on the middle line of the board. Keep your eyes looking up," he continued. It was simple and straightforward, and it seemed that no one had difficulty understanding.

Ikaika had us lie on our boards to practice swim strokes. "Dig deep into the water with cupped hands. Make sure your head is looking up, and when you're paddling into a wave, push your torso up with your arms like a yoga pose." Ikaika was a great teacher; he had a fun, positive attitude. I hoped I could channel his spirit the next day. "We've got the basics of our land lesson," he pushed, "so let's grab our boards and get out in the water!"

I had been waiting since childhood to try surfing. The waves were mellow, the sun was shining, the scenery was paradise, and the best part was that the crystal blue water was warm and comfortable. Carrying the board to the water wasn't so pleasant, though. It was painful to balance on my head, but otherwise, it's too big to cradle. I strapped the board to my leg before I threw it in the water.

I tried to apply the techniques Ikaika gave us, but paddling for fifteen minutes out in the ocean to catch a fifteen-second wave — *is it worth it?* I wondered. "Come on Daniel! Turn your board around. I'm going to push you when this wave comes," Ikaika said. My arms were too tired to think about stroking fast to catch the wave and then popping up on the board to ride it out.

"Here it comes! Start paddling!" Ikaika said. The wave was at least twenty feet away from me, but I did exactly as he instructed. My neck started to cramp, and I didn't bother to look back at the wave as it started to carry me. I felt a burst of speed from Ikaika's push, propelling me to stay with the wave. Just as rehearsed, I popped up, wobbling and stumbling, struggling to keep balance. As the wave died, I stood until I was thrown off the board. *Fifteen seconds and wow, it is worth it!* I thought.

All day, I practiced and observed the others, but I felt dehydrated in the sun. *Could I stay out here for five hours like the other instructors?* I wondered as a headache came on. I couldn't decide if the headache was from the saltwater or the sun, but I knew I couldn't go on. The rest of the day, I felt drained and dizzy, longing to go back to my room and sleep. At last, the time came. Tommy drove us home, but before I disappeared into my cottage, we picked papayas, mangoes, and avocados from his orchard. The next day, I studied my film and memorized Ikaika's lesson, just as I had studied football plays in Alabama. I felt refreshed and ready to instruct as I met the students from Germany and Portugal who would be in my group.

I came a few days early to learn how to surf from Tommy.

Tommy came over to watch my lesson, adding pressure for me to get it right. *This might be the only chance he gives me*, I thought. *I better not mess up.*

The land lesson was easy; no one had any questions. We went out in the water, and I tried to mimic Ikaika giving encouragement and instilling confidence, pushing my students with the waves. "Don't be afraid of falling," I yelled. It felt good to be coaching again, making the students comfortable and helping motivate them to keep trying. Soon enough, everyone caught a wave. Tommy and my coworkers were impressed by how well I caught on, and gave me another group to instruct.

For much of the week, the strenuous nature of surfing got to me; I felt as if I hadn't rested in months. Every day, I returned to the cottage in the early afternoon wiped out. I would guzzle water, call Kristen, and doze off soon after sitting down. In my jet-lagged, sun-drenched exhaustion, I felt like I'd been wasting time in bed, immune to the smell of sunscreen and wet shorts. Toward the end of the week, however, I built up the energy needed to hang out with the instructors after work.

"We're going to play basketball at the lit courts tonight," my coworker, Keoki announced. Everyone played in the same clothes they wore all day, board shorts, though hi-tops replaced sandals. After an hour of basketball, it was time to drink; for me, it was time to go back to my cottage and rest.

The next day, I was invited out again. "We're going to cruise the island and hit some surf," Keoki said. "We're all going to meet around 2:00 p.m." I was eager to see what surfing was like for the locals and agreed to go along. We loaded our boards onto the roof-top of the car and headed to Lahaina, where the waves are big and aggressive. Passing endless sugarcane fields on the drive, everyone in the car sang to the radio. *How come these song aren't mainstream?* I thought, as I admired their catchy rhythms.

That day, I tried surfing with an eight-foot board. It was hard to even lie on it without slipping off. I lost all control, and was swallowed by the waves. I thought of how paralyzing it could be if I hit a rock or the ocean bottom; it's scary to lose control, be forced underwater, where you can't breathe and can only hope to come to the surface safely. After a couple of hours, one of the guys asked the infamous island question: "What do you guys wanna do now?"

We started walking around as though we had a plan, though we didn't, and headed into a shaved-ice shop to enjoy the local specialty. After the surfing break, it came again: "What do you guys wanna do now?" We went back to the water, but drove to another location to hit the surf. Then we took a break to eat again. Then, like clockwork: "What do you guys wanna do now?" *These guys are wearing me out*, I thought.

At the end of the week, my flight from Honolulu to California was so early in the morning, I had to leave Maui the night before. I arrived at the Honolulu airport at ten o'clock and had to wait all night before boarding the plane to California. To pass the time, I called Kristen, planning to wait it out and nap in the airport until my early morning flight.

At 11:00 p.m., however, I was thrown out of the terminal. "Ever since 9/11, we don't let people sleep here," the guard told me. I didn't want to pay for a hotel room for five hours, so instinctively I wheeled my heavy bag out toward ground transportation and wondered what to do next, I spontaneously jumped on the rental car bus. "I'd like to rent a car for the night," I told the agent, selecting a good old-fashioned white Jeep Wrangler. As I pulled out of the parking lot, I was ready for my usual Jeep routine and scouted a place to sleep for the night. I drove to the nearest hotel parking lot and, in my usual fashion, climbed into the backseat to rest.

At 4:00 a.m., I returned the car. When I turned in my keys, the employee checked my mileage. "Two miles?" he asked, bewildered. He couldn't imagine why I rented a car to drive two miles. However I spent my night, it was my last in a "foreign" state. I was on my way back to the final stop, back to where it all began: my home state, California.

CALIFORNIA

WINERY CELLAR MASTER

I landed in Los Angeles and having left my Jeep in Massachusetts, was forced to rent a car again. As I came back full circle — one year since I started the project, one year since I hit rock bottom — I drove to that notorious Macy's parking lot where, a year earlier, I had felt "as low as a sober person could go." It was hard to believe that a vision born in curiosity and desperation had brought me so far and that what had been a dream had become a reality. I could barely recognize the man sobbing in the car in the Macy's parking lot waiting for an opportunity to come along, for someone else to choose his destiny. I was a completely changed man. I had more experience, more knowledge, more friends — and one last job in my final state, my home state: California.

I drove to Hollywood to reunite with the South Koreans. The same news team that covered me in Wisconsin was back to do a follow-up story on how I had managed to make it through all the states and how I had changed. In the twenty-seven weeks since I was in Wisconsin, I had become far more comfortable with strangers, and I learned from experience that there is always a way to accomplish any objective — whether directly or through other channels. When I started the journey, I had made goals for myself, and by the time I reached California, I had surpassed all of them.

When the news team arrived, I told the producer I wanted to film the parade for Nicaragua's National Independence Day. Having lived in Los Angeles during college, I'd grown accustomed to the area's ethnic cultural parades and festivals every weekend.

"Let's film you documenting the parade with your camera," the producer, Mark, suggested. I walked along the sidewalk, filming the dancers. "Get up closer, into the action," he urged.

As I filmed the loud, animated parade in the street, I felt the sudden pressure of a car rolling over my foot; within a moment, the car hit my lower back, striking my spinal cord like a bulls-eye.

"What the hell!" I yelled in pain. Spectators who had witnessed the accident yelled at the car as it drove slowly into the parade itself. As I held onto my back, I hobbled over to the car and knocked on the driver's window, yelling aggressively to the driver.

"You just ran over me!" I yelled, noticing an elderly woman behind the wheel. She ignored me; she didn't flinch, and needless to say, didn't roll her window down. She drove on through the parade, nearly hitting several people and even a horse. I took a picture of her license plate and hobbled over to the nearest policeman to explain what happened. Mark called an ambulance for me, but I knew it would be expensive and opted to ride in his car to the emergency room. Within minutes, I was in a hospital bed, getting a CT scan and praying there was no internal damage.

I could barely sit up in the bed; a nurse gently pulled me upright. "You're not from here, are you," I stated knowingly.

"No, not originally," she replied.

"You're from Iowa, right?" I guessed.

"Yes! How did you know?"

"You're too nice to be from here," I said, impressed and pleased with myself for testing my senses under such dramatic circumstances.

Mark and his crew waited for me in the emergency room, offering to let me stay with them that night in their hotel. "Don't worry Daniel, we'll find that lady. We're your witnesses," Mark comforted me. I couldn't believe how my return to California was going. Despite everything, I had to start my new job the next day. I had arranged to work in Hollywood as a producer with a movie production company. It had contacted me weeks ago, offering to help edit my documentary and even work on a feature film production of my journey. I didn't think twice about accepting the offer.

With a bruised back and a sore neck, I walked in to meet my fiftieth employer. In contrast to the previous forty-nine jobs, this time I was greeted by no one. From behind the glass door of the entrance, I looked for the office of Susan, my contact. I called her on my cell phone to let her know I had arrived.

"I see you out there, just give me a minute and I'll be right with you," she told me.

As I paced impatiently outside the office, Susan finally opened the door for me. "Hi Daniel, come into my office and we'll discuss what we can do this week; then I'm going to have you go down the street to get coffee for the meeting," she said.

I didn't mind getting the coffee for the snobby boss, but I thought I would at least be included in the meeting to learn about the industry. Susan neglected to introduce me to her four coworkers in their small office. I tried to overlook their haste and hostility, but I was starting to get a bad feeling for the week ahead.

Since the company had initially invited me to work on the video of my trip, I sat at my desk sorting through over four hundred hours of my own footage while the conference went on. An employee emerged from the conference room like a bear from its cave and handed me a five-hundred-page book. "Can you photocopy this?" he demanded.

I was bewildered. Skipping an introduction, he merely acknowledged me by giving me an order. "Sure," I replied, without any intention of doing it.

When Susan was done with her meeting, I popped into her office to talk about the South Korean film crew. It wanted to come in to film for their piece, but she refused permission. "I told you about this earlier," I reminded her. "You knew about my project; you invited me here. They came all the way from South Korea!" I was getting angry and with the pain in my back, irritable. Perhaps I could have swallowed the mundane office work, but being denied the welcome and hospitality I experienced in the past forty-nine states stifled my desire to stick it out at the office. No one had shown me any kindness or consideration. No one asked where I was staying while I was in town. At this point in my journey, I had been through a lot of strife: I had worked long hours, I had been through confrontations, I had been denied places to stay, denied money. And here I was, in my last state, my home state, and I just couldn't let it end like this, not when I was coming full circle to where I had been homeless, unemployed, mistreated, and struggling. California is where my tribulation began and where I would conquer it. With both frustration and ambition, I gave Susan my last words: "I quit," before walking off.

Though I was then jobless, quitting felt good. *I'd rather be jobless than treated like that*, I thought. It was midweek, and the Koreans were headed to San Diego for another assignment. When they returned to LA, they offered to give me a ride home to Northern California. In the meantime, until they returned, I stayed with a college friend. She blew up an air mattress for me, and I slept on it the rest of the week. My back was too painful to walk around or even sit upright for very long. I thought of finding another job, but I wasn't sure what to choose. *I'll put a survey on my web site*, I thought, *and let my viewers decide.*

I had all sorts of suggestions: Hollywood stuntman, plastic surgeon, picking produce, working in Napa Valley. And that was the winner; working in a winery earned the most votes.

Dumping recently harvested grapes into the press, an early stage to make champagne.

I desperately needed to let my back recover, so at home in Northern California, I rested as much as I could. I also needed a job so I spent some of the weekend calling wineries. By Monday, I was a cellar master with Domaine Carneros. I didn't want to work around alcohol again, but when I arrived at the vineyard's château, it was impossible not to appreciate the beauty of Napa Valley.

The cellar smelled just as good as the caramelized air in Vermont. *This is the right way to end it*, I thought, reflecting on the redemption of finishing strong after my false start in Hollywood. It was a relief to leave Los Angeles for the beautiful countryside of Northern California.

My coworker, Mrs. Hitchcock, had offered me a room in her house for the week, which I happily accepted. She and her husband made me feel like I was one of their own. They were loving and accommodating, even letting me borrow their car to drive to work every day.

Before starting at the winery, I watched a graphic safety film. I didn't realize people die from working in wine cellars; if you're not careful, cleaning the tanks may result in exposure to carbon dioxide, which can lead to death within seconds.

When I first opened the lid to the tank, I got a whiff of the gas and felt my brain wheeze. I could even see the gas, which looked like smog hovering over the grapes. I carried a fan to disperse it before I went in to clean the grape peels out of the tanks. The winery requires people to work with partners, in case someone has a problem. Every thirty seconds, my partner and I would check to make sure the other was holding up all right.

Despite the threat of CO_2, all the winery employees loved their jobs. It was like Monticello, with pleasant employees enjoying the outdoors as tourists filed through regularly. There were lots of tasks to complete, which helped reduce the monotony of day-to-day work. That week, I got to experience it all. I sorted recently harvested grapes — though working the grape-sorting machine, I got dizzy from all the rattling and felt out of it. I also shoveled grapes into the presser, making pure grape juice that was then stored in the tanks and mixed with yeast. I stirred it all together before cleaning the tanks. Finally, I put the finished product into wooden barrels to be aged into wine. I also had the opportunity to bottle champagne.

I was limited in the labor I could perform because my back ached constantly. I couldn't move as well as I used to. Nonetheless, I loved the job. I loved the smell of the grapes infusing the air and the views of rolling hills and grape vines surrounding the château, reminding me of the French countryside.

Later that day, I got a text message from Sasha: "Call me when you get a chance." My heart didn't jump out of my chest as it once had. In fact, I had become indifferent. But I decided to call Sasha, because I was still curious to see what she wanted. She told me she received the key I had sent to her in December — the key to the promised scooter — and that she had been keeping track of me on my journey. I had always wondered about that and finally got the answer. But it was too late to care anymore. I was at last with someone who was stable, dependable, and who cared about me as much as I cared for her. We understood each other, we could laugh together, we could share everything. I didn't have to walk on egg-shells around Kristen. It all just made sense with us.

Since the vineyard was so close to home, my parents came to pick me up on my last day at the winery. They were thrilled and proud that I had completed a mission that had seemed impossi-ble — logistically, physically, mentally, and financially. I handed my dad the check for $250 he gave me the day I left my driveway for Utah. I had done everything I could to make it through fifty jobs all on my own. And I did.

With that, breathing the sweet air and enjoying the warm sun was the ideal way to end a year of fifty jobs. Despite everything I had been through, I felt I had accomplished more than I intended. I thought of the many generous people who had opened up their homes to me and showed me their lives, granting me the chance to experience what brings Americans together — and what sets us apart. On my odyssey, I experienced our nation one state at a time, one job at a time, one family at a time.

Like a surf instructor riding out the wave, or a lobsterman reach-ing the shore, or a miner coming out of the cave, I made my last check of the wine cellar and walked out toward the sunlight. I took off my hat and took in a deep breath.

Land of opportunity, I thought. *No doubt about it.*

EPILOGUE

A LESSON FROM AMERICA

I was standing before a packed auditorium of eager college students uncertain about their future and hoping to get some answers from my lecture. I could have talked about anything and everything related to my fifty-week journey across America — from what I thought about my country before I started to how I came to realize that understanding other people helps you understand yourself. But I wanted to focus on the five critical elements of my success: perseverance, adaptability, networking, risk-taking, and endurance.

"Failing forty-plus job interviews was the best thing that had ever happened to me," I explained to the audience. I knew this sounded weird, but I would never have started my journey if I had not failed at all those interviews. I learned from those experiences not to fear failure, and that was my biggest success. Many of the students before me would go on to graduate, confident that they've followed a career path perfect for them. I'd been there, too; I had pursued economics, hoping it would be fulfilling to me. But as I explained to the audience, "After working fifty different jobs, I would never go back to economics. I realized that it didn't fit my personality." I wanted to offer the students who had come to hear me direct answers about how I found fifty jobs in fifty states and how they could apply my lessons to their own pursuits. But ultimately, the answers to their questions would not come from me, regardless of how much advice I could offer, they would be the ones to determine their destinies.

"As an athlete I had a close relationship with my coach," I continued. "He put me through exhausting workouts and gave me advice and strategies for competing. But when it came to the race itself, it was up to me to determine the outcome." Through athletics, I had developed the five elements essential for building confidence to carry out my idea of fifty jobs. "So you know my story. I had a vision, and people said 'no' to me from day one. Sponsors didn't want to help me, and my family thought I was crazy. But I found something I wanted to pursue. How did I do it? What did it take? What can you learn from my experience about pursuing what you really love?"

Perseverance – Dealing with Rejection

As a competitive athlete at an elite level, I learned never to give up. I had always set goals, both short-term and long-term, which drove me toward accomplishment. These goals fostered motivation and confidence, and pressured me to perform. Nonetheless, I still lost some of my races. Sometimes I lost even when I was sure that I had trained harder than the competition. What I learned is that you can't give up. You can't win every race. You won't get every job. You have to ask yourself: How would giving up improve my situation? The dedication, self-discipline, and resolve I developed as an athlete directly transferred to my experience in the job market. In all my job interviews, I would work hard to earn an offer, but I braced myself for rejection. In turn, I became accustomed to the rejection I later experienced when setting up fifty different jobs. Because of the goals I set, I didn't have the option of giving up, and I remained persistent until I met my objective. Over time, I came to love the word "no" or "you can't" – I saw them as a challenge, and they motivated me. Hearing those words just meant I needed to find another way. I had roughly 5,000 rejections over the course of my year on the road, but I was optimistic throughout the journey and focused on the light at the end of the tunnel. I learned that each rejection moved me closer to an acceptance.

Risk-Taking – Uncertainty

Often, because of fear of failure and the unknown, we don't follow our passion or pursue our dreams. We make excuses; we do what's safe and stay within our comfort zone because it's easy and we feel protected. I felt the same way, even at the very beginning. Leaving my parents' driveway for Utah, I had no money and no promises. I knew that if this project didn't succeed, it could set me back should I continue to pursue my field of study. At the same time, I had my mind set on pursuing something I knew was worth doing. I wasn't sure how things would go, but I owed it to myself to give it a shot. I had faith that the risk would be outweighed by the outcome.

On the road, I dealt with unanticipated risks. I learned that no matter how much you prepare, you'll be thrown curveballs. Uncertainty became an everyday experience, because each day meant different environments, different people, and different jobs. I couldn't predict weather, crime, or even how dangerous jobs could be. Despite that, I never second-guessed myself. I knew that taking chances was worth it. It would make me a better person because I could learn and grow from facing risks.

Adaptability – Engaging Yourself/Finding Solutions

You won't realize new opportunities unless you're adaptable to changing circumstances. Throughout my journey, I met and lived with cowboys, Indians, rednecks, Jews, Latinos, Arabs, Hawaiians, African Americans, and Amish. I constantly adapted to different religions, foods, hobbies, and living arrangements. I lived in a trailer, in a cabin, in mansions. Further, I had to adapt to an almost unimaginable variety of jobs. I wasn't sure how comfortable I would be descending into a coal mine or slaughtering cattle or even serving alcohol. There comes a point when people have to acclimate, be flexible, and try new things in order to achieve their goals and make the most of their situations. Not everything is straightforward, but there's more than one way to pursue your objective. It is essential to always have a Plan B because you never know what could fall through.

Networking – More People, More Opportunities

I quickly learned that if you prove yourself and your capabilities to people, they will remember you and connect you with others. Essentially, networking is dependent upon marketing yourself, your idea, your business. You meet people, present your best self, and build relationships. During my trip, such relationships were vital. People I met at work in one state connected me with people who could host me in other states; in turn, those people connected me with still others who could take me on a weekend adventure or help me develop a professional idea or strategy.

Colleges also emphasize the importance of networking to create job opportunities. Sure enough, as I was on a train in New York City, I saw a gentleman wearing a shirt with my college logo. When I mentioned that I went to USC and told him about my project, he immediately offered me a job in Massachusetts.

Endurance – Active Mind and Body

To endure fifty consecutive weeks on the road, it was essential to prepare mentally and physically. I drove 28,000 miles and flew roughly 20,000 miles, but downtime was only possible during lonesome drives. I had to be constantly alert, focused, and engaged, usually after just four hours of sleep. It was vital for me to find ways to keep balance mentally and physically to endure the project.

When I set out to make the trip, I didn't know how much I could endure or what challenges I would encounter. For that reason, I chose to do the project over fifty weeks — one job per week. I had to consider what my mind and body could handle — the long drives, missed meals, the attention required for each job, the agility needed to learn and adapt every week.

● ● ● ● ●

After the fifty-week odyssey was complete, not only did I learn about fifty different jobs and states, but I learned about fifty different lives. I realized all America has to offer. From living at a resort in South Carolina to sleeping in the back of my Jeep through bitterly cold nights to passing out from exhaustion every afternoon in a bamboo cottage on a Hawaiian beach, I had been there. Singing in a Baptist choir, riding a buggy with the Amish, and walking on stilts at a theme park — I had done that.

I had dug up artifacts and learned about America's history; I waded in rivers and learned about its resources; I met our country's people and found its lifeblood. That's where the true discovery lies. At the heart of my journey, I learned about people. I learned of a stranger's inclination to help another, a family's willingness to take someone in, and employers' willingness to train others. I had never expected to rely on the kindness of strangers. It boiled down to reliability — being able to depend on people to fulfill promises to myself and to others. Employers were skeptical of hiring me, but they took the risk to fulfill the promises they had made. And because I could rely on people to do that, I was able to fulfill my greater goal. Without reliability, everything falters.

I also learned about myself. I was capable of doing things I didn't understand and triumphed over hardships I didn't foresee because I had made the commitment to myself and to my goals to persevere. I realized that we can all pursue our vision in life if we accept the challenges with tenacity.

By the time nearly every workweek ended, I was offered a full-time position. I could have pursued any job I tried, but instead, I wanted to help those who found themselves in the position I was in when I graduated from college. When entering college, students should be aware of the different careers and opportunities our country offers. For that reason, I have developed a college semester program, enabling students to get exposure to different careers and industries in order to find the field that is most fitting to their interests and future.

When I finished my presentation, hundreds of thoughtful faces stared back at me. "I found something I wanted to pursue, and today I shared with you the five elements essential to fulfilling my vision. If there's a goal you are committed to, you too are capable of reaching it if you embrace the elements of success I have described."

There are lots of nightmares you need to get through before you reach your dream. I had been through years of them, and even as my dream was becoming true, I continued to go through rejection, doubt, and struggle. I ran the race, but there were still barriers and water pits. I slipped, stumbled, and hit the ground, and at times people walked away from me.

"If you find something worth the risks, then open your mind and use your network; adapt to the challenges and maintain endurance," I urged the students. "The bottom line is: Your ideas mean something, and if you find something worth pursuing, take the risk."

In the end, even if people walk away from you, ignore you, tell you no or shoot your dream down, the power lies within you to create an opportunity for yourself. I had been through a lot of nightmares, but when I finally realized my dream, I knew the struggle was worth it.

ABOUT THE AUTHOR

Daniel Seddiqui was born and raised in the Bay Area of Northern California. Throughout his life, Daniel has been an avid athlete, training and competing in cross country and track and field. In college, he was first recruited to participate in these sports by the University of Oregon, before transferring to compete for the University of Southern California, where he graduated with a B.A. in economics.

Upon earning his degree, Daniel struggled to find a job in his field and failed countless job interviews. After a year without luck, he decided to pursue his interest in sports and took a position as a volunteer coach at Northwestern University with the women's cross-country team. The following year, he volunteered as a coach for the University of Virginia football team. In the meantime, Daniel struggled to make ends meet by taking odd jobs and working in retail, soon concluding, however, that he needed to find a more permanent career.

After having lived in various states and experiencing some of what our country has to offer, Daniel conceived the idea of working one job at a time for one week in every state. His goal was to learn about America by crossing borders and working alongside its people. He sought work representative of each state's culture and economy — at a theme park in Florida and as a surfing instructor in Hawaii, for example.

To turn his vision into reality, Daniel had to return to California first. There, he attempted to fund his project through sponsorships, but again met with constant rejection. So he decided to pursue his journey independently, setting up fifty jobs in fifty states over fifty consecutive weeks.

Though Daniel's journey was initially publicized only through his personal web site and social networks, it gained national and international media attention as he proceeded, and millions followed him on his remarkable quest. He has been featured on *World News Tonight*, CNN, Fox News, *The Today Show*, MSNBC, National Public Radio, and in the *New York Daily News* and *Los Angeles Times*, among many others.

Since fulfilling his all-American resume, Daniel has been on a lecture tour, speaking at universities, conferences, and with organizations, inspiring others to pursue their own goals amid adversity. He has developed a college semester program that empowers students to make informed decisions about their course selections and future career paths by exposing them to a variety of authentic work experiences during an "on the job" summer college semester. Daniel is now based in Chicago, Illinois.

Berrett–Koehler
Publishers

Berrett-Koehler is an independent publisher dedicated to an ambitious mission: *Creating a World That Works for All*.

We believe that to truly create a better world, action is needed at all levels—individual, organizational, and societal. At the individual level, our publications help people align their lives with their values and with their aspirations for a better world. At the organizational level, our publications promote progressive leadership and management practices, socially responsible approaches to business, and humane and effective organizations. At the societal level, our publications advance social and economic justice, shared prosperity, sustainability, and new solutions to national and global issues.

A major theme of our publications is "Opening Up New Space." Berrett-Koehler titles challenge conventional thinking, introduce new ideas, and foster positive change. Their common quest is changing the underlying beliefs, mindsets, institutions, and structures that keep generating the same cycles of problems, no matter who our leaders are or what improvement programs we adopt.

We strive to practice what we preach—to operate our publishing company in line with the ideas in our books. At the core of our approach is stewardship, which we define as a deep sense of responsibility to administer the company for the benefit of all of our "stakeholder" groups: authors, customers, employees, investors, service providers, and the communities and environment around us.

We are grateful to the thousands of readers, authors, and other friends of the company who consider themselves to be part of the "BK Community." We hope that you, too, will join us in our mission.

A BK Life Book

This book is part of our BK Life series. BK Life books change people's lives. They help individuals improve their lives in ways that are beneficial for the families, organizations, communities, nations, and world in which they live and work. To find out more, visit **www.bk-life.com**.

Berrett–Koehler
Publishers

A community dedicated to creating
a world that works for all

Visit Our Website: www.bkconnection.com

Read book excerpts, see author videos and Internet movies, read our authors' blogs, join discussion groups, download book apps, find out about the BK Affiliate Network, browse subject-area libraries of books, get special discounts, and more!

Subscribe to Our Free E-Newsletter, the *BK Communiqué*

Be the first to hear about new publications, special discount offers, exclusive articles, news about bestsellers, and more! Get on the list for our free e-newsletter by going to **www.bkconnection.com**.

Get Quantity Discounts

Berrett-Koehler books are available at quantity discounts for orders of ten or more copies. Please call us toll-free at (800) 929-2929 or email us at **bkp .orders@aidcvt.com**.

Join the BK Community

BKcommunity.com is a virtual meeting place where people from around the world can engage with kindred spirits to create a world that works for all. **BKcommunity.com** members may create their own profiles, blog, start and participate in forums and discussion groups, post photos and videos, answer surveys, announce and register for upcoming events, and chat with others online in real time. Please join the conversation!

SUSTAINABLE FORESTRY INITIATIVE
Label applies to the text stock
Certified Fiber Sourcing
www.sfiprogram.org